# Government, Evaluation and Change

# Government, Evaluation and Change

Mary Henkel

Jessica Kingsley Publishers
London

First published in the United Kingdom in 1991 by
Jessica Kingsley Publishers Ltd
118 Pentonville Road
London N1 9JN

Copyright © 1991 Mary Henkel

**British Library Cataloguing in Publication Data**
Henkel, Mary
    Government, evaluation and change.
    1. Great Britain. Public administration. Management
    I. Title
    354.4107

    ISBN 1-85302-524-0

Printed and bound in Great Britain by
Biddles Ltd, Guildford and King's Lynn

# Contents

# Foreword

This book is an account of a study of evaluative bodies in British government. It owes its origin to an initiative taken by the Economic and Social Research Council to fund research into the management and efficiency of central government.

The approaches taken in the pages that follow make it part of a sequence of studies undertaken in public policy in the Department of Government, and its Centre for the Evaluation of Public Policy and Practice (CEPPP) at Brunel University. In work on decision making, evaluation and policy development in higher education, science policy and the health and social services we have followed two main lines of analysis: the authority base from which institutions work, and the kind of knowledge that they bring to their aid or which serves as a basis for critique of their actions. It is also compatible with our other studies in its attempt to exploit careful field work in the service of conceptualisation about the nature of government.

Such approaches leave the author heavily in debt to many colleagues and friends. The ESRC grant made the study possible. The Audit Commission, the Social Services Inspectorate, and members of management consultancy firms -evaluators all- were helpfully open to my enquiries, even when they involved being continuously observed and interrogated on a five day inspection of secure accommodation for young people. The directorate and staff of the Audit Commission and inspectors from the Social Services Inspectorate headquarters and two regions took immense time and trouble to facilitate the fieldwork studies and to provide material. The local education and social services authorities in which the field work was carried out were unfailingly hospitable and helpful.

In acknowledging these debts I should record that the case studies of the Commission and the Inspectorate were undertaken at particular points of time when they were changing rapidly. Both organisations believe that this, and the limited number of case studies, should be taken into account in assessing the conclusions derived from cases. Both were, of course, fully consulted about the choice of cases, and the generalisations in the book are based on a combination of case studies and institutions' published material.

The Health Advisory Service had already patiently submitted themselves to our evaluation (Henkel et al.,1989) and I was able to further internalise our findings from that set of encounters in Chapter Eight. That earlier study was supported jointly by the King Edward's Hospital Fund for London and the DHSS, whose officials, and particularly Robert Maxwell of the Fund, were exemplary research sponsors.

Several colleagues from my home department were invaluable guides and mentors, and, indeed, direct contributors to my research. Tim Whitaker, now of the ESRC's staff, undertook the bulk of the field work and the primary conceptualisation and writing up of the case study of management consultants (Chapter Four). He set up and carried out the fieldwork for the first half of the Audit Commission study (Chapter Three). He was also a member of the team, together with Maurice Kogan, Tim Packwood, Penny Youll and the author, who undertook our study of the HAS. In producing that work, my colleagues contributed to part of this book.

The Department of Government was fortunate in having as a visiting teacher an outstanding theorist of policy analysis, Mary Hawkesworth, Professor of Political Science at the University of Louisville, Kentucky. Her rigorous and creative critique of an early draft was indispensable.

My greatest gratitude goes to Maurice Kogan, my colleague grantholder. He provided insight and critical support through the stages of project conceptualisation until the book reached publication stage. My intellectual debt to him, accumulated over many years, is incalculable and without his encouragement the book would not have been finished.

Evaluative studies, and studies of the substantive policy areas most open to evaluation, have bred strong international networks. Because of my earlier studies of higher education, I was privileged to complete part of this work at the Center for Studies in Higher Education, University of California, Berkeley whose former and present directors and associate director, Martin Trow, Sheldon Rothblatt, and Janet Ruyle provided a most hospitable haven.

Finally, all who know our department and faculty will not under-estimate the prodigious efficiency which Sally Harris has applied to the administration of our research and other academic needs over the years. This book was no exception. I am also indebted to Tom Kogan and Carole Buller for bibliographic assistance.

*Mary Henkel*
*Brunel University, September 1990*

Chapter One

# Politics, Knowledge and Evaluation

This is a study of diversity and change in public sector evaluation: in its practices, its epistemologies, its institutional frameworks and its functions in government. At the same time it is a study of government in action during a period of major change - change in conceptions of government itself and of the relationship between public and private enterprise.

During the six years covered by the study, 1983-1989, evaluation and the institutions through which it was carried out acquired a new and more sharply defined public profile to the point where one authority could refer to the 'Rise of the Evaluative State' (Neave, 1988). Government had identified evaluation as a significant component in its strategy to achieve some key objectives: to control public expenditure, to change the culture of the public sector and to shift the boundaries and definition of public and private spheres of activity.

New evaluative institutions and practices were installed, based on new assumptions about the knowledge and expertise they required, the values they should endorse and the authority they should carry. Old institutions were scrutinised and, in some cases, reconstituted. Evaluative machinery in the public sector at the end of the 1970s was vulnerable to criticism from the government and others (Hartley, 1971; Rhodes, 1981) on a number of counts: preoccupation with needs, input and process at the expense of assessing the management of resource constraints or output and outcomes; a lack of agreed and explicit targets and standards; unambitious conceptions of what could and should be measured and made the subject of conclusive judgement; and failure to achieve results.

A key change in the approach to evaluation sponsored by government was to emphasise its technical and instrumental nature and purpose. Government aimed to reduce the influence of service oriented professionals and to install management criteria and expertise. The study was structured round that shift. It focused on evaluative machinery located at different points on a professional ... managerial continuum. It was based on an intensive investigation of four institutions at different stages of evolution.

This made it possible to analyse the complexities of evaluative practice and its impacts and to indicate the range of expectations placed upon it in a period of continuous policy change. Evaluation was seen variously as providing tools to be used in the assertion of either centralised or local managerial accountability and control, as a component in programmes of change and as making it possible for public regulation to replace public provision as a symbol of collective responsibility.

The four selected institutions spanned a range of governmental contexts and displayed differing degrees of independence and dependence on government for the power to act. The Audit Commission, set up in 1983, the Social Work Service, redesignated the Social Services Inspectorate in 1985, and the Health Advisory Service, under review in 1988-89, were examined, along with the extended use of management consultants by central government departments. Thus evaluative practice in central and local government and in the health authorities was included.

## The Government and Political Evaluation

The 1980s were a period in Britain when the government succeeded in restructuring the framework of ideas, institutions and authority within which political options were determined. It did so on the basis of a radical political evaluation.

The Conservatives were returned to power in 1979 with a mandate to tackle Britain's problems through major economic change. Keynesian economic theory was disavowed and policies were pursued within a monetarist framework, implying maximum freedom for the market, a reduced role for the state and enhanced freedom for the individual. The foundations for that line of development were laid in the 1970s when political economy reemerged as an important source of analysis and critique of the policy systems of the Western world.

Strenuous attempts by governments to intervene to manage the economy were perceived as compounding its unmanageablility. Theorists from the right and the left (eg Bacon and Eltis, 1976; public choice theorists such as Mueller, 1979 and Breton, 1974; Marxist analysts such as O'Connor, 1973; Gough, 1979) combined to persuade that the tensions between capitalism and welfare had reached breaking point, that investment in the public sector was draining the life blood of the private sector or that the public investment required by capitalist enterprises to sustain them was actually undermining them.

The dominant voices were from the right. It was argued that democracy itself was threatened by a combination of rising individual and collective expectations and the disruptive effects of the pursuit of coercive group self interest in the market place (Brittan, 1975; see also King, 1975). Rising expectations were, in part, the fault of politicians competing for power and using lavish promises to as many sections of the electorate as possible. The result was that 'an excessive burden was placed on the sharing out function of government' (Brittan, *ibid*). It was faced with incompatible demands to keep inflation in check, to maintain full employment and to control the balance of payments. The problems were seen as an inevitable outcome of the development of democracy and the breakdown of various forms of authority. The ideology of equality, the loss of an inherited sense of the limits of what could be contested (for example, the decisive but unobtrusive command of power by the owners of and traders in capital (Lindblom, 1977)) and the abandonment of belief that any moral or political question could be settled by reasoned argument (see also MacIntyre, 1981) were diagnosed as the underlying causes.

The bureaucracies through which the public sector was administered were said to be dominated by self serving interests, bureaucrats, professionals and unions, whose main concern was to enlarge their own power. In consequence, bureaucracies got bigger, consumed an increasing proportion of the gross national product and at the same time became progressively less manageable or responsive.

Government moved towards corporatist solutions, attempting to secure policies through bargaining and negotiation with powerful functional groups: relationships in which 'favourable policy outcomes are traded for cooperation and expertise' (Cawson, 1982). But it found them unworkable as some of those groups were unable to guarantee compliance by their members.

However, it was argued by some (eg Winkler, 1981) that the requirement to manage the economy which led to the failed corporatist solution remained. The impetus to centralise power was strong.

Certainly, the new government's approach suggested that this was so. If its ultimate objectives were retreat from government and a radical shift from public to private enterprise and responsibility, the means were stronger central government control of priorities and institutions, reinforced by the setting up of management as the key to internal institutional change and the depoliticisation of the public arena.

Government insistently structured political debate within economic imperatives ('There Is No Alternative' was for a time in the early 1980s the government's most favoured slogan). Vigorous attempts were made to establish economy, efficiency, value for money, effectiveness and performance as incontestable values, essential to the sustainment of political order.

At the same time, a particular culture of management was installed, first in central government, and then in other areas of the public sector, based upon economic concepts of rationality (Minogue, 1983; Bromley and Euske, 1986). Central to it were either linear-rational or simple closed systems models of decision making in which unambiguous objectives are established, action upon them flows in predictable ways through established implementation structures, outcomes are monitored against them and objectives themselves may, in consequence, be reformulated. Supporting management technology was a host of quantitative techniques derived predominantly from accountancy (Gray, 1986). Expenditure control and the reduction of the money supply were, at least at first, the overriding objectives. Strenuous efforts were made to break down large bureaucracies, reduce the size of their staff and locate accountability more precisely within them. The burden of taxation rather than the need for enlarged or better services dominated the concept of accountability.

In central government the Rayner scrutinies of departments' expenditure, the broader based Efficiency Strategy and the Financial Management Initiative (FMI) were designed to produce efficiency savings and tighter managerial control of resources through the delegation of financial accountability to cost centres and through an improved financial information system for ministers (MINIS). Numbers of civil servants were to be reduced.

In the National Health Service (NHS), an entire tier of management was removed and, following the Griffiths report in 1983, management by interdisciplinary consensus was replaced by appointing one general manager at each level in the service. The performance of district health services was reviewed annually by reference to centrally determined performance indicators and resource allocation was tied to the reviews. Economy and efficiency were the principal performance criteria.

The control of local government expenditure was seen as central to the Conservative strategy. The scope of local government action had greatly but incrementally expanded in a period of enabling legislation and public sector growth in the 1960s and early 1970s. Some argued that in a period of economic constraint following rapid inflation it would inevitably confront problems. Many of its new responsibilities were mandatory. Moreover, as Sharpe (1979) points out, it was dependent for its revenue on central government grants combined with 'an unbuoyant, income-inelastic property tax'. Therefore it could increase its revenue only by increased government grant or by revaluation of the taxed property or by raising rates. A disproportionate rise in public expenditure ascribable to local government would be almost inevitable under the circumstances prevailing in the late 1970s and early 1980s.

But central government action to reduce local authority expenditure was mounted on a quite different set of propositions: that such expenditure was out of control and that local government management was inefficient and had resulted in massive failures. More fundamentally, the government also began to challenge the legitimacy of some local authority activities and to attack the role of local government in British democracy.

The first steps were to reduce the proportion of local authority funding contributed by the Rate Support Grant and to control the raising of rates through financial penalties and then direct rate capping legislation.

Evidence of contemporary literature (Bramley, 1984; Greenwood, 1983 and 1987; Stewart, 1983) tended to support government strictures on the quality of local authority management and financial control, although the verdict of the Audit Commission, created in 1982, was mixed. (St.John-Brooks, 1983; Audit Commission, 1987b) And critique was often based on broader and more dynamic conceptions of management than the linear- rationalism emphasised by government. Local authorities were chided not only for the low level of their information and analytic capacities and their reactive approaches but also for their tendency to conformity and uniformity (Stewart, 1983) and for the absence of anticipatory or 'prospector' modes of management (Greenwood, 1987). They were ill-adapted to manage change (cf Audit Commission, 1988b).

Local authorities were also vulnerable to attack on grounds of performance. In the fields of education, housing, personal social services it was easy to characterise local authority intervention as ineffective, if not disastrous and illegitimate: the education system had produced an undertrained and undereducated labour force; local authority flats fell down, their housing constituted health hazards and their estates were prey to escalating vandalism and violence; children under social work surveillance died; vulnerable people were uncared for. In these circumstances, government condemnation of left wing authorities for spending money on what were widely perceived as marginal groups and causes fell on ready ears.

But government went further and challenged head on the power and political significance of local authorities at large, first through the abolition of the metropolitan counties; later through the reorganisation of local government finance, the introduction of compulsory competitive tendering and the reduction of local government's role in the provision of housing, education and personal social services.

During the 1960s and 1970s, local government had been useful to central government as a provider for increasingly broadly conceived needs and as a source of learning and policy development in the meeting of such needs. In exchange it had got a rapidly increased share of national income and enhanced influence in the policy system. Such developments were marked in a growing literature on the local state (eg Cockburn, 1977), even if the implications for the national pattern of political power had not been fully addressed in public debate.

Local government had become increasingly politicised (Widdicombe, 1986; Stoker, 1988). In some areas in the 1980s it became the focus of organised opposition to the conservative government. In some, predominantly but not exclusively, inner city areas it provided a base of hard left opposition also to the mainstream of the Labour Party. Mainly in these latter areas, but also in some Conservative authorities, a new breed of young, politically committed and usually radical councillors emerged, some of them full time politicians. They were not willing to let their officers make strategic policy; they wished to impose a mission of their own on their authorities (Laffin and Young, 1985).

But in some authorities political links were being established which were criticised as undermining the proper functioning of local democracy (Bush et al. 1989). Councillors in one authority were employees in another. Some were appointed to key positions as much for their political commitment and experience as for their other qualifications. Strong links were established between councillors and union members at all levels in the organisation, so exacerbating management and industrial relations problems.

Such developments led Walker (1983) to write of a newly emergent 'public service class' which threatened the accountability of authorities to the general public. They gave the conservative government the occasion to reduce the role of local government in the more politically significant of its responsibilities and to reassert the principal-agent model of central-local government relations.

## Professions and the Public Sector

If the harnessing of professional power, values and knowledge had been a key strategy in the development of the modern state, particularly in its Welfare State emanation, doubts about the efficacy of that strategy were growing by the end of the 1970s. In the UK and elsewhere, confidence in the validity and usefulness of professional knowledge faded as evidence of the failures of the state accumulated; demand grew for professionals to be more publicly accountable; professional expansion came to be seen as a cause of the impotence of public sector organisations and, as resource constraint tightened, the tension between traditional and service oriented professionals and newer management based professionals increased.

By the end of the 1970s, professionals at the head of many local authority departments were experiencing a shift of identity and role. As the tasks of the authority widened, and the problems of management deepened, they began to see themselves as corporate managers and politicians as much as professional advisers to their authorities or professional leaders in their organisations (Laffin and Young, 1985; Young, 1989).

Against this background, the Conservative government sought more decisively to subsume professional under managerial authority or to recruit professionals to managerial roles. The nature of, for example, health service and higher education organisation was redefined in managerialist terms (Griffiths, 1983; Jarratt, 1985). Professionalism came to be associated with growth and the economics of demand. It had now to yield to managerialist priorities of economy and efficiency or supply side economics.

## Reconceptualising the Public Sector

Government action outlined above can be described in terms of its establishment of new degrees and forms of control, following a period of question about the governability of Britain (King, 1975). Government not only aimed to control public expenditure. It also redefined institutional boundaries and roles in such as a way as to reduce the diffusion of institutional power. It restructured the terms of political debate and it created new normative and conceptual frameworks for public sector activity.

Constriction of the scope and power of local authorities and the professions was paralleled by attempts to reduce the political functions of trade unions and to confine the public role of the churches, in the former case through stressing their responsibility to negotiate the rewards and conditions of labour, in the latter case through asserting a distinction between (legitimate and necessary) moral leadership and (illegitimate) political intervention.

More fundamentally, thinking in the UK about the interdependence of the public and private sectors was reshaped so as to ground the working of the public sector firmly in the norms, methods and mechanisms of private enterprise and the market. For example, the aims of higher education and science were subsumed under those of the economy, leaders of private industry were allocated key roles in their governance and their institutions were recast in a managerialist mould (Jarratt, 1985; Croham, 1987).

Not only were the technologies and concepts of management seen as key to the reform of public organisation but public sector functions were to be relocated in the private sector. A reduced public sector was then to be subject to the laws of competition, demand and supply and to set up internal markets.

These changes required shifts in the meaning and operation of public accountability. Accountability was now conceived as being primarily to taxpayers and secondly to individual users of services, mirroring the shareholders and customers of private enterprise. Externalities and notions of public good or collective responsibility receded in importance.

Accountability was to be based on a model of rational man seeking to maximise his own individual interests in an economy aimed at the dominance of private over public expenditure. In such a model individuals need maximum disposable income, not enlargement of public provision. On these assumptions, the public as taxpayers, would more unequivocally than at present (Judge et al. 1983) wish to minimise taxation. As users or customers, they would call providers to account through opportunities to exercise choice and obtain services or goods from alternative sources.

For their part, providers would be required to concentrate on maximising output from limited resources and an important aim of management would be to locate responsibility for performance on these criteria more precisely and, as far as possible, with individuals.

Thus a radical political agenda centred on the values of individualism and economic freedom was established by strong assertion of central authority and the installment of rationalistic management.

## Evaluation and the New Order

These developments may now be linked to the central concerns of this book. Many of the government objectives described depended for their achievement on effective review and control mechanisms. Managerialism assumed internal feedback systems on success in meeting objectives. Linkage of the control of resources with the renewal of government support meant monitoring resource use. Economy, efficiency and effectiveness had to be measured and compared between as well as within organisations. And help was deemed to be required if public sector bodies were to analyse and improve their performance.

But did the kind of monitoring, evaluative and change institutions required to achieve these objectives exist at the beginning of the 1980s?

## Change Objectives in Central Government

Various reforms aimed at rationalising the policy process in central government and placing greater emphasis on monitoring the relationship between resource allocation, policy output and outcome had been tried in the 1970s and apparently failed. Of the various techniques tried, Programme Analysis and Review (PAR), Planning, Programming and Budgeting Systems (PPBS), Cost Benefit Analysis, PAR was probably the most systematically applied (Gray and Jenkins, 1983). It failed for technical reasons (departments had insufficient analytic capacity) as well as for political reasons. Powerful interests, the Treasury, the CPRS and spending departments had conflicting objectives for it and it ultimately lacked ministerial support. Its aims of maximising outputs for given inputs were overtaken by the imperative to reduce inputs (Gray and Jenkins, ibid.; Garrett, 1972; Bourn, 1989).

Accounts of the progress of the 1980s initiatives, the Rayner scrutinies, FMI, MINIS (eg Richards, 1987; Gray and Jenkins, 1983) suggest that both technical and bureau-political obstacles to implementation remained and were tackled slowly in the course of the decade.

## Evaluative Machinery and Other Change Initiatives

### Inspectorates

Concern about the strength and meaning of democratic government under which there was widespread failure of policy implementation had led to calls for reform and reappraisal of inspectorates by the middle of the 1960s (Hartley, 1972; House of Commons, 1967-68). A study was commissioned by the Royal Institute of Public Administration (Rhodes, 1981). Interest centred both on the adequacy of existing inspection practice and on the potential to strengthen and extend the use of inspectorates in the public and private sectors.

Amongst the different kinds of inspectorates, Rhodes identified two main categories: *enforcement* inspectorates established to regulate the operations of private industry in the interests of public protection and *efficiency* inspectorates designed to promote efficiency and standards in the public sector. Enforcement inspectorates, unlike their efficiency counterparts, had recourse to the law and the courts to secure compliance. In practice, however, both relied heavily on persuasion and collaboration in pursuit of their objectives and had as a result to be content with compromise. Meanwhile, some inspectorates (eg those for education and for children's services) mainly in the efficiency category had enforcement powers in limited aspects of their roles.

Efficiency and some enforcement inspectorates tended to comprise professionals inspecting other professionals. They were often thought to have become too close to those whose work they were evaluating. Their practice shared many of the characteristics of peer review and was in consequence vulnerable to criticism.

*Peer Review*

Peer review carried important functions in a period of high delegation of responsibility and authority to professionals or experts. Evaluation and decisions on resource allocation were handed over to professionally based institutions such as the University Grants Committee (UGC) or the Council for National Academic Awards (CNAA) or were made on the recommendations of peers, as for example in the Chief Scientist's Review of Research Units in the DHSS (Kogan and Henkel, 1983).

Peer review assumes a closed system of shared values, knowledge, criteria of merit and standards of performance. There is a premium on selecting as evaluators those with acknowledged reputation and authority of knowledge. In consequence, the criteria and standards on which they base their judgements are often not made explicit; there is a general assumption that they are known and accepted.

Peer review systems are likely to come under attack from outside if professional or expert knowledge is perceived as flawed. The absence of clear norms or measures makes it difficult for lay managers to compare professional performances, set targets or exact accountability independently of the professionals.

Peer review may be attacked from inside as well if there is a breakdown in professional consensus, prolific or fragmented specialisation and substantial stratification within the peer group. Attacks are likely to be more acute if peer review is used as a basis for the allocation of resources (Kogan and Henkel, *op. cit.*).

*Audit*

The District Audit Service was primarily concerned with financial regularity when the Conservatives came to power in 1979. The Layfield Committee (1976) had thought it necessary to make value for money and poor financial management in local government more central but had received no clear response from the Labour government.

As far back as 1966, Normanton had commented that, by comparison with other Western countries, the British state audit system was 'severely restricted in scope and expertise and not fully independent from the executive'.

A later review of audit arrangements in six Western countries revealed that all except Britain had set in place audit arrangements to monitor efficiency by the end of the 1970s and at least two were tackling the problem of assessing the effectiveness of resource use in the public sector (Glynn, 1985).

In the USA the General Accounting Office devoted a minority of its time to regularity audit and was actively concerned with the use of resources and with the outcomes of public spending programmes, indeed to the point where there was some criticism that its traditional regularity function was being neglected. At least half its staff were trained in professions other than accountancy. Normanton had also commented on the low level and narrow range of qualification of audit staff in Britain as compared with the USA, France and West Germany. These countries recruited graduates and post graduates in a range of disciplines, while recruitment to the Exchequer and Audit Department in the UK was predominantly post GCE A level (Garrett, 1986).

It would thus seem that evaluative machinery perceived by government as relevant to its purposes in central government and local government was not ready to meet many of its purposes.

## Epistemological Context and Government Assumptions

The shift from professional to managerial authority and values was accompanied by changes in the kind of knowledge exploited in evaluation of services. Government policies now promoted evaluation as a contribution to the control of the periphery by the centre, particularly in the management of resources. It stressed values of economy, efficiency, 'value for money' and effectiveness or performance. As a corollary, it assumed that evaluation would be summative, delivering authoritative judgements, based as far as possible on performance indicators or quantitative measures of input-output relationships and outcomes and set against predefined targets and standards.

The language was that of economics as used in management theory and practice. The underlying theory of knowledge was positivist; it assumed that social phenomena could be divorced from their context and that objective knowledge about them could be achieved through empirical observation and quantitatively expressed; that facts were distinct from values and means from ends; that concepts and methods of 'good management' were applicable to the pursuit of any values.

Those assumptions were at variance from the dominant theory and practice of evaluation in the 1970s and 1980s. They were more like the working assumptions of policy evaluation in the 1960s, except that they were based on a different concept of the role of government. In the 1960s government, at least in the USA, the home of evaluative theory and method, thought that social scientists could help it solve social problems through the application of economic, sociological and psychological theory in public programmes. In the 1980s government wanted to leave as much as possible of that task to the market and to harness expertise to the management of public resources and the reduction of the public sector. Concepts of what constituted 'good value' in the public sector came to be resource led rather than needs led.

Evaluation theorists in the 1960s believed that they could make generalisable judgements about the impact of social programmes. The perceived ideal methodology at the time for the evaluation of social programmes was experimental, based on randomised control. And although the idea that experiments could yield authoritative generalisations useful to policy makers gradually lost ground in the face of their limited external validity and the complexity of the social problems to be tackled, the experimental analogy was robust. Social reforms themselves came to be conceptualised as experiments (Rivlin, 1971; Campbell, 1969), as social scientists adopted a Popperian notion of evolutionary knowledge, based on trial and error and provisional solutions. (Dunn, 1982) Popper himself put forward ideas about social engineering, social reforms that would be subjected to the test of pluralist political argument and practical empiricism (Popper, 1966).

Rationalist and synoptic models of policy making assuming a single, final locus of decision making and the possibility of value consensus gave way to incrementalist models. In those, complementary, competing and conflicting interests bargained and negotiated their way to provisional solutions.

At the same time models and methods of evaluation multiplied. Conflict developed among evaluation theorists. Some saw themselves as value free social scientists in the Weberian tradition applying rigorous methods of inquiry and analysis within a framework of values and objectives set by policy makers. Their contribution was argued by Rossi (1982) to be based on a clear distinction between evaluative research (which they offered) and evaluation by connoisseurs. He contended that there was then a separate argument to be conducted about the usefulness of social science to policy makers and practitioners. That had already been engaged by, for example, Lindblom and Cohen (1979), in their contention that the utility of social science was limited and more importance should be attached to social learning, in which all could participate.

Others expressed more radical doubt about the nature of social science and the authority of the knowledge derived from it. Some based their arguments on a distinction between science and social science, following the line taken by, for example, Winch (1958) that the idea of a social science was a mistake: that human action, organisation and association could not be based on immutable scientific laws; rather they should be understood as subject to rules, norms and ideals conceptualised and selected by cultures, societies and governments.

More radical post positivist theorists conceived of scientific knowledge and the disciplines subsumed under it as identifiable knowledge traditions, with no more claim to truth or authority than any other knowledge traditions. All knowledge was constructed and shaped by different ways of conceptualising or representing experience developed by different communities. Correspondence theories of truth had therefore to be replaced by coherence theories (Hawkesworth, 1988).

Evaluation theorists representing both of these views agreed that values were central to the activity of evaluation. Evaluators should recognise this and ensure that the value base of their work was made explicit and exposed to rigorous analysis (See, eg, Rein, 1976; House, 1980).

Major models of evaluation were identified and classified by House (ibid.), who belonged to the more radical school outlined above. It is notable that he does not include experimental or quasi-experimental models (for which, see Cope, 1981; Davies and Challis, 1981) which are identified with concepts of objective and generalisable knowledge. The classification assumes that policies and programmes subject to evaluation have multiple stakeholders, and that evaluators must choose to which of them their evaluations should be addressed (see also Wholey, 1983; Stake, 1982; Scriven, 1980; Cronbach, 1980; Patton, 1978).

Models based on systems analysis imply that programmes could aim for logic and predictable relationships and outcomes. They could work according to bounded rationality, determined from the top. Evaluators accepting problems as defined by managers could assess the resulting systems on conceptual and operational adequacy. Or they might propose alternative definitions and models of response.

Grimwood and Tomkins (1986) suggest that different evaluative models may be systematically associated with either positivist/scientific or naturalistic/critical epistemologies or methodologies. House and others, however suggest that they are more importantly associated with concern for different stakeholders. Certainly, evaluations are addressed to limited rather than general audiences and their aims and outputs are defined by reference to stakeholders and audiences.

As ideas about the applicability, authority and robustness of evaluations became more circumscribed, their purposes were more readily defined as formative rather than summative or combining elements of the two. Evaluators collaborated with those evaluated to identify criteria and standards and to share judgements. These would then form the basis of planned change.

In this context, the analogy of experiment was replaced by that of argument. House suggested that evaluation was best conceived of as argument, designed to persuade more or less limited audiences (House, 1977). Later Dunn (1982) proposed that social reforms be seen as arguments, using Toulmin's transactional model of argument (1958). The task of the analyst or evaluator is then to disaggregate and map the argument, identifying its justifications and the tests to which its knowledge claims ought to be subjected. These are categorised as truth, cogency and utility tests. These authors assume that facts and values are integrally linked and that both together can be subjected to rigorous test but in a framework of a coherence, as against a correspondence, theory of truth.

In the context of ferment in the field of evaluation, theorists have adopted two main kinds of strategy. One is to accept that there is no point in attempting anything like a comprehensive evaluation even for the purpose of producing a provisional statement. Rather evaluations should be undertaken with precise and limited objectives and audiences in mind. In this case evaluation is part of a pluralist and partisan decision making process and can serve to enhance the quality of the arguments on which it is based (cf Weiss, 1977).

A second strategy is to attempt some synthesis of multiple evaluative methods and approaches. Cook, for example, proposes careful and complex systems of triangulation (Cook, 1987), while Glass et al advocate meta analysis, which involves weighting and synthesising similar types of study based on different samples and varying degrees of methodological rigour (Glass et al., 1981; Cook and Shadish, 1987). Cronbach suggests various techniques for qualitatively integrating single evaluative studies with findings from previous research (Cronbach et al, 1980; Cook and Shadish, ibid.).

The assumptions of the British government in the 1980s gave no heed to these complexities. The stakeholders were, at least in the first half of the decade, those at the top of the system, who were assumed to be able to set clear targets based on limited evaluative criteria. The government had itself not only weakened pluralism and the institutional arrangements on which it was based. It had also confronted the epistemology underpinning it.

In the face of a society that had seemed to take for granted that no set of moral or political beliefs could be authoritatively asserted and that reason could not decide between matters of value which were ultimately emotively based (cf MacIntyre, 1981), it built a framework in which the scope for contested values and beliefs was reduced. It had installed economic imperatives as central to political order and seen first managerialism and then a more wholesale commitment to market values and institutions as its prime goals. It appealed in debate either to facts or to 'common sense' or to incontestable instrumental values such as economy, efficiency and effectiveness. As time went on, and government became more confident in widening the boundaries of consensus, the market values of choice and responsiveness to consumer demand assumed a higher profile.

## Government, Evaluation and Change

The 1980s saw government give a higher profile to evaluation but one based on assumptions that flew in the face of contemporary, post positivist critiques of policy analysis and evaluative theory. Evaluation could be founded on distinctions between means and ends, the technical and the normative, instrumental and substantive values and it could be definitive. Circumstances dictated that primacy be given to instrumentalism. Management and control of resources were prerequisites to creating and maintaining good services, whatever criteria were used to determine goodness and whatever context specific expertise was deployed in those services.

The rest of this book explores how strong a hold instrumentalism or managerialism gained in four forms of evaluation in the public sector and how effective as instruments for control and change these forms of evaluation were. It does so on the basis of detailed case studies supplemented by more comprehensive documentary analysis and more broadly based interviews.

The four chosen forms or institutions are as follows: the Audit Commission, a body created by the conservative government in 1982 to monitor and promote the instrumental values of economy, efficiency and effectiveness in the management of local government; the use of management consultants in central government departments, substantially increased in the 1980s; the Social Services Inspectorate (SSI) whose redesignation in 1985 was intended to regulate and promote the values of instrumental management in what was formerly a professional advisory service in government; and the Health Advisory Service (HAS), created in its original form in 1969 and based primarily on the values and methods of professional peer review.

Chapters Two to Eight provide the empirical meat of the book: they comprise discrete case studies set in the context of a critical institutional analysis in the case of the Audit Commission (Chapters Two and Three) and the Social Services Inspectorate (Chapters Five, Six and Seven) and collated case studies in the case of the use of consultants (Chapter Four) and the Health Advisory Service (Chapter Eight).

Chapters Nine to Eleven take an overview. They examine developments and changes in evaluative objectives, knowledge base, methods and values as evinced in the chosen institutions. They consider how clear and coherent were the assumptions on which they worked, how much convergence there was between them, and how consistent they were with key government objectives. They analyse their impacts and how they linked with forms of authority, exchange relationships and power. The picture that emerges reveals some clear trends towards instrumentalism and managerial values and away from professional assumptions and modes of evaluation. But it also demonstrates the complexities and ambiguities of evaluative practice and the difficulties of containing it within predetermined boundaries.

Chapter Twelve considers the role of evaluation in the 1980s, as government priorities shifted from promoting managerialism to the broader objectives of making forms of market more central to the public sector.

Chapter Two

# The Audit Commission

The first case study is of a body created to promote the instrumental values
of economy, efficiency and effectiveness in the public sector. The Audit
Commission was a major product of the shift in governmental objectives
for evaluative practice in the 1980s.

It did not, however, spring fully armed from the head of Michael
Heseltine, Secretary of State for the Environment, in 1982. An independent body, 'an audit commission', to take responsibility for the local
government audit function was first proposed by the Chief Inspector of
the District Audit Service in 1970 (Nicholson, 1986) at a time when local
government powers were growing rapidly and before local authorities
were given the right to choose their own auditors in 1972.

The idea was taken up by the Layfield Committee (1976) as part of
its concern to tackle value for money issues and to eliminate bad practice
in the administration of local government finance. However, it was
strongly resisted by local government, and the Labour Government of the
day did not pursue it. Government response to continued concern, expressed in the reports of three Parliamentary Select Committees in the
years 1976-1979 about the need for more effective monitoring of local
government use of resources, was to set up the Advisory Committee on
Local Audit shortly before the general election. The Expenditure Committee, the Public Accounts Committee and the Procedure Committee of
the House of Commons wanted to make local authority expenditure
subject to parliamentary scrutiny and to establish the right of Parliament
to follow public money wherever it went. They advocated transferring
the audit of local authorities to the Comptroller and Auditor General to
create a more integrated system of public audit (Robinson A. and Webb
A, 1987).

The conservative government elected in 1979 resisted parliamentary
scrutiny of local authority expenditure and a more integrated system of

public audit. Some shift in these directions was achieved but through a private member's bill, eventually passed as the National Audit Act, 1984. The Comptroller and Auditor General was to remain an officer of the House of Commons and in practice to continue to be recruited from the civil service. But he would be the head of a powerful National Audit Office (to succeed the Exchequer and Audit department) and have broader powers to examine the efficiency and effectiveness of central government departments. The system was not fully comprehensive, as local government and the nationalised industries were excluded.

Meanwhile, the proposal to establish an independent commission to oversee local government audit had been revived when Michael Heseltine took over at the Department of the Environment. He soon made it clear that he wished to toughen the audit function and make value for money a key objective. The proposal had the support of the Advisory Committee on Local Audit set up by the previous government.

The Audit Commission was eventually established under the Local Government Finance Act, 1982. It was to be independent of central and local government. But it was seen as part of a package of measures to impose more control, including sanctions, by the centre over local government expenditure. It assumed the responsibility to ensure an effective audit of fiscal probity in local government, but its scope was to be far wider than that. It was to promote economy, efficiency and effectiveness in local authority resource management.

## The Legal Framework

The 1982 Act laid the following main duties on the Audit Commission:

* to appoint auditors to local authorities and other local public bodies in England and Wales. Local authorities thus lost their power to appoint their own auditors;
* to prepare a code of audit practice;
* to give an opinion on a local authority's accounts and to satisfy themselves by audit and in other ways that it had made proper arrangements for securing economy, efficiency and effectiveness in the use of resources; (a new duty; Section 15)
* to undertake or promote comparative and other studies designed to enable it to make recommendations for improving economy, efficiency and effectiveness in the provision of local government services' (Section 26);

- to carry out studies on the impact of legislation and ministerial directives on local authority economy, efficiency and effectiveness (Section 27).

Section 27 contained an amendment to the Act introduced against the government's wishes. It went back to an earlier parliamentary concern to establish a means through which it could monitor local government expenditure. The Comptroller and Auditor General would have access to Audit Commission reports compiled under this section and would lay them before the House. These reports have been an important mechanism for the Commission in demonstrating its independence from central government and thus breaking down the hostility of local authorities to its creation. Three early reports published under this provision high- lighted the obstacles to coherent local authority resource management and policy development implicit in central government machinery and policies (Audit Commission, 1984c, 1985 and 1986e).

Local auditors had the power to refer an expenditure which they considered unlawful to the courts, though only post hoc. Sanctions available to the court included disqualification for up to five years under certain circumstances, if those responsible were councillors. The court could also require the sum to be made good.

In some cases of deliberate misconduct or failure to account for money, auditors could themselves take action to secure repayment and disqualification of members who were implicated, if the sum were substantial, although there was a right of appeal to the court.

The Commission started work in April, 1983.

## Objectives

At the end of its first term of three years, the Commission offered its own appraisal of its achievements in its Annual Report of 1985-86 (Audit Commission, 1986c). It identified its main objectives as to secure com- pliance with the law in local authority expenditure; to help local auth- orities achieve better value for money; to ensure that audit fees are competitive for comparable service and so demonstrate in its own practice that public services do not need to be more expensive than private; to strengthen local accountability. But it made it clear that it interpreted its duties to oversee economy, efficiency and effectiveness in local govern- ment in wide terms, to include a remit to help improve local authority management and so to exert a fundamental influence on it.

The audit function was basic to the work of the Commission. The law extended that function from probity or regularity to 'value for money' audit, and in so doing made it clear that the two aspects were to be connected. This was part of a longer term trend, at least as far as the work of the Comptroller and Auditor-General was concerned (Normanton, 1966). The expectation was incorporated by the Commission in the Introduction to the Code of Practice it laid before Parliament in 1983:

> 'The auditor's concern that the authority has made proper arrangements to secure economy, efficiency and effectiveness should influence him throughout his audit.' (para 3)

By 1987, the Commission claimed to have established an 'overall methodology' for 'integrated audit' of economy, efficiency and effectiveness. This comprised a number of components: the use of Commission profiles of local authorities and performance measurement statistics; (these provided a quantitative framework for inter-authority comparisons of performance); special studies under Section 26 of the Act, which would be translated into local 'audit flavours' administered by auditors in their own authorities; local value for money projects identified collaboratively by auditors and their authorities, probably using material from profiles and performance measures; and reviews of overall management arrangements of local authorities.

Audit had thus been extended in two main ways: the scope was far broader and it became a vehicle for promoting change. Audit was no longer simply a monitoring or evaluative mechanism.

## Structures and Staffing

The Commission was to comprise 15 members appointed jointly by the Secretary of State for the Environment and the Secretary of State for Wales, initially for a three year term. They were drawn from industry, local government, the accounting professions and trade unions. They included some Labour appointees. A small central staff would be mainly based at headquarters in London. Its 550 or so auditors were either directly employed and based in the regional offices of the District Audit Service (DAS) (approximately 70 per cent) or employed by private firms. It was to be self financing; its income, once the Commission was underway, was to derive almost entirely from fees for audit work.

There were four directorates under the Controller of the Commission: finance and administration, concerned with the Commission's own resources; operations, accountable for regularity audit and accountancy;

special studies, responsible for the design and execution of the Commission's studies under sections 26 and 27 of the Local Government Finance Act, 1982; and management practice. This directorate combined the development and dissemination of models and advice on overall management arrangements in local authorities with the production of local authority profiles and work on performance measurement.

Although within that central structure responsibility for regularity audit was kept separate, local auditors were expected to develop the extended audit function through an integrated approach, as described above. Under the Commission's Code of Practice (1984 and revised in 1988), it was made clear that the traditional auditing methods and standards were still needed to conduct a regularity audit. The importance of systematic analysis based on adequate information and alertness for irregularities was emphasised. But 'value for money' auditing was to be incorporated into the concept of audit. Auditors must be concerned with arrangements for securing economy, efficiency and effectiveness in the use of public funds as well as with the form and regularity of accounts.

The aim was not to recruit other staff to carry out the new tasks but to enlarge the capacities of auditors, up till now almost universally based on the audit training of accountants. In tackling their tasks, auditors were required by the Code of Practice to take a broad based holistic approach. Their analysis must be informed by an understanding of the overall characteristics and responsibilities and the strengths and weaknesses of individual local authorities. They must take into account the complexity of the public interests involved.

The enjoinders to independence on the part of auditors were no less rigorous than had always been applied. They included the avoidance of official, professional or personal relationships that might impinge on the nature of the audit. Auditors should not involve themselves in decision making in the authority. They must be prepared, if necessary, to use the instruments available to them to highlight and so deter bad practice, waste and inefficiencies (qualification of reports; reports in the public interest; use of the auditors' annual management letter to their authority to draw attention to perceived problems or inaction). At the same time, they were expected to be 'concerned for action' and constructive: willing to assist members and officers. They were also to disseminate good practice.

In short they were to recast their conception of their professional role and incorporate values, attitudes and modes of thinking and action that might not only be new to them but also difficult to reconcile with existing characteristics.

A study by Tomkins, undertaken in a private firm during the Commission's first year of operation, found that in fact there was a division of labour. Staff with management consultancy training who might or might not be accountants were undertaking value for money audits. Regularity audits were carried out by the audit division, in which auditors all had the audit training given to Chartered Accountants. They did not at that stage think the tasks could be combined. They insisted that the difference between the skills of the two groups were critical and, in the case of value for money auditing, far more important than previous local authority experience (Tomkins, 1986).

## Special Studies

The link between the audit function and the special studies authorised under section 26 of the enabling Act was established from the beginning and was regarded at the Commission as a powerful mechanism for installing value for money as a central criterion.

The District Audit Service (DAS) had laid some foundations for the development of special studies in the 1970s. They originated in part from comments in the Layfield Report (1976) drawing attention to the need for comparative studies to promote efficiency and value for money. Government response to this call had been to place primary responsibility on the Local Authority Management Services and Computer Committee (LAMSAC). However, the DAS started to use comparative statistics to identify performance measures. And although there was widespread resistance to anything like league tables of statistics, a few authorities worked with the DAS to identify measures they could use to examine their own performance. The DAS then went on to initiate some fieldwork-based comparative studies using statistics as a starting point. They engaged teams on a consultancy basis to carry out these studies. These included management consultants from private firms as well as people from local government. The DAS secured agreement from relevant professional associations and the local authority associations to advise on and monitor the studies. This eased the problems of persuading authorities to participate.

These early studies were in three areas: the fire service, further education and the personal social services. They laid the foundations of the Audit Commission special studies. Their aim was described by a contemporary senior member of the DAS as ' to produce a methodology to assist auditors in their work, and to explore and publish information about how different practices at authorities affected economy, efficiency and effectiveness' (Langley, 1986).

Special studies carried out under section 26 of the Local Government Finance Act, 1982 were the responsibility of the Special Studies Directorate. They employed staff with quantitative analytic skills to specialise in certain areas of local government activity and to form the nucleus of the teams for the individual studies. By 1988, the directorate was mounting usually three (the original number was four or five) studies each year. They formed the basis for the local auditors' annual programme of 'audit flavours' or value for money projects in their own authorities.

By 1988, the organisation of special studies teams had evolved. Team structures were conceived in circular rather than linear terms. At the centre was the project manager, who was as much a coordinator as a manager. At least two people worked full time on a study alongside the project manager, a senior projects officer and an auditor seconded from the DAS. Each team might have one or two part time advisers, an academic and/or someone with substantial expertise in the field. Teams might also have advisers representing 'the great and the good', nominated from the field, who would typically give one or two days of their time per quarter.

Special studies were planned on two year cycles (although they often had to be completed more quickly) and followed a broadly uniform pattern. The Commission identified an aspect of a local authority activity with potential for substantial increase in the economy, efficiency or effectiveness with which it was managed. A team was appointed, which first developed a specification for a comparative study by intensive networking and pilot studies in a few selected authorities. 'By analysing the way in which the activity is tackled (in those authorities), the study team identifies the vital elements of good management practice and the performance indicators which will help to point the way towards improvements' (Guide to the work of the Audit Commission, undated, p.10).

Preliminary findings were tested in a larger sample of authorities and a national report published. The data and analysis were used to produce, by the end of the second year, an audit guide, which auditors in each local authority could use as a basis for analysing that activity and specifying a programme of improvement. They thus applied the findings of a nationally mounted exercise to the particular circumstances of their own authorities. The authorities were responsible for using that programme as they determined but the auditors were encouraged to follow up the impacts of the study.

By the end of 1988, the directorate had overseen 17 section 26 special studies. The areas covered included: further education; teaching costs and non teaching costs in secondary education; refuse collection; vehicle fleet management; purchasing; cash flow management; energy management; housing supervision, management and maintenance; highway maintenance; property management; services for the elderly and people with a mental handicap.

If financial management and technical areas such as highway and property maintenance predominated in the first years of the special studies, the Commission moved into the more diffuse and professionally based work of social services departments and education quite early, initially following up studies carried out under the old order. Soon the Special Studies directorate grew more confident about what they could offer in such fields.

The main purpose of special studies was to use systematic analysis and evaluation as instruments to promote learning and change. The Commission itself and its auditors were intended to learn, as were the prime beneficiaries, the local authorities. The team members in our case study spoke of describing and disseminating good practice. Teams also identified and quantified measures of performance, which could feed into the Commission's continuing work on performance indicators and performance measurement.

The Commission linked the work of these studies with its aim to enhance local accountability in local government. It saw its role as heightening awareness among electors of the main issues it sought to address. And its reports laid stress on the ways in which it could keep the public well informed about matters which ought to be brought to their attention. The Commission ensured that reports effectively marketed its work. And locally the results of all forms of value for money projects were included in the annual management letter to the authority.

In practice special studies in the first years of the Commission focused primarily on economy and efficiency, but in the 1987 review of its work (Audit Commission, 1987d) the Commission announced its intention to undertake more analysis of effectiveness and the quality of services. From then on the emphasis shifted. We shall consider this more fully in the discussion of the case study that follows.

Chapter Three

# Evaluation and the Instrumental/Political Boundary:
## A Case Study of the Audit Commission

Special Studies extended the audit function of the Audit Commission and constitute the nearest point of comparison of the Commission's work with that of the Social Services Inspectorate and the Health Advisory Service.

The special study selected for our analysis was the second of two on secondary education mounted under section 26 of the Local Government Finance Act, 1982, by the Special Studies Directorate of the Audit Commission.

The national study was carried out during the years 1984-1986 and focused on some key aspects of managing teachers. The report published in May 1986 under the heading *Towards Better Management of Secondary Education*, together with the Audit Guide derived from it, formed the basis for value for money projects carried out by local authority auditors in 1987.

This chapter analyses the objectives, processes, outputs and impacts of the study at national and local levels from 1984 to 1988. The analysis of the national level is based on relevant documents and interviews with the team and key members of the policy community. The local project analysis is based on work in three local education authorities, a metropolitan district, a London borough and a shire county. A detailed account of the methods of this and other case studies is given in Appendix A, but the Commission's view should be recorded here: that the size of the sample, together with the fact that the proportion of authorities audited by private firms to those audited by the DAS was the reverse of the national norm, mean that the basis of the analysis of the local projects is narrow and unrepresentative.

The limited number of authorities was dictated partly by resources but largely by the case study method. This is designed to enable researchers to get inside processes and understand the multiplicity of factors affecting impacts, to a degree unattainable by survey methods based on a representative sample.

The research focused on the coherence of the methods and values pursued in the exercise and the factors affecting its impacts. Was the internal logic of the exercise strictly that of instrumental evaluation? It so, how far was it sustained?

## Special Studies: Topic Selection

Special Studies are selected by the Commission in collaboration with the Controller and the staff of the Special Studies unit. The Commission plays an active role in this task and is clearly 'the owner' of the studies.

The rationale behind the choice of topic was perceived by almost all respondents to be that education was a big consumer of local authority resources in a context where the issue of economic and efficient use of resources was made acute by falling secondary school rolls.

This study was billed originally as 'Secondary Schools Teaching Costs' and was carried out two years after a study on non-teaching costs in LEAs. The management of teachers, as professionals, was thought to constitute sensitive territory for the Commission, but most team members and half of the respondents from the policy community thought the Commission had established some credibility with the teaching profession in the earlier study on non-teaching costs.

Team members saw the management of teachers as at the heart of the study. They agreed that they did not start with definite hypotheses but they wanted to produce a study that would tackle hard practical problems such as principles of teacher allocation, teacher redeployment, and conditions of service. One member emphasised that this was not a straightforward comparative study; it was designed 'to compare an authority with itself'. Two of the 'policy' representatives mentioned the role of the special studies in disseminating good practice.

Most respondents felt that enhancing efficiency was the study's main purpose. No one thought it was a cost cutting exercise; it was concerned with value for money but tried to focus on educational impacts.

## The National Study

*Process*

The study required a long lead time. The topic was settled early in 1984; the national report published in May 1986. The timetable was broadly as follows:

| | |
|---|---|
| *Spring 1984* | Topic agreed<br>1st specification written<br>Team selected |
| *Summer 1984* | Preliminary paper written by academic consultant<br>Consultation on specification with the field |
| *Nov 1984* | 1st team meeting |
| *Early 1985* | Team work on specification, hypotheses<br>Preliminary data collection<br>Sample of LEAs selected for fieldwork |
| *May 1985* | Fieldwork |
| *August 1985* | 1st draft of report written |
| *October 1985* | 2nd draft of report written Discussed with HMI and DES |
| *December 1985* | 3rd draft of report written<br>Sent to Controller, four AC members,<br>TUC and some unions, professional<br>associations, two CEOs, some sample LEAs |
| *February 1986* | 3rd draft submitted to full AC meeting |
| *Spring 1986* | Final report written |
| *May 1986* | Report published |
| *November 1986* | Course for local auditors on the Audit Guide |
| *January 1987* | Course for LEA liaison officers on Audit Guide |
| *Oct-Dec 1987* | Local reports ready for presentation to LAs |

*Selection of the Team*

The team comprised a project manager and six other members. The secretary was a permanent member of Audit Commission staff. There was an auditor on three year secondment from the District Audit Service and an academic consultant, who was a specialist in industrial relations,

education and local government. There were two local authority education officers and a head teacher seconded to the study for two terms.

All the team members from outside the Commission were interviewed
before they were selected. The academic was chosen after competitive
tendering with management consultants; the decision to go for expertise
in the study area rather than in management consultancy was made partly
as a result of experience on earlier education studies and partly because
management expertise was already available in the Audit Commission
itself. The members selected from the field were recommended, two by
the Society of Education Officers and one by a previous external consultant on a study.

Both of the Audit Commission permanent headquarters staff had
previously worked in the public sector. Their expertise included statistics,
computer consultancy and operational research as well as management.
Neither had any specialist knowledge or experience in education, apart
from work on previous Commission studies in the case of one.

Team members described working relationships as based on mutual
respect for the contribution of each person. There was a broad consensus
of purpose but more detailed agreement was reached through quite
rigorous argument. There was not a sharp divide between the educationalists and the other members of the team, although the latter group more
often provided the 'hawks' on specific issues and they were more likely
to think in terms of efficiency and costs. The educationalists did not
always share similar perceptions or priorities and at least one felt he had
changed his views on some things through his work on the team. External
team members were contractually free to dissent publicly from aspects
of the report and some did, although all felt that the report as a whole was
a good piece of work.

## Methods of Work

Preparatory work of different kinds had been completed before the team
had its first meeting. The project manager had consulted informally with
some parts of the field, the academic consultant had recently published a
book on the management of teachers, based on government funded
research, and he wrote a preliminary paper for the team. Yet the team did
not start with firm concepts, issues or hypotheses for the study, let alone
a worked out model of good practice in the management of teachers.
Indeed they were well into the six month formative period of the study
before they changed the title from teaching costs to one incorporating the
larger and more action oriented concept of management.

Throughout, the study was exploratory. The team used existing research but its impact on the study was slight. The more influential factors were team discussion and argument and collective knowledge of practice in the field. Within the first few months they undertook a trawl of all LEAs in the country to gather information about existing practice and policy in the management of teacher deployment in the current context of falling rolls. But the process of establishing their methodology and conceptualising the project was iterative. Some concepts were not fully clarified until they began the work of writing the report. And throughout, the task was to conceptualise for action as well as analysis. They were moving towards commitment as well as clarification.

The trawl for information was used along with personal knowledge of the field to identify a sample of authorities in which they would conduct fieldwork. The final selection of 12 was determined partly by choice and partly by where it was politically possible to go. They aimed for a mix of LEAs on the dimensions of size, type of authority, geographical location, political control, good and bad practice and the existence of innovative schemes.

The fieldwork itself was based on a detailed aide-memoire. The work in each authority was carried out by pairs of members of the team, although the pairings were not the same throughout. Officers in the Education department, members of education committees and head teachers of schools were interviewed. The purpose was to get further information, to test some developing ideas and hypotheses and to make others more explicit and clear.

The approach was broadly that of the case study. The aim was not so much to generalise from the findings, either statistically or analytically. It was to identify conditions affecting teacher allocation that could be changed, and approaches to the task of managing teaching resources that could solve problems. The proposals in the report had to be feasible and convertible into effective action by authorities with a range of educational philosophies. They were to go beyond the identification of alternative perceptions or even models. They had to make choices about what would be most effective. They also had to assure themselves that their methods afforded a good enough spread of contexts and systems to make their ideas recognisable and credible to the great majority of education departments.

Thus within the team members had to make their own ideas more explicit and expose them to people with different perspectives and critical minds. The Audit Commission staff's background and practice were based on quantification and empiricism. Ideas would have ultimately to be accommodated within those frames, even if specific values of economy or efficiency might not be strongly emphasised. Educationalists, even if they were managers and thus used to building bridges between professionals and others, were used to a world in which objectives and values were often expressed in more diffuse and ambiguous language.

The team operated according to well publicised rules about the boundaries of their work. They were to concern themselves with management, not professional practice or policy. And as one team member pointed out, the educational context was a particularly difficult one for the Commission. The educational world is sensitive to encroachment; it is also articulate and so likely, at least at the time of the study, to be adept at repelling boarders.

The majority of team members found this a problem and of these some felt the distinction to be unreal in practice. Making judgements about the management of teacher resources inevitably entailed educational judgements. The presentation of facts could not be free of educational values. (An example might be the report's tables showing different percentages of teacher time spent in direct contact with pupils. Some would argue that the selection of such an indicator as significant was in itself a judgement about what affected pupils' educational experience). One team member felt that the educationalists on the team were there partly to put down the markers for the education - management boundary, but it was not always possible.

But the team certainly felt bound by 'the rules of the game' and they did prevent them from making their own analysis of some issues. For example, they were confined to quoting HMI on class sizes and although they were critical of the statement by HMI on the extent of mismatch between teacher qualification and educational need, they could only set a survey of headteachers' views against it. They also would have liked to address the issue of teacher effectiveness. They had to find measures that could be asserted by non-educationalists.

However, two members of the team found that in practice the boundary issue was less difficult than they had expected. One said that their concern was with the process of management and not with what went into the curriculum.

Whatever the views of the team, the very fact that they aimed not simply to reduce waste and cut costs meant that the boundaries assumed in the rules were more difficult to determine, let alone maintain. If they were also to address best use of resources and effectiveness, they would find it hard to avoid entering educational territory. They were concerned with the implications of teacher deployment for the range and choice of curricula and they certainly referred to curriculum disadvantage in their report.

### Emerging Concepts and Evaluative Criteria

The key problem that the team addressed was how to allocate the right number of teachers at the right time in order to maintain a satisfactory curriculum. The team agreed from the first that the Pupil-Teacher Ratio (PTR) was an inadequate tool. They identified the practice followed in a few authorities of Curriculum Led Staffing (CLS) as more promising: it related teacher numbers to what teachers did. In the course of their work, they modified this, partly through their own thinking and partly drawing on work done by the Secondary Heads Association (SHA). The result, Activity Led Staffing (ALS), was a central concept in their final report.

Other tools of management which team members identified as robust in the course of their work were teacher redeployment, effective pupil forecasting, good in-service training. Throughout they were seeking feasible solutions.

As far as measures of efficiency were concerned, they were looking for positive and well-informed approaches to ensuring schools had the teachers they considered they needed. But they did not identify any absolute measures. For example, a team member pointed out that a school could have a perfect match between pupils and staff and still be ineffi- cient. They were looking at cost criteria but from the first broadened this to value for money.

## The Report

### Constructing the Report

The team intended to write individual reports on each LEA in the fieldwork study. In the event they wrote reports on nine out of 12 and cleared them with the authorities concerned.

A first draft of the full report was written by the academic consultant and submitted to the DES and HMI for comment. During the next few months the team took the draft apart, hammered out agreement about recommendations, restructured it and rewrote it. They modified the language of the first draft; they thought it was too academic. Individuals took responsibilities for different sections.

Meanwhile the auditors' reports from the value for money studies at local level on the Non Teaching costs study were coming in and providing new evidence for some of the team's work. These may well have influenced the attitudes of the then Controller to this study.

The secretary to the team quickly followed up the second draft with a third, based on a different structure again. 'The order is important...you need to make it attractive and hardhitting, yet also coherent and logical.'

This draft was submitted for comment to local authority associations, selected local education chief officers, professional associations and the TUC. They received it at the same time as the Controller and three members of the Commission.

The Controller made substantial criticisms of the draft and, when it was submitted a few months later to the full Commission, he broke with custom and appended a note containing critique and recommended changes.

Team members thought that the Controller's intervention made a major difference to the nature and substance of the final report. In the words of one, the original was concerned with 'sound management issues and recommendations - all good stuff which would have been welcome in the system.' Most members of the team perceived the Controller as wanting the report to have more impact and visibility. He injected his own style into it and also introduced large strategic issues. In particular, he stressed that teaching costs must be viewed in the context of falling rolls and the urgent need for school reorganisation, and he underlined the urgency of the problem. He also put greater emphasis on the problems created by central government policies for the management of teaching resources.

The result was that the report did achieve a higher profile than it might otherwise have done. In doing so, it may have obscured some of the local managerial issues. But it was felt perhaps to be more relevant 'if you were trying to influence elected members' (Interview with team member).

It also changed the empirical base of the report, which in its final form strongly continued the theme of the earlier study of non-teaching costs. It introduced material which had not been researched by the team and relied on, in one case, a recently published book and some new analyses of other data. It included some views with which the team disagreed.

The Commission was in consequence subject to some criticism that the report on which it had consulted was substantially different from the final version.

The Commission itself considered the draft report along with the Controller's recommendations at a meeting early in 1985. One of the members who had received an advance copy was also critical of it. He saw it as expansionist and insufficiently concerned with management.

It was not then surprising that the Commission asked for a rewrite of the report from the team. They made particular points about delegated management, underlining that it should be a long term plan that needed careful preparation. It would require attention to the selection of head teachers and changes in the local authority management framework for schools. LEAs should draw on the experience of Solihull and Cambridgeshire. LEAs should retain control of Activity Led Staffing (ALS); otherwise the educationalists might use the formula to produce larger than warranted workforces. They also thought a clear distinction in local management should be drawn between the roles of heads and governors. They did not want governors to have too much power.

The Commission had some ideas about property management. But they did not favour earmarking receipts from the sale of schools for the use of the education service alone.

These points had to be taken on board, together with the reorientation of the report by the Controller. But by this time the team had disbanded. The two permanent members of the Special Studies Directorate did the remaining work, after going through what had to be done with the Controller. The report was finally published three months after the Commission had given its views on the third draft, that is in May, 1986.

In the event, therefore, the Commission members and the top executive retained control of the output but potential for conflict was inherent in the procedures as described. The special studies team had a long discretionary rein. They were left to convert the specification into an operational document, in this case in a policy environment which was rapidly shifting, to formulate the key concepts and instruments, and provide the empirical base, without reference back to the top until the document was already out for consultation with the policy field.

In this instance there was a new complication. The team had incorporated the perspective of the professionals into their work more decisively than in previous studies. Some of the Commission's comments might be seen as an attempt to redress the balance towards the managerial perspective.

Since that time, procedures have changed to ensure greater integration of the views of the directorate and the Commission members in special studies. Formal three monthly reviews of progress include the special studies director and sometimes the Controller, as well as influential representatives from the field. Each special study has a Commission panel with three or four members. They see the first draft of reports and then a revised version before reports are submitted to a full Commission meeting.

There was never any doubt that ultimately the report was the Commission's: team members were free to dissent from it in public, if they wished. On this occasion, some did. Also, the educationists within the team felt that the summary which went out with the report obscured the useful instrumental material in it and was essentially a public relations document. They thought this a serious problem, because authorities each received only two copies of the full report. The ideas might therefore remain unread by some key people. Two of them offered to write a more executive summary and this was published by the Industrial Society under the Audit Commission colours.

## *What the Report Said*

The report was firmly presented as having a key contribution to make in the context of falling rolls and the urgent need to release the resources being used to sustain too many schools and too much plant. It was divided into three main parts.

The first sought to demonstrate how LEAs could better manage teaching resources within the existing legislative constraints. The arguments here focused on both the strategic level (school reorganisation) and the operational level: ALS as an instrument of teacher allocation superior to either Pupil Teacher Ratio (PTR) or Curriculum Led Staffing (CLS); the place of redeployment, the use of part time teachers, early retirement and voluntary severance schemes in more efficient teacher allocation; the need to increase in-service training to enable teachers to adjust to changing demands. There was also a substantial section on delegating responsibility to local level and its implications for the way in which heads were selected and trained for their jobs.

The second part outlined more fundamental changes thought to be required in the system: in central government controls of local authority expenditure; in the machinery for negotiating teachers pay and conditions. The abolition of Burnham and the integration of pay with conditions in new machinery were advocated. There should be regular performance assessment of teachers and ways should be found to provide more flexibility at local level so that teachers could be recruited to the shortage subjects and adequate cover arrangements made for teaching staff.

Finally the report outlined in more detail the next steps that should be taken by both central government and LEAs.

*Verdicts on the Report from the Policy Community*

Despite the impression given by the education press at the time of publication, the reactions of those interviewed for this study from the policy community were broadly favourable. Apart from the representatives of the most senior local authority education administrators, most people thought the main thrust of the report to be based on sound analysis and to contain useful advice.

Most respondents thought the report a relatively successful attempt to describe and disseminate good practice in the management of teaching resources. Although a senior administrator thought the report was often 'teaching grandmothers to suck eggs', and a head teacher representative thought the report was based on a limited concept of educational management, almost all respondents thought it contained useful management tools.

Some respondents felt that it was not a coherent whole and that the management message was partially obscured by the enjoinders on school reorganisation and closures. And although some acknowledged that schools had to be closed, the general view was that the report oversimplified the problems, underestimated the political complexities of the issue and failed to acknowledge the implications for longer term need and for existing communities of taking out schools. Respondents felt that the Commission had moved into the policy area here and although they did not necessarily object to that, they thought that the policy analysis was weak by comparison with the management analysis. And while some support was expressed for the report's proposals for change in central government's role and powers on closure, they were not thought to have had any impact.

The weight of opinion among the respondents was in favour of the advice on ALS; it included head teacher representatives, and others concerned with management. A senior LEA administrator described that part of the report as 'manna from heaven' for LEAs and valuable support for the kind of model he himself was seeking to introduce in his own authority. A colleague, however, was less enthusiastic: the Audit Commission was promulgating as new initiatives that were already taking place in the field. Local Authority Associations were also less enthusiastic.

Other management advice in the report was less generally commented on. There was some support for greater delegation of management to heads, although some doubted their readiness to take this on. One person felt that advocacy of local management was in conflict with the support for greater control by local authorities of the system as a whole and particularly of school closure.

There was little comment on teacher redeployment or the abolition of 'ring fencing' in appointments or teacher appraisal. While there was some support for appraisal, there was little evidence of any willingness to move towards performance related pay.

Only one respondent objected to the proposals to abolish the Burnham Committee and there was some feeling that it was necessary to introduce more flexibility into pay and conditions negotiations.

### *Values Underlying the Report*

Respondents from the policy community were almost unanimous in thinking that efficiency was the central value underlying the report. Some mentioned cost efficiency; others thought the concept broader than that. They talked about the 'best use of resources' or, in one case, 'systems efficiency'. Only two people saw it as narrowly based on economy.

A number of people were concerned about undue emphasis on efficiency at the expense of effectiveness. And one representative was also concerned about the neglect of equity in the current evaluative frameworks. But none thought that effectiveness of education provision could be appropriately tackled by the Audit Commission; that was beyond the bounds of their competence.

A representative from the local authorities thought the report reinforced the value of local as against centralised management. His view that the trends in local authority management were also largely supported was not shared by others. This could, however, be partly explained by the particular policies of his own authority which were more evidently in tune with the thrust of the report than was widely the case.

A union representative was pleased that the commission was prepared to ask awkward questions and to deal in plain speaking, implying that criticism of local authority management was welcomed.

### *Impacts of the National Report*

The report was said to have been largely welcomed by the bodies represented by the respondents to the study, although some were worried about how it was interpreted in much of the press: as a stick beating the LEAs.

However, it was generally felt that the impact of the report was much reduced, if not nullified, by the government's radical new proposals later to be incorporated in the Education Reform Act,1988. 'The parameters of the system changed'. A representative of head teachers thought that while the report might have resulted in rational reductions of school places, educational change was now to be effected through a market. The basic assumptions of the Audit Commission were thus, it was felt, undermined.

Curriculum Led Staffing and its derivative, Activity Led Staffing were central concepts in the report. But the Audit Commission's view was not always accepted and neither CLS nor ALS was encouraged in the DES Circular (7/88) which gave guidance on the implementation of the Education Reform Act, 1988.

Although the report was felt to contain some useful criticism of central government, there was no discernible response to the critique. The Commission's early public support for a form of local management in schools was recognised but thought to have been absorbed in more radical reforms. Only one person thought the report might have been the impetus behind the abolition of the Burnham Committee on teachers' salaries. A respondent fairly close to central government thought the report was seen there as 'competent not exciting'. The report was in some respects useful to government. It could reinforce criticisms of the failure of LEAs to close schools or demonstrate effective management. On one issue government was thought to have acted in direct contradiction to the report. Far from contracting its powers, as recommended in the context of school closure, in a number of areas it expanded them.

The response to the report in LEAs was said to have been mixed. While it might have been an impetus for change in some, and speeded some changes already underway in others, for the most part it was overtaken by events. Some education officers did use it as ammunition against reluctant politicians in the context of proposals for school reorganisation and others quoted from it selectively to committees on particular issues of management such as staff allocation, to get support for changed approaches. They knew that the Audit Commission had credibility with their members. But evidence of impact was limited. The change in climate to which the Commission had contributed had now moved ahead of it.

It was noticeable that our respondents talked as much about the use made of the report by different interest groups and levels of government as its impact upon them. And groups representing quite disparate interests seemed to have found some political usage for it: central government, local authority officers, and even teacher unions critical of LEA management and/ or central government. But the dramatic emphasis given to the falling rolls issue by, for example, the reference to 1000 empty schools, fell victim to government's changed thinking about solutions once the immediate impact died away, as did most other parts of the report.

## The Local Audits

### The Audit Guide

Once a national report is completed there is a second task to be carried out by the Audit Commission staff on a Special Studies Team: the production of an *Audit Guide*. The guide is the tool with which the auditors for each local authority are expected to exploit the special study to examine and help enhance economy, efficiency and effectiveness in areas of activity covered by the national study and thought to be amenable to local authority action.

The aim of writing the guide was said by one member of this special studies team to be 'to pick up useful and appropriate issues and construct a logical framework' within which they could be reviewed. The task of producing it required considerable rigour and discipline and was quite distinct from carrying out the study. This guide was thought by one of its authors to present a new challenge because the issues which it required auditors to address bordered on professional expertise and local educational policy.

The authors assumed that its users knew how to carry out an audit but had little knowledge about the educational management issues. The document was divided into a number of sections, most of which provided questions auditors could ask to elicit the required information and establish a basis for assessing how well the authority was managing its provision of schools and its teaching resources. It gave detailed technical advice about, for example, Curriculum Led Staffing (CLS) and Activity Led Staffing (ALS) models, rules for curriculum construction and the relationship between school size and teacher resource allocation.

But it went beyond introducing auditors to the specialist information relevant to the exercise. It was a handbook on how to approach an exercise involving some elements of consultancy. It assumed that at least some of its users would be inexperienced in this kind of activity, although it also counselled that senior and experienced staff should play a significant role in the work. It offered guidance on planning the exercise and identified issues to be included in the report. It pointed out the pitfalls of working on the boundaries of professional and political territory. 'The auditor will need to tread warily so as to make constructive statements on management while at the same time avoiding accusations that he or she is interfering with policy or professional judgements about educational quality.' It also warned that there were no reliable national norms against which to measure good practice in resource allocation.

The guide was selective in the issues to be taken up from the national report. The main thrust of the exercise was to ensure that authorities had rational systems for the allocation of teachers to schools, that they had continued to address the need to reorganise and reduce provision of schools, as recommended in the 1984 Non-Teaching Costs study, and that they were making effective use of methods of reducing and redeploying their teachers. A substantial part of the guide was devoted to justifying and explaining ALS as the recommended method of setting teacher establishments. The inefficiency of small schools was a second major theme. Neither delegated management nor teacher appraisal was mentioned.

The local auditors reported that they used the *Audit Guide* selectively. One commented that it was useful for his team who were inexperienced. He also summarised it and sent the summary to the authority to establish with them the methods and objectives of the exercise. However, another said that he had to do quite a lot of work on it before his team could use it effectively. He tried to develop a number of tools by which to measure educational effectiveness of curriculum organisation in order to assess the implications of the authority's disposition of schools and their allocation of teachers. But he said that almost without exception they were thought to be fatally flawed by the authority's educational advisers and had to be abandoned. He was highly conscious of the need to respect professional boundaries but this had not deterred him from trying to establish some criteria of effectiveness.

The same auditor felt that the guide itself had drawn the auditors very near, if not over, the boundary of management and policy in the computer model they offered them for assessing local reorganisation plans for schools. In any case he thought the model too complicated and they managed what assessment they considered to be feasible without it. Another criticism, acknowledged in the guide, was that it did not take account of the variety of secondary school organisation.

A more general comment on the *Audit Guides* was that they were well tested and their credibility with the education profession was high because they were based on advice from experts from the field. This one marked a departure from earlier practice in that it moved away from authority profiles and was more concerned to provide a framework in which authorities could test their management of resources against their own objectives.

The Audit Commission mounted two courses on the guide before the inception of the local audits: one for auditors, effectively on CLS and ALS, which those who commented found useful. The other was for officers from the LEAs designated as liaison officers for the study. Liaison officers are usually third tier officers, and some auditors considered the course to have been pitched at too elementary a level for them. 'It was a basic instruction course on CLS.'

## The Auditors

All the auditors were accountants, trained and experienced in public sector work. The private firm had had a substantial history of public sector work extending from before 1983 and was expanding this side of its operations. It was now doing its own training for CIPFA qualification. It employed CIPFA trained staff with experience in local government and the NHS. The managers of audits usually had this kind of background. But they also employed people on Audit Commission work with either general management consultancy training and experience or with specialist knowledge in the sector of work being investigated, for example educational finance, local government personnel work and engineering.

Of the two auditors from this firm who participated in our study, one identified himself clearly as an accountant, the other as a management consultant. But this person had initially trained as an accountant and his kind of career development was seen in the firm as desirable. They were moving away from a clear separation of the two kinds of expertise.

The two members of the District Audit Service noted similar trends. Staff with MBAs were being recruited and they found themselves needing to develop personal skills of collaboration and negotiation now, whereas before they had simply needed auditing expertise and a thorough understanding of local government.

None of those interviewed had experience of education and all were wary of overstepping the professional boundary, an attitude which clearly conveyed itself to the education staff with whom they worked on this exercise. As managers of the audits, for the most part they impressed the educationalists with their general understanding of the field, their ability to work with heads of schools and the willingness of themselves and their junior staff to listen and learn.

Local authority staff did, however, perceive their lack of professional educational knowledge as having disadvantages. In one of the authorities the auditors had put a lot of time and thought into developing measures of effectiveness which they could not sustain in the face of professional critique. And their consciousness of their lack of knowledge, while appreciated, was thought to blunt the critical edge of their reports. And although authority staff thought auditors' collaborative styles were appropriate, one commented that their relative lack of knowledge meant that they had no choice but to be collaborative. In one case they gave managerial advice the following of which was thought by the authority staff to have had serious consequences for the educational opportunities offered to children.

### Approaches to the Audit

The organisation of the audits was in part a function of the size of the authority. In the London borough most of the work was undertaken by one auditor with good experience of the authority working to a senior member of the service. In the shire county a senior manager had a team of three working with him, one of whom was fully qualified and of relatively senior status. In the metropolitan borough, the team was managed by a highly experienced and skilled person who spent between 35 and 40 days on the project but it contained a large group of junior staff.

The approaches to the exercise were, to some extent, a matter of personal style but they were also responsive to the differing contexts. All four described their approach as collaborative. The audits in the shire county and the metropolitan district were structured round the audit guide and the terms of reference sent to the authority taken direct from that. By contrast, the London borough exercise was organised round the unique strategy that the authority had evolved to cope with the problem of falling rolls.

### The Local Authority Contexts

In each of the authorities both officers and members had long been aware of the need for school closure and rationalisation to meet the problem of falling rolls. The largest had undertaken a major exercise to reduce places in the early 1980s, before the non-teaching costs study, but by 1986 still found itself with a surplus of over 6000 places according to DES targets. In two of the authorities the viability of small schools was an issue, in one case because of the traditional investment in small rural schools and in the other, because the population was shifting as well as declining, some relatively new schools had drastically reduced numbers of forms of entry. The political sensitivity of school closure had been heightened by the judicial reviews on consultation and in each of the authorities politicians had been reluctant to grasp the nettle. Any closure exercises tended to be strongly influenced by the electoral timetable.

Each of the authorities had a central unit for evaluation, although with different emphases, and two of the departments had their own capacity for research, planning and evaluation. The Education Department as a high spender was under pressure in all the authorities, but most evidently in the metropolitan district. It was underresourced according to the Grant Related Expenditure Assessment (GREA) formula but the competing demands on the budget were intense and the political environment was marked by conflict within as well as between parties. It was thus not surprising that the officer-member relationship was also particularly sensitive and that relationships with the teacher unions were difficult.

One of the authorities whose reputation had been enhanced by success in the national league tables of examination achievement (Gray and Jesson, 1987) decided on a novel approach to the problem of falling rolls at about the time of the publication of *Towards Better Management of Secondary Education*. Instead of closing an additional school, as had been thought necessary at the time of the non-teaching costs study, it adopted an aggressive marketing strategy to attract children from across its boundaries and out of the private sector.

While the Audit Commission had identified ALS or CLS as the key to managing teaching resources, the view from the authorities was slightly different. One of them was operating a fairly successful CLS model and was more concerned about teacher redeployment. Another was also using a CLS model. It was encountering some problems but there were other far more intractable issues to resolve on teacher allocation, such as the timing of the annual setting of staff establishments, redeployment, ring fencing and the mismatch of resources to needs. The third had tried a CLS based system but abandoned it in the face of opposition from the heads and had set up a working party to explore a modified form.

## Scope and Objectives

The auditors were all aware of the political constraints upon change in their authorities. They took seriously the requirement to provide a rigorous and independent review of the management of teaching resources in secondary education, but they saw the overriding objective as to achieve change. According to one, the objective was to 'carry out the exercise and write the report in such a way as to cause maximum impact'. Another judged that there was more likely to be political support for movement in the right direction if he tempered criticism. In the authority with the expansionist strategy, the auditors saw their task as to provide an independent test of it but to support the authority in their objectives if they could do so with integrity. The general approach of all the auditors was to support officers in their endeavours to implement more efficient management; to lend them weight in any attempts to assert rationality in the face of the pressures in the system for compromise and delay. They saw themselves as collaborative change agents, although they were clear that their tasks were those of analysis and recommendation. Responsibility for implementation lay with the authorities.

Education department officers interviewed tended to see the Audit Commission exercise as something they could use to support their own strategies or to highlight issues they thought to be high priority. In one authority a newly appointed Chief Education Officer decided to appoint himself as liaison officer to maximise impact. There had been a shift of emphasis from falling rolls to questions about the educational viability of small schools of which there were many in the authority. Plans for school reorganisation in the authority had to take this into account. He wanted to tackle inertia on some issues such as teacher redeployment and persistent overestimation of pupil numbers in some schools. He saw the exercise as a formative evaluation, although the auditors had the right to make summative judgements at the conclusion of the work. Officers in another authority saw this special study audit as an opportunity to get movement on some longstanding and, in their view, predominantly political obstacles to better management. Some feared that the Audit Commission could only propose managerial solutions to these essentially political problems but they could open them up and thus exert pressure for them to be tackled.

Heads of vulnerable schools tended to see the exercise as a threat and teacher unions thought it was going to be predominantly economy and efficiency led. But some heads did see the Commission as concerned with educational impact, even if their schools were vulnerable.

## Methods

The exercise had a clear methodological framework provided by the *Audit Guide* and had to be completed within a specified time. The Audit Commission course on the Guide for auditors took place in November,1986 and that for authority liaison officers in January,1987. The local audits were expected to be completed in time for the 1987-88 management letter to authorities. In the three authorities in our study the reports were completed by October,1987, although one was revised in December and in another case the presentation was delayed until April,1988.

In the two authorities where the audit was carried out by a private firm, a detailed account of the methodology based on the audit guide was sent to the authorities in advance, including the information that would be required from the department. The DA working in the third authority did not appear to have done that. But that may have been because of the unorthodox nature of the authority's approach and the decision to adjust the audit accordingly.

One auditor provided a clear outline of his timetable. The collection and analysis of the information were carried out in the first two months. From there the team could structure and plan the rest of the work. They selected a sample of schools on which to base their fieldwork and conducted a series of interviews with head teachers. They produced a first draft of the report for discussion with the CEO and the relevant Assistant Director and a draft for the Chief Executive and the Treasurer was ready in July.

They made a number of corrections most of which were matters of emphasis and were accepted by the auditors. The final draft was completed in October 1987 in time for submission to the authority's Finance and Management sub-committee that month. The main recommendations of the report were included in the management letter. In the course of the exercise the auditors also, at the request of the Chief Education Officer (CEO), made a presentation at a regular departmental seminar. The aim was to maximise the impact of the exercise in the department, particularly on staff who had been slow to recognise the need for reorganisation and more rigorous management.

All the auditors started their work by meeting the CEO and other senior officers in the department. This was advised by the Audit Guide but was in keeping with the collaborative approach adopted by them all.

The *Audit Guide* gave clear and detailed guidance on the information to be collected, and the data requested were perceived as relevant in the authorities. This part of the exercise was obviously important for the auditors not only as a basis for their own analysis but also in helping them to assess the managerial capacity of the authorities. In one case the inadequacies of the information technology available to the department were underlined. In another weaknesses in pupil forecasting were highlighted.

The rationale for selecting the sample of schools to be visited was left to the auditors. They selected a mix of large and small schools and high and low recruiting schools; in one authority a special study was made of the schools in one area with a particularly urgent need for reorganisation. In two of the three authorities the sample was larger than recommended by the *Guide*.

Probably the central features of the methods developed by the Commission for its special studies were the identification of well defined management issues, the development of tools of performance measurement and analysis and the selection of formulae within which problems could be addressed in all sorts of authorities. The criticisms most commonly levelled against the Commission in interviews conducted in local authorities were directed at the limitations of this across the board, formulaic, approach. Sometimes criticisms were directed at the execution of the method. Auditors, perhaps particularly those from the private sector, were thought to rely too heavily on young and inexperienced staff who had been well briefed but had little understanding of the context in which they found themselves.

But it was also thought that the method was too rigid to address the particular problems confronting authorities; it was too precisely focused. Some respondents would have preferred the Commission to function more like consultants, formulating their brief in conjunction with individual authorities. Auditors had no answers to the implementation problems faced by many authorities.

This touched on a key characteristic of the Commission's mandate: that it was concerned with management and must not trespass on policy issues. Moreover, it had a limited concept of management. Auditors were given no appropriate model of needs assessment, planning, evaluation and the links between them, particularly how these might work in a political environment. According to some they inevitably produced narrow managerial solutions to political problems. Underlying the complaint was a critique of the conceptualisation of public services as businesses and the authority of officers as that of managers. It raised the question whether the Audit Commission could be concerned with public organisational development or with only limited aspects of organisational analysis. Officers pointed to the limits imposed by politicians' assessments of what they could do without losing their power, by the relative autonomy of heads and/or by the pressure exerted by teacher unions. Some felt their room for manoeuvre further restricted by the Education Reform Act, in particular the opting out clause.

In fact one of the authorities in our study demonstrated that auditors could be persuaded to adapt to particular circumstances. The audit carried out in the London borough was predominantly concerned with their preferred solution to school reorganisation, although the auditors also analysed and made proposals on teacher allocation.

Officers also almost universally denied that the Audit Commission had any technical capacity that they themselves did not possess or have available, although some said they lacked the necessary information technology. Some also said that they did not have the time to do what was done in local audits.

Undoubtedly school closures did present huge political problems and there was evidence in all three of the authorities in this study of members procrastinating or drawing back from agreed solutions. There was also evidence of industrial relations problems, collective resistance to change by head teachers, together with failures to grip problems such as persistent over estimates of pupil numbers, inadequate supply teaching systems and redeployment schemes that effectively subverted any forward planning of the teaching force. These may not be wholly management problems but neither are they wholly political.

*The Reports*

We examined the final reports on the three authorities against the *Audit Guide* and against the critique made in interviews of auditors' methods and outputs.

The *Audit Guide*, while drawing back from proposing a tightly prescriptive 'model' report, identified three key components: reference back to the Non-Teaching Costs audit of 1984-85, linking it, where appropriate, with the current exercise; school reorganisation, including the action taken in the authority and an analysis of what might be achieved by existing plans or new action; next steps, indicating that the auditors would check on future progress.

All three reports reflected major concern with the need for school reorganisation, the problems posed for equitable and effective teacher allocation by small schools, the importance of rational methods of setting and implementing teacher establishments and the advantages of CLS and ALS. Two discussed in some detail the possible curriculum deprivation which might result from failure to confront these issues and commented on the accuracy of forecasts of pupil numbers.

All three picked up from the *Audit Guide* what appeared to be definitive normative statements on size of schools and sixth forms from the DES (1985). They acknowledged that such norms could not be applied without reference to other constraints and local circumstances. But their analyses were clearly influenced by the norms.

The reports, particularly those on the metropolitan district and the shire county, were based on substantial quantitative analyses, many, though not all, derived from the *Audit Guide*.

However, the reports differed considerably from each other in length, presentation and content. It is difficult to make more than tentative comparisons between the reports of the private firm and that of the District Audit service since the local circumstances were so different. The DA service had to depart radically from the *Audit Guide* to respond to the authority's policy. The private firm reports were more crisply presented and their recommendations were summarised with quantified savings opportunities attached to them together with a timetable for action.

The reports undoubtedly reflected the differing circumstances and preoccupations of the education departments. They also varied widely on the number of issues tackled; none tried to cover all the issues identified in the *Audit Guide*. The report which dealt with the largest number of subjects demonstrated the linkages between them and the main themes of school reorganisation and the allocation of teacher resources. The claim that auditors were strongly influenced in their approach by the incentive to identify the maximum number of opportunities for cost savings was weakly substantiated.

Two reports discussed school reorganisation in some detail; in one case the authority's expansionist strategy, agreed in principle by officers and members, was analysed and four questions identified to which, in the auditor's opinion, the authority must provide satisfactory answers if the strategy was to succeed. The other report predicted the savings that would be achieved if a particular form of reorganisation of one area were implemented.

The third report noted that the department had developed, but not yet published, major reorganisation plans and reinforced the urgency of rapid action on these. Their importance was linked with the analysis in other parts of the report of how small schools affected the use of staff resources and the range of school curricula.

All the reports reflected issues identified by officers as key preoccupations. Often they could be read as providing independent evidence, frequently quantitative, of problems causing officers anxiety or external support for strategies developed by officers. But they also identified failures of managerial monitoring and, at least in one case, proposed changes to staffing models against the judgement of officers.

One report made it possible to discern how the education department and many of the schools coped with an underresourced education system. The department operated a CLS model judged by the auditors to be simplistic. The report showed that it discriminated against small schools more powerfully than the department realised. But small schools now constituted a majority of the authority's provision and nothing had been done to counteract this development for five years. The response of the schools had been consistently to overestimate pupil numbers, so mitigating the worst effects of the model. The department had done little to stop them in a context where political obstacles to mounting any major reorganisation were high.

Thus the responses of the department and the schools to a serious problem had been implicit and incrementalist. The auditors, while recognising the problems facing the authority, cautiously advocated explicit and rationally planned strategies. They were introduced into a volatile political environment but one in which new solutions would have to be sought, if the local authority was to continue to have credibility. In such circumstances there is always the risk that partially implemented rational solutions backfire and yet wholesale recourse to linear rational models are even more unlikely to succeed. It may be therefore that entirely different models, perhaps based on systemic or microeconomic theory would be more appropriate.

## *Formal Authority and the Local Studies*

The auditors were generally thought to adopt a collaborative approach but to be clear about boundaries of responsibility. They proposed; the local authorities disposed. Reports did not necessarily go to committees. It depended on their salience as perceived in the authority. In only one of the authorities in this case did the report go to a committee, the finance and management sub-committee, but they were thought by officers not to be particularly interested. In the other authorities the report was brought to the attention of the Chairman of the Education Committee.

However, in all three the study and its main recommendations were incorporated in the auditors' management letter to the authority. In two cases the auditors commented favourably on the efforts of the authority on the main issues. In the third, reference to the study was relatively brief. The letter noted the authority's slow progress in improving financial management and information systems and stressed their importance. While recording that much had already been achieved in addressing falling rolls and that there was now a new initiative, it emphasised that further rationalisation of secondary schools was urgent. The point was made but in a relatively low key.

An officer in this authority doubted the value of the management letter for exerting pressure on the council to act on special studies. In his view, such issues tended to get swamped by political conflict about matters nearer to fiscal probity. This particular letter included a comment about a 'perceived trend towards increasing non-compliance with ... [the authority's]... own Financial Rules and Regulations'.

## Impacts and Implementation in the Local Authorities.

Officers in the Education Departments described the reports as broadly confirmatory of their own thinking and providing support for what they wanted to achieve.

They tended to play down any criticisms or to demonstrate that the auditors were wrong in judgements or proposals with which officers disagreed. Criticisms that bordered on educational judgements were described as crude applications of norms or ideas about, eg, curriculum disadvantage; if they were felt to be justified, the problem was attributed to shortage of resources.

But in one authority senior officers conceded that the report had highlighted more sharply than they had themselves the problem of teacher establishments in small schools. Slightly more junior staff in another authority conceded that a report's criticisms on three important aspects of the department's work had been telling.

Opinions in the departments about CLS and ALS were broadly favourable, although none of the officers thought that the Audit Commission had provided them with new thinking on approaches to staffing models. All the authorities had tried some form of CLS, although one had abandoned it, at least for the time being. Opinions about such models among teachers were divided. Two thought they did not take account of developments in educational thinking about integrated teaching. But the weight of opinion was in favour of them.

In one authority, an officer from outside the education department was more forthrightly complimentary about the Audit Commission exercise. He thought it had picked up a key issue in the need for school reorganisation to tackle falling rolls, confronted the inertia of officers and 'given the politicians backbone'.

Both officers and politicians considered that the credibility of the Audit Commission as an external, impartial body, whose work was based on sound management principles and well-researched and targeted projects was an important political support. Their work contained, for the most part, sound technical analysis and advice, within the constraints of their mandate and expertise, but its importance to them was that it could be used: by officers negotiating with schools; in intra-authority negotiations on resources; in discussions with politicians; and by politicians in their turn, who could argue that their unpopular decisions on such matters as school closures and teacher reductions were based on recommendations of an authoritative external body.

In only one of the three authorities in this study had there been a formal follow up by the auditors one year on. There the follow up report showed progress on all the main recommendations made and achievement of three concerned with the planning and execution of teacher allocations. Significant action had been taken on school reorganisation and substantial reviews made of the number of small schools in the authority and their impact on curriculum development.

In this authority a major organisational review had been carried out in collaboration with the auditors and a medium term strategy agreed with them. The audit on secondary education had the active support of the recently appointed CEO who acted as liaison officer and was committed to a rationally planned approach to school reorganisation and the allocation of staffing resources. While it could not be claimed that the study caused a major change, it did sharpen analysis and therefore consciousness of problems, and was part of a longer term strengthening of rational organisation in the authority. There had been conflict between the authority and the auditors on issues other than education; members had resisted the auditors on some strategic issues and the political environment was unstable. But members had given sufficient support to plans that included school closures and rationalisation for progress to be made.

In the London borough, the auditors had allowed the exercise to be led by the authority's strategy for recruitment to schools. The introduction of CLS was receiving attention in the department but there was no evidence that the study had had any impact on progress. CLS did not have the priority accorded the strategic exercise. But overall the policy environment here, while unstable due to uncertainty of political control, was one in which members and officers were jointly committed to rational planning and the enhancement of efficiency and economy.

The third authority, the metropolitan district, provided a contrast. The publication of the auditors' report was delayed until after the local elections in May 1988. School reorganisation was a highly sensitive issue and the authority was coming forward with its own plan. There was political reluctance to allow it to become part of the election campaigns.

In a political environment dogged by resource problems, inadequate information technology to provide a strong information base, and political conflict and volatility, officers tended to regard the Commission as one of a number of means they could use to further their ends. Auditors had to make difficult judgements about how to make an impact and strengthen rational approaches to planning and management. They had to hold the tension between the requirement to make a critical and independent judgement of the management of falling rolls and teaching resources, supporting the department in its attempts to enhance efficiency, and maintaining credibility with politicians.

Following auditors' criticism of the inadequate information base and technological resources available to the department, the department was allocated improved computing facilities. This meant that it could improve its organisation of supply teaching, also criticised in the report. Resources were also released to increase the numbers of supply teachers. That was as much to do with the impact of industrial action by teachers and negotiations with teacher unions, according to one member of staff, but the auditors' report was at least a significant contributing factor.

Not all the auditors' proposals for change were as well received. Suggestions about changing the timing of the annual teacher establishment setting exercise were thought to be unrealistic. The timing was locked into a historic agreement with the selective schools, which was politically impossible to break. One officer thought it important, nevertheless, that the issue was opened up - no one other than the auditors could have done this. Another thought their proposal constituted a clear example of an attempt to apply managerial solutions to a long ingrained political problem.

Another solution to the problem of matching teaching resources to children's needs was considered to be an over simple accountant's solution to a complicated educational management problem. When the department decided to impose it in a cash crisis both the officer responsible and heads of schools on whom the consequences fell thought it to be disastrous. It might, however, illustrate the difficulties of introducing piecemeal rationality into a situation held in check by incrementalist adjustments and compromises.

In this kind of environment it is unrealistic to expect an external agency, based on a relatively narrow technical foundation, with objectives derived from a different conceptualisation of public sector activities from those assumed by powerful insiders, to achieve directly attributable changes. Its influence is far more likely to be percolative and based on quasi-political judgement than the strength of its analysis or clarity of its prescriptions.

Respondents to the study suggested that the Education Reform Act, 1988 might fundamentally undermine the Audit Commission's base. It was established, they suggested, on assumptions that it could persuade local government to become more economic, efficient and effective by adopting a more rational framework and more rigorous application of management techniques, particularly of financial management. The recent act, however, was strongly influenced by the idea that clearer central government direction together with the operation of market forces would exert more effective control over educational resource allocation and management. In all three authorities, it was suggested that the solutions developed in this special study of the Audit Commission had been overtaken by new laws and were either no longer relevant or had been replaced by different priorities.

### Follow up Action by the Commission

The Commission demonstrated its own concern about the implementation of this study's recommendations. It made its own review of progress by LEAs in reducing school capacity (Audit Commission, 1988). It did not accept the suggestions of irrelevance made by the authorities, although it did acknowledge that the opting out clauses of the 1988 Act made the task of school reorganisation more difficult. It emphasised the obstacles that had to be overcome by authorities regardless of the Act, particularly those linked with the political sensitivities of the issue: the problem of incorporating clear commitment from the authority into the electoral timetable, the length of parental consultation processes and, worst in terms of time that might be lost, the uncertainty of central government response.

The Commission reviewed progress not for the period since its own work on falling school rolls began (1983) but since 1979. It showed that while the number of secondary schools had been reduced, the average school size had also fallen; that approximately 50 per cent of all secondary schools were below the size recommended in the DES's *Better Schools* (1985), while over 75 per cent of sixth forms fell short of DES guidance. Spare school capacity was still being reduced at a slower rate than the catchment population.

The review did not attempt any close analysis of the figures. In effect, it was not so much a progress report as a determined attempt to continue and reinforce the case for school closures.

Indeed, this review highlights the importance of argument in the Commission's conception and execution of Special Studies. It presented not only the financial, but also the educational costs of failure (lack of choice for pupils in small schools and lack of stimulation in small classes); it criticised authorities' tendency to emphasise the financial costs of reorganisation itself and their relative neglect of the opportunity costs of keeping unneeded schools open; and argued that the costs of inaction would increase under the new legislation.

The review drew attention to some of the weaknesses of the Audit Commission itself. As an independent body, it could not compel action by LEAs and the review illustrates the difficulty experienced by the Commission in producing significant change through its own audit processes. Its willingness to criticise central government might be effective in sustaining its reputation for independent comment. But even that risked easing the pressure on LEAs while having no real impact on a government which hoped that the workings of the market would solve the problems where the local authorities, and Commission itself, had failed.

The review was also interesting for the limitations it exposed in quantitatively expressed argument and apparently hard data. Apart from the arguments about which costs should be calculated, the Commission showed that some schools by altering definitions of school places had managed to present themselves as having after all no spare capacity, where on the Commission's calculation it was abundant. Its own presentation of the educational and financial advantages of rationalisation shows too that they were not as self evident as might be expected. The relationship between size of school, choice of curriculum and unit costs was shown to be generally but not necessarily valid.

## Conclusions

The case study illustrates well the dualities inherent in the special studies of the Audit Commission and the problems of clearly distinguishing between instrumental and political evaluation. Special studies were designed to evaluate and to change. They had national and local dimensions and addressed both strategic and operational issues. They deployed the skills of argument and persuasion as well as those of analysis. They were perceived by those evaluated as carrying the external authority of an independent body and as part of a policy system that could be used to achieve internal goals.

The debate within the Commission about the style and emphasis of the national report showed special studies as designed both to make a political impact, that is, to persuade local authority politicians to change their policies, and to offer technical evaluation and advice to improve local authority management.

The objectives of special studies were to improve local authorities' economy, efficiency and effectiveness. They were a key means of extending the *audit* or *regulatory* function of the Commission to include *change*.

In order to meet these objectives national studies were undertaken which identified target areas of activity, priority objectives within them and significant means of achieving them. The results of the national exercises were then translated into guidance designed to enable local auditors to apply them systematically in their own authorities. Implementation was worked out through a rigorously integrated method: national and local exercises were strongly linked.

Special studies teams constructed ideal models for aspects of management from the first part of the study. Local auditors evaluated local arrangements against those models with a view to inducing change within the models' parameters. The mode of operation at both national and local levels was one of prescription based on analysis and argument. In this case, the problem of falling rolls was analysed within a political framework of resource constraint requiring economy, efficiency and effectiveness. The Commission used vivid imagery and quantitative material to demonstrate both the seriousness of the problem and the logic of its own solution. The argument was continued from the earlier study of non-teaching costs (Audit Commission, 1984) and repeated in the Commission's follow up study.

At the local level, although auditors were told that the prime criterion against which they were assessing LEAs was whether they had installed a rational system of teacher resource allocation and planning, they were advised on the arguments through which to persuade authorities of the merits of CLS and ALS.

The national and local components of the studies had distinct functions, outputs and audiences. In the first, the Commission had strong political meta-objectives to be pursued in addition to its search for effective and acceptable problem solving strategies. It must present itself as a national body fulfilling a significant mandate and possessing the credentials to succeed. The national reports were one of the most important public faces of the Commission and they had multiple audiences: central government, local authority members, local authority chief officers, professional bodies, the media and the general public. Through them the Commission established and sustained its reputation for independence, particularly of central government, and its credibility with the policy communities whose fields it entered.

Special studies reports were intended to enhance local government accountability to the electorate. One of their purposes was to help reframe the expectations of the electorate, in tune with the extended audit function carried by the Commission, as well as to inform them about what was being done by their representatives. The electorate had to be convinced that economy, efficiency and effectiveness were priority objectives for local government, which could be reconciled and met. National reports must give direct, uncomplicated messages about strategic problems and solutions.

But the studies were also intended to give substantial technical guidance to local auditors and local authority officers. This team was not atypical in thinking it could provide robust, detailed answers to long term managerial problems. The audit guide emerged as an important technical document which in some cases was regarded by the Commission and local authority departments alike as definitive operational guidance on aspects of their work. But the rationale for clearly differentiating the audiences for national reports and audit guides had not by the time of this study been fully made or appreciated. The national report was long and contained detailed, quite technical material, as well as presenting a forceful argument on the strategic nature of the problems it addressed.

The audit guide's target audiences were more evident. It constituted a detailed protocol for the implementation of the national exercise. This suggested that auditors needed a collection of fairly finely honed analytic tools, from which they could choose those most appropriate to their particular area; and that the key to achieving change lay in more effective systems analysis.

The auditors carrying out the local studies certainly detected areas in which defective models of practice were being used, where reliable basic information was lacking and where predictions were faulty. But the reasons for these phenomena were more varied than simply lack of technical expertise. Many had more to do with the nature of the managerial environment constituted by local authority education departments. And the auditors tended to talk about achieving change in terms of collaboration and assessments of where to apply pressure, persuasion and support, in what combination and at what times.

The auditors too had to combine rational-technical approaches to managerial problems with a recognition of the complex structure of political, professional, managerial and industrial relations of which education departments and schools were a part.

In turn, the auditors were perceived by a number of officers as themselves constituting one component of a policy system that worked primarily by partisan mutual adjustment on the part of a range of actors.

This particular study represented a new direction for the Special Studies Directorate in one respect. The management of teacher resources was felt to come close to areas of professional expertise such as curriculum content. The team appointed for the study accordingly contained more than the usual proportion of outside members, partly to ensure that the Commission held the line between management and professional advice. But that line, too, was artificial. The team and local auditors thought they were staying within it. Inevitably they crossed it. But in trying not to, they were inhibited from broaching the issue of effectiveness, which they had hoped to do. Ironically, the second factor inhibiting them was the virtual absence of any criteria of effectiveness developed within the profession itself.

It was generally agreed by respondents to our study that the dominant value for the Special Studies team was, in the event, that of efficiency. However, two teams of auditors in our study quantified the savings they thought the LEA could make through school closures. It seems that although they too thought the study to be broader than a money saving exercise, the economic value framework was a powerful influence on their perceptions.

The study was structured by economy and efficiency and by the restricted concept of management they represented: an instrumental concept in which means and methods are developed in isolation from ends and substantive values and in which links between the analysis of resources and that of needs, policy options and policy processes are given less priority.

## The Broader Context

Our case study was a relatively early example of the Audit Commission special studies. The Commission was developing in a period of enormous political, economic and social change to which it was responding. On average, it carried out four special studies a year in the first years of its life and special studies constituted only one of its main activities. What can be learned from one such study is inevitably limited.

The Commission marked the first five years of its existence by publishing *The Way Ahead* in September, 1987. In it it claimed some achievements and declared itself satisfied that its broad strategy continued to be appropriate. It did, however, set out some new emphases for its work.

A key task that the Commission had set itself in 1983 (Annual Report, 1984) was to establish its independence and so gain the confidence of local government. Its claim that by 1987 it had succeeded in this was widely upheld in the local government world. Its willingness publicly to criticise central government was appreciated. It had also established a reputation for penetrating analysis and begun to make a practical impact on local authority management.

The changes it intended to make in its 'operating methods' included paying more attention to implementation of the potential savings identified by local auditors, giving more emphasis to analysis of the effectiveness and quality of services and adopting a 'positive and anticipatory approach' to assessing central government policies for local government (Audit Commission, Annual Report, 1988).

The case study showed that early in its history the Commission was inhibited from evaluating against the criterion of effectiveness partly by its respect for professional boundaries. It had, therefore, given priority in this exercise to gaining the confidence of professional educationalists and included three in the special studies team, an unusually high number of external specialists. A participant in the study thought the Commission needed to maintain the boundary between management and professional knowledge. Without it some of its auditors would have found themselves in territory they could not negotiate.

But as time went on, the Commission became far more confident. That special study itself exposed the poverty of professional thinking about criteria and measurements of effectiveness in the education field. And when the Commission undertook a special study of services for people with a mental handicap (Audit Commission, 1987; 1988; 1989), it received positive encouragement from the professional managers of personal social services to develop relevant criteria and measures of effectiveness.

At the same time, the Management Directorate of the Commission had begun to develop performance indicators as part of its work on performance review. Its first guide to local authorities was published in 1986. It was cautious about performance measurement, in particular stressing the limits of quantitative analysis: 'the art in assessing performance lies in knowing when to allow political and professional judgement to extend, or counter, the objective measures available' (Audit Commission, 1986). It warned that measures of efficiency or effectiveness can rarely be absolute; they can be used as comparators in a number of different ways.

It offered only a few performance indicators in the fields of local authority activity normally dependent on soft forms of knowledge. And it defined effectiveness in terms of authorities' success in achieving their own objectives.

By 1988 it was bolder. It showed that it was prepared to use specialist literature in education and personal social services to make normative statements about service philosophies, policies and standards and to identify measures of performance. It had exploited previous work of the Management and the Special Studies directorates to identify more indicators of economy, efficiency and, in a few cases, outcome. It also in a separate document attached values to the indicators. And It had constructed a framework in which indicators of input, process, output and outcome were diagrammatically related to each other. It stopped short of making any efforts to offer performance indicators in the more established professional fields of law, engineering and architecture. But it made it clear that it regarded the management-professional boundary in education and personal social services as far more permeable.

The Commission's statement in 1987 suggested that it was prepared to be more robust about the management - policy boundary too. It coincided with the start of the Conservative government's third term of office and hardening determination to shift the public sector more decisively towards the norms and mechanisms of the market.

The local authorities included in our case study, together with key members of the wider education policy community, thought that *Towards Better Management of Secondary Education* had been overtaken by this shift. Some considered that the Commission's own rationale had been undermined by it and that it would be forced to confront the government on this issue in order to maintain its credibility.

But the Commission, while criticising the government and some specific elements of the Education Reform Act, also enthusiastically welcomed the broad trend of policies that exposed local government, although it included Labour and union leaders, to market forces, and particularly the introduction of competition into the public sector (Audit Commission, 1988 and 1989). It abandoned its stance of value neutrality and became explicitly value committed.

Was this a new departure for the Commission? The management-policy boundary was, if anything, more strongly asserted by the Audit Commission in its early self denying ordinances than the management-professional boundary. It insisted that it could not make judgements or recommendations about policy. The case study evidence apart, there was general recognition, however, that it did, although there were different views about whether it should (Neilson, 1986; Whitehead, 1986; Public Money, 1984).

It involved itself in policy issues in a variety of ways. At minimum, the Commission took some policy statements or targets from central government departments for granted as providing best guidance on the policy framework within which local authorities would have to operate; examples were targets for the number of school places to be taken out of the system. In *Managing the Crisis in Council Housing* (1986) the Commission went further by commenting on desirable rent levels and rent structures, an issue left to local choice by legislation, and by assuming that there should be partnerships between the public and the private sector in housing and identifying a range of methods by which this could be implemented, 'many of which have a strong ideological content and have not been proven to be cost effective' (Whitehead, ibid).

In the non-teaching costs study (1984) they had been bolder, effectively recommending a curtailment of political involvement in the closure of schools. In this instance, and there were others, the way in which the Commission presented themselves as remaining on the right side of the management/policy line was itself politically based. The Commission explicitly or implicitly converted what had been seen as political questions, for example the source and distribution of resources or processes of decision making, into managerial questions, in many ways a more fundamental attack on the existing policies and politics (Audit Commission, 1984a).

Local authority officers and other professionals interviewed for our study for the most part considered that it was inevitable that the Commission did make policy statements. Few objected strongly, if at all, to that in principle, although Neilson points out that local authority members often did (Neilson, ibid.).

The criticism was more frequently that the analysis did not recognise the complexity of the needs, the relationship between education and communities or electorates or the nature of the political environment, and that they were apt to propose managerial solutions to what were essentially political problems. The implication was that the solutions were technical and could not encompass the complexity of power and interests involved or the range of options that might need to be considered.

Such critics perceived the Audit Commission operating in the managerialist mould set by the government when it came to power in 1979: relying on accountancy or economics based techniques to modernise the public sector. Our case study showed it working in that way but also, at the top, demonstrating a more expansive and proactive style, one strongly endorsed in the products of the management directorate. They proclaimed good management to be essentially concerned with challenge, change and experiment and dependent on understanding and harnessing human motivation (Audit Commission, 1984b).

This second mode was more consistent with the picture painted by McSweeney (1988) of the Audit Commission in the early years of its work. He argued that the Commission was a major force in changing the culture of the public sector in this period. It succeeded not so much through the quality of its managerial or planning technologies as through its (political) success in creating or reinforcing a climate of crisis; and establishing a decision frame in which the choice for local authorities was to follow the line of economy, efficiency and effectiveness as elaborated by the Commission or face disaster. Plenty of traces of such a formula can be found in the Commission's literature. 'Councils ... face conflicting demands for more and better services, but all at lower or no greater cost to ratepayers. Unless these challenges are tackled effectively, the outlook is bleak: frustrated councils, disillusioned residents and demoralised employees' (Audit Commission, 1984b). '...the alternative [to establishing a competent system of performance review], at its bleakest is an authority where services are deteriorating, staff are frustrated, the needs of future client groups will not be met, and there is a lack of conviction that local government is worth having' (Audit Commission, 1986b).

In embracing the government's ambition to impose the disciplines of market forces more directly on the public sector, the Commission was maintaining the position it had already established in a number of ways. It was developing its key policies in line with those of government; it was modelling an organisation adapting to and retaining control of a turbulent environment; it spelt out the strategy it was recommending to local authorities within the same conceptual structure that it had advocated from the beginning: a structure developed by McKinsey, the firm from which its first two Controllers were recruited. Its earlier success in securing the confidence of local government made it possible for it to state its position unequivocally. Local authorities should not resist the new policies; rather they should adopt the more flexible and anticipatory styles of management that informed successful companies in the private sector.

The Commission could now be said to be contributing to a political culture in which the distinctions between management and politics were being further eroded. That it was in a position to do so within five years of its creation showed the distance it had established between itself and the previous arrangement for district audit.

Chapter Four

# The Public/Private Sector Boundary:
## The Use of Consultants in Government*

### Introduction

The Audit Commission is a permanently established body working within traditions, structures and modes, many of which it has created itself. An entirely different option for government, and one exercised increasingly in the last decade, when evaluating its policies and management is to commission external consultants to carry out specific pieces of work (Hogwood and Peters, 1985).

Consultants differ in a number of important respects from other sources of evaluation used by government. They are brought in at the discretion of the department or public body concerned, as and when they are required. Unlike inspectorates or audit bodies they do not have a formal statutory role. They are independent practitioners who enter into a contract with the department concerned to perform a specific assignment.

Their contribution to evaluation in government can therefore be expected to be different from either the mechanisms internal to departments or other formal external mechanisms. But their use raises some issues similar to those addressed in the previous chapter. As predominantly 'management' consultants their role might be to strengthen technical expertise and instrumental rationality in government or they might be regarded as a means to install managerial perspectives and norms in

---

* This chapter is based on a fieldwork report researched and written by Tim Whitaker.

government, to change its culture. They operate at the boundaries of government and may provide a way of bridging ideas and values from the private and the public sector. A study of their work in government may throw further light on the feasibility of drawing clear boundaries between management, policy and politics in evaluation and on the relationship between externality and independence of judgement.

## The Research Study

We analyse here their role within the policy making and management process and in particular their contribution to evaluation. We explore why consultants are used, how they are recruited, how they evaluate management or policies, the relationships between consultants and departments, and how their findings are used. We draw on the available literature on management consultants in government as well as research carried out with a range of consultants and civil servants in departments that have used them.

We interviewed a range of management consultants working in firms which have carried out assignments in the broad field of evaluation and policy analysis for government and other parts of the public sector. They included the different types of firms within the management consultancy range - the large accountancy based consultancies, the more traditional consultants, consultancy firms with an emphasis on organisation and human relations, and smaller specialist firms. Civil servants were interviewed in five departments - the DHSS, Customs and Excise, Defence, Environment, and Trade and Industry - and in the Cabinet Office and Treasury. These were selected because they had expertise in using consultants for a wide variety of assignments.

In choosing which assignments to study it was necessary to decide what counted as policy evaluation. Assignments were rarely couched in the terms of a formal evaluation. Those concerned with implementing information technology or accounting systems were not included in the study. The assignments studied covered a number of different policy areas ranging from social policies to more technical areas. Most of them were concerned with the provision of some service by that department and in some cases involved another agency such as a local authority or governmental body. A number were concerned with management structure and functioning. Some not only included an element of evaluation but were also concerned with presenting and implementing alternatives. Although most followed the traditional consultant- client relationship, in some instances consultants were seconded to a department to work on a particular project with civil servants.

## The Nature of Management Consultancy

The Management Consultants' Association defines the management consultant as, 'a person or firm whose principal activity is to provide to business, public and other undertakings, assistance in identifying and investigating problems and or opportunities concerned with policy, organisation, procedures and methods, recommending appropriate action and helping to implement those recommendations as necessary'. This definition covers a whole range of different activities. Kubr (1980) in a guide to the management consultancy profession identifies what are seen as the main features. First, consulting is an independent service provided to a range of different clients. The consultant is detached from the employing organisation and has to retain a degree of objectivity. Secondly, consulting is an advisory service. The consultants' recommendations do not have to be implemented; they give an objective account of the problems that are seen to exist and then provide advice. The third feature mentioned by Kubr is that of consulting as a professional activity, providing professional knowledge and skills which are applicable to problems of management. The distinctive values and knowledge that are common to management consulting will be examined later in this chapter.

The definition of management consultancy outlined above is broad and conceals differences between the many firms operating as management consultants. There are a number of registers that list the types of management consultants. The Management Consultants Association covers 30 of the large and medium sized firms in this country but does not represent all of the major firms. The management consulting 'industry' has sometimes been sub-divided as follows:

- The large multi-national generalist consulting firms operating in a worldwide market.
- The management consulting divisions of the large chartered accounting firms, for example Coopers and Lybrand.
- Generalist consulting firms that have a wide range of consulting services, such as PE Consulting.
- Large specialist firms who focus on a specific market but who operate on a worldwide basis.

- Small to medium sized firms which concentrate on one particular sector.

- The small firm and individual practitioner engaged in a variety of services.

- The intermittent consultant, for example an academic involved in consultancy work.

It has been estimated that in the UK there are 5000 management consultants working in consultancy firms and a further 2000 who work part-time. It is thus a large and well differentiated industry. Management consultants started operating as early as the 1930's in such fields as work study and management but it was in the 1970's and 1980's that the growth rate increased dramatically (*Management Today*, 1983). Now many of the largest management consultants are based on the major accountancy firms. The management consultancy industry is a highly competitive one with a concern to develop new markets including government (Peet, 1988).

## Management Consultants in Government

Although expenditure on management consultants has increased most dramatically over the past five years, central government departments began to use them in the middle of the 1960's. In 1965 an inter-departmental working party under Treasury chairmanship presented a report on when and how to use them. (*O & M Bulletin*, 1966).

By 1970 contracts with consultants were becoming more widespread; the Civil Service Department held a seminar on management developments in central government that referred to the range of consultancy tasks and emphasised the use of management consultants. Consultants at this time were most often asked to apply new management systems in the fields of Organisation and Methods, costing schemes, computer application and management accountancy. The management ideas came from operational research, work study, management by objectives and management accounting. The Fulton Report on the civil service (1968) had argued for more in-house management services units with a wider range of responsibilities than before.

One significant use of consultants was in undertaking reviews of civil service organisation. It was thought that teams of civil servants drawn from different areas of management services could, in conjunction with management consultants, mount reviews of organisation and policy making of a complete department or sub- department. The origins of this approach lay in the notion of company appraisal which was being undertaken by consultants. It was accepted that these review teams should also include outside consultants.

While respondents in our study thought that consulting had increased with the Thatcher administration and its concerns with efficiency, there had been gradual growth since the early 1970s. It was a feature of the reforms of the Heath government (1970-1974). Conservative governments have favoured bringing in management consultants from the private sector more than Labour governments which tended to use other ways of evaluating the government machine and its policies.

The type and range of assignments were listed for each department in the journal *Management Services in Government* from 1967 to 1980. Analysis of this information reveals that the largest users of consultants were, in the order of the number of assignments commissioned: Trade and Industry, Environment, Health and Social Security, Defence, The Home Office and the Civil Service Department. Other government departments used them much less often.

In the 1980s management consultants were increasingly used as measured by both the volume of assignments and expenditure. Exact information on this trend is hard to obtain because the government no longer releases information on all assignments except through written Parliamentary Questions. However, in 1984-85 expenditure on computer and management consultants was over £27.5 million (excluding the Home Office). By 1986-87 it was £70 million. This figure includes computer consultancies which multiplied with the development of information technology in the civil service, in particular, in support of the DHSS social security operational strategy.

There were two principal reasons why the present government favoured using consultants. First, some of the government reforms emphasised new skills in the area of value for money. For example, the introduction of the Financial Management Initiative led to an increase in their use in implementing budgetary and financial systems. Similarly the introduction of information technology into the civil service led to management consultants implementing computer systems in a number of departments. Developments in particular departments were also seen to require the use of management consultants. For example, in the Ministry of Defence the introduction of MINIS involved management consultants. They were said to have been brought in because the management skills required were predominantly of a technical kind - accountancy, operational research, investment appraisal, and information technology. Assignments were mainly in the areas of management accounting, purchasing, budgeting, accommodation and the costs of these activities. The management consultants interviewed thought their role comparable to those of other specialists in the civil service except that they provided these services from the outside.

They added that civil servants were becoming more accustomed to using consultants and were beginning to recognise that they possessed 'management' problems. Some of the civil servants stated they had become less wary of bringing in consultants into the policy making process; this was becoming accepted practice in many, if not all, departments.

The second broad reason for their use rested on their external status and the credibility of their advice. In the words of one senior civil servant using management consultants 'might indicate that the department was aware of what was going on in the outside world'. In particular exploiting external expertise and techniques that had originated in the private sector was seen as important.

## Reasons for Using Management Consultants in Evaluation

Civil servants saw consultants as just one of the means of evaluation open to a department. Views on why they were used were related to the type of assignment.

The main reason given was the match between the expertise they were seen to possess and the particular problem. They could be used to develop, as well as to evaluate, projects. Again, this expertise was mainly technical, especially accountancy, financial appraisal, communications and purchasing skills. Other skills mentioned but less emphasised were organisational or of a traditional management kind. In some cases consultants were seen to be expert in a particular area. For example, consultants in the Department of Environment reviewed the use of private resources in industrial regeneration; civil servants were thought not to possess appropriate skills and they lacked the capacity to undertake these types of exercises.

Cutbacks in civil service staffing were thought to have reduced the availability of skills particularly in the fields of information technology. It was emphasised that some departments brought in consultants for certain tasks rather than employing existing staff or appointing new staff.

Often consultants were used because there was not the staff time to undertake a review and employing consultants was cheaper than employing new staff. Some respondents were critical on the grounds that policy analysis was being sub-contracted to the private sector because of a shortage of civil servants. But some civil servants saw the use of consultants with this expertise as a way of training their staff, particularly where consultants worked as part of a departmental team. Such teams might require the addition of a consultant with particular types of skills.

Consultants were thought to provide independent advice for the analysis and evaluation of policies. Some civil servants saw them as able to provide a detached perspective and assessment of issues where it would be difficult for the civil servants themselves to conduct such an evaluation. They needed 'credible' solutions to problems. For example, the DHSS used consultants to determine the scales of general managers' pay in the NHS. Some also noted the difficulty of civil servants reviewing certain practices or policies because of their own self-interest: outsiders would provide an impartial perspective.

Sometimes purposes were more utilitarian; consultants could be used by civil servants to 'test' a policy or management issue before another outside body, such as the National Audit Office, undertook a formal review. Civil servants could thus demonstrate that they had addressed the problem. A slightly different use was to investigate the performance of public bodies outside the department's boundaries. This was used as a strategy in some departments to monitor programmes indirectly, so that it would give the image of independent review by evaluators detached from the department.

Management consultants might also be brought in where ministers wanted a review independent of the findings of the department; there were cases where ministers had distrusted the official analysis. One example was the review of the Defence School of Music where civil servants had already presented policy alternatives but ministers wanted a new review because there was conflict between the services and politicians over the possible site of a new School of Music.

External consultants were, therefore, used to fill gaps which departments themselves could not fill. Internal units tended to be used only in traditional organisation and methods type reviews or in small scale efficiency exercises.

Nevertheless, some departments had to demonstrate before commissioning consultants that the work could not be undertaken 'in house' by internal units or specialists such as economists. The availability of other resources varied between departments. Some had established bodies, including inspectorates, which might be used to review a problem or carry out developmental work. A department might also commission its own study team to carry out a piece of work composed not only of civil servants but also specialists from the field. This was also a means of including different stakeholders, as when the Ministry of Defence in reviewing the proposals for a new defence school of music formed a study group composed of representatives from the three services.

A further alternative was to use specialists because of their experience of the field rather than their technical skills, though management consultants might not have this type of knowledge. Finally, a few civil servants mentioned the use of bodies within government but outside their own departmental boundaries which could, in theory, be used for evaluation: for example, the National Audit Office, the Joint Management Unit, or the Efficiency Unit of the Cabinet Office.

## Management Consultants' Views on Their Use in Government

Consultants who had carried out assignments for government departments held similar views to those of civil servants on the growth of management consultancy in government. They thought the Financial Management Initiative meant that departments needed the technical skills of consultancy firms. The new approaches in government were felt to have provided a rapidly growing market for management consultants. The consultants saw it as applying their technical expertise and experience of similar problems in the private sector: these types of skills were in short supply within government. In particular, departments lacked the expertise to review the cost effectiveness of policies and programmes and other bodies such as the NAO could not take on such tasks.

Consultants also recognised that sometimes they were used because staff with those particular skills were not available. Some questioned whether this type of service constituted 'real' management consultancy. By management consulting they meant bringing to bear expertise in systems of management and solutions to problems based on the experience of the consultant.

Some noted other motives for using consultants; their role was not just simply to solve a problem or apply particular techniques. One common view was that consultants were commissioned in order to 'park a problem'; the assignment would demonstrate that the problem was receiving attention. They may have been recruited reluctantly perhaps because of a ministerial instruction.

Consultants might provide legitimated expertise, in the words of one consultant, to allow the civil servants 'a way of getting off the hook'. Finally, some consultants spoke of a 'genuine motivation' for the use of consultants where a department recognised that they required help in order to address a problem and come up with a review and possible alternatives.

## The Selection of Management Consultants

Management consultants were recruited for most assignments in central government departments through competitive tendering. This stage was important: the selection of a particular consultancy firm might have implications for how the work was to be carried out.

The growth of management consultancy assignments in government, together with the impact of FMI, brought change in the way they were recruited. The old Civil Service Department (CSD) operated a centralised system. A department would formally request an assignment. The CSD would give advice on how to select and manage the assignment. Since 1970 it had produced a booklet for departments which was regularly updated on when and how to use management consultants. Now, however, departments were given responsibility for recruiting consultants.

Departments shared similar structures and procedures for dealing with management consultancy assignments. Most had a small consultancy unit responsible for the selection, management and evaluation of assignments. These might also be responsible for types of assignment other than those given to management consultants, including specialisms such as legal advice, merchant banking and computing, depending on the nature of the department concerned. In some departments policy branches wanting to commission work from management consultants had to seek permission from the unit, which then advised on selection and administered the process of recruitment. In other departments each policy branch had its own budget which could be used for consultancy assignments; in this case the department's consultancy unit simply advised and administered the assignment. But in each case the policy branch was responsible for framing the idea for the assignment.

A department's consultancy unit usually sent out requests to tender for assignments using their knowledge of the consultancy field. Most departments maintained their own list and the Management and Personnel Office (MPO) kept a computer index of management consultants who had worked in government departments in the last four years according to specialism.

Departments had their own contacts with consultants. It was also practice for 'invited' consultants to talk with the policy branch about the specification of the assignment. Civil servants in some departments tried to invite some of the smaller management consultancy firms or those that had not carried out work recently for government in order to create more competition. Once tenders were received they were submitted to the policy branch and the selected firms were then shortlisted for a presentation. The tenders included details of how the firm would carry out the assignment, the methodology they would adopt and their costings. In one department costings were submitted separately to a finance branch and neither the policy branch nor the consultancy unit knew the costings until they had chosen on the basis of their technical evaluation of the firm's tender. The selection meeting was normally chaired by a civil servant from the branch and involved a formal presentation and answering questions.

The selection of the consultants was a crucial stage in an assignment. The type of assignment affected which criteria were felt to be appropriate. Costs were clearly important. Yet a contract would not be automatically awarded to the cheapest firm; they would have to be competent to carry out the work. The reputation of the firm counted. Departments possessed their own formal records of assignments carried out by consultants which in some cases included an evaluation of the performance of the firm. Civil servants had their own views about the reputation of the firms, their particular expertise, the quality of the personnel and their 'track record' in government. The 'grape vine' between departments was thought to influence choice, particularly concerning the reliability of firms. Most of those interviewed felt that a firm's reputation was important, at least in ensuring that it got on the short list to be interviewed. Some departments preferred firms that had worked for them before or had experience of a similar area of work.

The specific expertise of the firm was another important factor. Those civil servants that had been involved in a number of assignments recognised that the methods and approaches of firms differed. This was especially important in cases of policy evaluation where the approaches and methodology were likely to influence the outcome. Some felt that these issues were more significant in cases of 'loose' assignments than where consultants were being used to supply a specified service to the department. Civil servants' views on the techniques and methodologies of management consultants are explored later in this chapter.

Consultants' knowledge of the public sector was considered by some but not all civil servants to be important. It was felt that management consultants were learning fast about the nature of government. How government worked was thought to be important: recommendations would have to be feasible.

The personal attributes of the team were assessed at the interview stage of the selection process. Consultants must be able to work with the department. Civil servants preferred those consultants who would actually be carrying out the assignment to be present at the interview rather than senior consultants who often formally presented a firm's proposal. The composition of the team and how much time would be spent on the assignment by senior consultants were also considered, together with the firm's written proposal giving their approach and perception of the problem.

Departments differed in how systematic were their processes of selecting consultants. The MPO's guide to recruiting consultants gave advice on these. One department which employed a large number of consultants used a formal points system in interviews which allocated the following marking system:

| | |
|---|---|
| Understanding of the project | 30 per cent |
| Methodology and approach | 20 per cent |
| Staff expertise and capability | 20 per cent |
| Allocation of resources | 20 per cent |
| Corporate capability | 10 per cent |

There were cases of assignments which did not involve competitive tendering. An individual senior partner of a firm known to the department might be invited to carry out a high level piece of advice or an evaluation. A second example would be where a firm possessed a particular expertise which was appropriate for the assignment. Finally in cases of implementation or follow up studies then competitive tendering was waived.

## Consultants' Views on Selection

Most management consultants accepted the principle of competitive tendering: it enhanced the departments' choice. Some however thought that it added to the cost of an assignment because of the additional costs of firms having to tender for all jobs.

Consultants' assumptions about criteria for selection broadly matched those mentioned by the civil servants interviewed. There was frequent dialogue between firms and departments. In some cases unsuccessful shortlisted firms were told why they had not been selected. Those interviewed discussed some of the factors that influenced the selection process.

Some mentioned the close links between their firms and various departments but recognised that civil servants might not sufficiently differentiate between their interests and expertise. Others felt that departments' knowledge about firms varied. A number of consultants thought that factors such as the firm's reputation and image were important in getting them onto the shortlist but after that personal attributes and costs became important. Some felt that departments were meticulously fair in selection even to the extent of having a rotation policy for inviting firms to tender, so as not to be accused of favouring one particular firm.

The selection process was seen to vary between departments. Consultants preferred negotiation and collaborative framing of the problem. One consultant felt that departments tended to treat commissioning in the same way as the purchase of any service: they concentrated on the inputs to an assignment rather than the outputs. It was felt that the type of assignment affected which firm would be chosen. For example, assignments that were politically initiated required one of the major firms that had a reputation in that particular field. Some consultants criticised the lack of rationality in choosing firms.

Management consultants had to decide whether they wanted to tender for an assignment. This depended on the nature of the firm and their other work commitments. Several firms were selective in assignments they would tender for. Others mentioned the type of considerations which affected whether they would tender. The first were commercial: did they want to be known to be carrying out an assignment for government? There were the professional issues: could the firm carry out the particular assignment? And sometimes there were ethical considerations.

## The Process of an Assignment

We examined different types of assignment performed by management consultants in different departments. Some were concerned more with the development of policy or management than with evaluation. But all had some element of evaluating or assessing practice. The variety of assignments makes it difficult to generalise about the activities of management consultants in this sphere. However, it is still possible to make some points about the way that assignments were carried out using examples from the research.

## Briefs for an Assignment

The first stage was the departmental brief which specified the nature of the problem and the aims of the assignment. Briefs varied both within and between departments in the level of detail they contained and their format. Guidance from the Management and Personnel Office was that they should be precise in identifying the problem and the product expected from the assignment. Those departments such as the Ministry of Defence with a long experience of using consultants tended to use highly specific briefs.

The views of management consultants about briefs illustrates how they approached assignments. Most noted that briefs varied from being highly precise to unclear. The majority of management consultants interviewed preferred working to briefs that were 'loose' rather than 'fixed'. The reasons for this varied. Some welcomed the opportunity to negotiate the problem posed by the department as this might be wrong to begin with. In some cases consultants were asked to consider the problem itself. Other consultants stated that a 'good' brief made clear what were the ends of the assignment and left the consultants to develop the means. Consultants emphasised the importance of 'engaging with the client at an early stage' in order to identify such issues as the underlying questions in an assignment, the motivation behind it, the pressures facing the department and the chances of success of the assignment. In some cases, following this discussion between consultants and departments, the brief was renegotiated.

## Models of Consultant-Department Relationships

Underlying the views of consultants were implicit models of the relationship between consultant and client. The literature on management consultants discusses these in some detail (Kubr *op. cit.*). Those consultants interviewed made a broad distinction between what they saw as 'engineering' and 'process' type approaches to assignments. The choice of approach was dictated by the type of assignment and the nature of the management consulting firm.

In the 'engineering type model' the consultant provides an expert service for the employing organisation based mainly on analytical skills such as economic analysis, information technology, accountancy skills, and computer analysis. These assignments tended to start with a problem that the consultant was hired to solve.

In contrast, the process (or marriage) model was based on a looser style of relationship characterised by one consultant as the consultant acting as a 'guide, counsellor and friend'. Here consultant and client worked together to solve the jointly discussed problem. The skills possessed by these consultants tended to be based on behavioural and organisational techniques.

## The Methodologies and Techniques of Assignments

Our research explored both consultants' and civil servants' views on how assignments were carried out. We examined their general views based on experience of a range of assignments. We also studied particular assignments, where we analysed the final reports and supporting documentation.

Of particular importance was the methodology of assignments and whether distinctive techniques were employed. Some were assignment-specific. An evaluation of information systems in a department would use particular techniques. And consultancy firms had their own distinctive approaches, techniques and 'house styles'.

However, there were patterns in the way that assignments were carried out. The first stage was the delineation of the problem, whether or not it had been clearly identified in the assignment brief. Given the opportunity, consultants liked to adapt and negotiate the boundaries of the problem, which they did in discussion with the departmental officials responsible for the assignment. This also allowed the consultants to explore the context of the problem.

At an early stage in most assignments the consultants gathered information both on the background and more factual data. In certain cases they used questionnaires to identify views more systematically. Some consultants saw this essentially as a research stage where the emphasis was on the empirical and scientific mode of analysis.

In some cases consultants felt that techniques might be emphasised in the bid for an assignment if the department was keen on methodologies. Most techniques used were derived from quantitative management - operational research, statistical analysis, and modelling-techniques. It was stated that these were used to aid judgements and test particular findings. At a broader level theories or techniques of management or strategic policy making used in other contexts were applied to the field of government. Certain consultancy firms had their own philosophies about management, although several consultants noted that techniques were rather like a 'fashion game' and were constantly changing. The notion of total quality management designed to examine all aspects of an organisation's performance was cited as an example.

Apart from management techniques, consultants also emphasised the consultancy skills they possessed which gave them a distinctive role within the organisation. It was noted that their presence might have an effect in inducing change.

## *Interaction*

The literature on management consulting lays strong emphasis on the process of assignments and how the consultant should engage with the client. Yet these formal prescriptive accounts inevitably present a rather stylised view of how the consultant interacts with their clients. The research explored through interviews with both consultants and civil servants the main stages of an assignment and the main issues that arise.

Once a consultancy had been commissioned to carry out an assignment, there was usually some negotiation over the brief and a timetable was set. Normally, a civil servant was appointed as a project officer to act as a point of liaison and to monitor progress. For larger assignments a steering committee was set up composed of representatives from the different branches within the department and other interested parties. The steering committee co-ordinated the work and met regularly to receive progress reports from the consultants and to guide the work. The final report would normally come to this committee for discussion. Departments were advised by the MPO to set up proper formal procedures for monitoring.

At the outset, consultants had to identify who was the real client of the assignment. In some assignments, this was difficult, particularly where there were potentially a number of stake holders. That might produce problems in gearing advice and recommendations. There were several possible clients: those who had commissioned the assignment; the project officer; senior civil servants or the steering committee. The problem was more acute when there were different interests such as when an assignment was across departmental boundaries. Civil servants interviewed felt that the client of an assignment in most cases was the official who had requested the assignment. It was very rare for ministers to be involved with the consultants during the course of an assignment although they frequently saw the final reports.

For consultants, identifying the client of the assignment was a crucial task. It was the key to discovery of the power and values of the organisation. Most assignments started by exploring the different views about a problem in order to assess who exerted influence and what were the boundaries of a problem. For example, it was noted in some assignments

that senior staff had a particular view of a problem and wanted a certain
type of response whereas those lower in the hierarchy had different views.
For some civil servants responsible for commissioning assignments and
ensuring that the consultants worked within the structure, this posed a
problem. In one assignment the civil servant stated that 'we give the
consultant a good steer about what we want at the beginning of a project'.
For the consultant the problem was knowing how to reconcile the often
conflicting views within the department. Where assignments were in
contentious areas consultants had to cope with demands and lobbying
from different stakeholders within the department or policy field.

Such political interaction raises the question of the objectivity of the
consultant role. The management consultancy literature emphasises that
the value of consultants is that they provide an independent and objective
account of problems and are able to offer appropriate advice. It is further
argued that their repertoire of consulting skills enables them to be
effective as they relate to different parts of the organisation.

Yet those management consultants interviewed, whilst promoting
their role as a neutral adviser, also noted the political and organisational
context outlined earlier. The effects varied between consultants. Some
felt they should have a degree of sympathy and identification with the
client and produce realistic recommendations. Others questioned whether
it was right always to produce what the client would want. Instances were
given of consultants who had been used to legitimate policy proposals
advanced by civil servants and were thus not viewed as completely
independent.

There was also disagreement about whether consultants should ask
civil servants their preferred solution to a problem at the beginning of an
assignment. Some felt that this was permissible; others took the opposite
point of view. One consultant emphasised the need to be constantly
reflective about advice; in his words, 'Can we apply a test to our
conclusions to demonstrate that they are right?' He felt it important to
have an analytical base on which to evaluate conclusions.

The issue of objectivity was also raised in connection with the formal
position of the consultant with the department. It was felt that consultants
who worked too long in the same department could be incorporated into
the dominant values and assumptions, and thus their independence might
be diminished. However, some departments tended to prefer to use the
same consulting firm; they had developed a relationship over time with
that firm and were used to its way of working. Independence also became
an issue with consultants that were seconded to work with a department.
This was becoming more common where consultants would work full

time for a period as part of a team composed of civil servants. Those departments that preferred this style of relationship felt that it allowed the department to benefit from the experience of consultants and therefore had an educational function. The critics of this practice pointed not only to some of the commercial difficulties but also to the possibility that the consultants would be 'captured' by the department or develop conclusions that were not objective enough. In contrast departments felt that the close working relationship was a source of strength; it allowed the consultants to appreciate fully the organisational and policy context and hence be more realistic in their advice.

Civil servants also commented on the commercial interests of management consultancy firms which were seen by some challenge their professional objectivity and integrity. They were regarded as business organisations selling their expertise and skills in a market. Critics argued that this influenced their decisions to bid for assignments, the extent to which they specialised and the lengths to which they would go to differentiate their specific expertise from those of other firms.

## Recommendations

The formal output of an assignment was normally a report to the department accompanied by a presentation to civil servants. In a few cases the steering committee would clear the draft version of a report before it was finally released to the sponsor. Some civil servants believed that a report's conclusions ought to be 'squared' with all those concerned before it was released.

The interviews with management consultants revealed a number of issues in connection with the production of recommendations. These were linked with beliefs about the role of consultants in the organisation and types of assignment. For example, in assignments with a technical aspect such as the evaluation of information systems the role of the consultant might be to provide technical advice which would be non-controversial and authoritative. In contrast assignments more concerned with the evaluation of policies or management arrangements within a department might be treated by civil servants as one input only into their own evaluation.

Management consultants faced problems in deciding on their advice. They differed in their attitudes to providing solutions that were 'required' by the department. Some felt that they had a responsibility to provide an objective assessment rather than producing advice that was wanted by the department for political reasons. Some gave examples of assignments carried out by other consultants which were not felt to be independent in that they were used for political reasons. This view of objective advice was based on a notion of the professional expertise of management consultants; their claim to be acting in the best interests of their clients rested on that expertise. Some consultants also felt that they must preserve their reputation in the future. Their capacity to do so would depend partly on the legitimacy and success of their recommendations. A contrasting view was that consultants should indeed be acting in the interests of their clients and that meant taking into account the preferences of the department.

A second factor was the need to gear a solution to the problem faced by the department. It was argued that recommendations 'should not be too far outside the boundaries of what the client department wants'. Some options that were judged by consultants to be appropriate because they had experience of seeing them work in, for example, private sector organisations, were ruled out by civil servants.

Civil servants emphasised the need for close monitoring of the process by which conclusions and recommendations were reached. Consultants who attempted to bring in 'off the shelf packages' and to sell these to departments regardless of the particular circumstances were criticised. Some consultants felt that they had 'to sell' recommendations to civil servants because officials were reluctant to take risks.

A linked point was that recommendations must be feasible. In the words of one consultant, 'there is no point in producing an ideal solution which has no chance of being implemented'. Feasibility, it was argued, required the consultant to identify the constraints and preferences in a department and take these into account in the conclusions.

Civil servants preferred reports which contained only a small number of recommendations which were straightforward and could be implemented easily. The formal end of assignment presentation was felt to be of particular importance in communicating findings to the department. Some civil servants commented how presentations were made and noted that the presence of a firm's senior partner might affect the degree of importance attached by the department to the recommendations.

## The Utilisation of Consultants' Recommendations

*Consultants' Views*

Departments' implementation of recommendations mattered to the consultants concerned. Some did not like to see the results of their activities wasted. There were also commercial considerations: a 'successful' assignment might lead a department to use the same consultants again and mention them to other departments.

Consultants' attitudes to the implementation process were, however, linked with the model of the consultant-client relationship to which they subscribed. If a consultant's role was purely to advise, then it was for the department to make what use it wanted of their recommendations. The client was seen to be responsible for implementation and it was no part of the consultant's role to be involved in policy making.

A contrary set of views favoured the consultant becoming involved in implementing findings and acting as a 'change agent' in the organisation. This was more common in assignments dealing with management and organisational change than in those with a technical orientation. Some assignments were extended to include an implementation phase which involved the consultant in working with civil servants. One firm of management consultants felt that the customary practice of producing reports was a waste of effort. The long term impact of their recommendations was what mattered to them.

Most consultants recognised that the success of their assignments depended on whether senior civil servants or ministers agreed with their recommendations. Some took the view that their presence in the department might stimulate civil servants or indirectly contribute to 'better' decision making. Impact lay there rather than in having their recommendations automatically implemented.

*Civil Servants' Views*

It is difficult to estimate with accuracy the extent to which consultants' findings were implemented in departments. This is in part due to the different motives behind using consultants. For example, some assignments were deliberately commissioned to review a problem and thus to provide no more than an outside perspective. Others of a more technical nature were expected to provide solutions which could be implemented.

Those responsible for assignments felt that a number of factors affected the use of consultants' findings. Most important was the extent to which they accorded with the views and expectations of civil servants.

The credibility of findings was also critical; the recommendations should be seen to be worthwhile and based upon a thorough analysis which also showed signs of recognising the particular circumstances of the department. If an assignment led to discernible savings it would be favourably received. Some were felt to be useful because they had indirect outputs such as spreading expertise within the department. It was recognised that consultants often expected recommendations to be implemented quickly but this was not always possible.

Some departments actively used management consultants in implementing changes because of their skills in inducing change, and their experience of other organisations. Civil servants recognised that consultants wanted to be involved in this type of work. One remarked that in the past consultants 'used to take the money and run' but now they frequently included plans for dissemination and implementation in their bids for assignments.

## The Evaluation of Assignments

The interviews with civil servants and management consultants examined how both groups evaluated consultancy assignments in government.

Most departments had no formal system of evaluating assignments. Those that did tended to have a form which was completed at the end of each assignment and kept centrally for future use. One department had started an exercise in examining the impact of consultants' recommendations, mainly from the standpoint of costs and whether the department was making best use of consultants.

Despite the absence of formal evaluation, civil servants did possess views of how they judged assignments. Objective criteria included basic factors such as whether the assignment kept to time and kept within its budget. One of the important subjective criteria was whether the recommendations were felt to be both useful and acceptable to the civil servant responsible for carrying out this work. 'Did it take us forward in our thinking?' commented one civil servant who had used a large number of management consultants over time. Civil servants also assessed such factors as the rigour of the analysis and the degree of innovation and the personal attributes of the consultants were given prominence.

Management consultants clearly felt that assignments were successful when their recommendations were implemented. Some used the criterion that assignments should be 'productive'. According to one consultant an assignment was successful 'when the civil servants take on board the consultant as a partner and the assignment leaves behind a particular approach or methodology'.

## Conclusions

There has been a rapid growth in the use of management consultants by government in the 1980s, although its origins lie in the 1960s with the onset of 'management reform' in government. All parts of the public sector are now regarded as growth areas for consultants.

The practice of commissioning management consultants for policy evaluation and other purposes was most commonly justified by reference to their technical skills and expertise. Government departments often lacked such capacity and where they possessed it demand for it outstripped resources. Consultancy enabled departments to obtain external judgements based predominantly on quantitative, financial, commercial, information and communications expertise, but in some cases on more general management experience. And consultants were a flexible resource: departments could select according to specific needs. Overall, the dominant arguments for their use were rational.

However, it is clear that they were also used for political reasons: to 'park a problem', to divert pressure for action, to legitimate a desired solution, to resolve conflicts of interest or sometimes to generate alternative proposals that would carry authority. The use of consultants gave credibility partly because they came from the private sector. They brought into government values and methods from industry and commerce, a major underlying objective of ministers.

If they provided external judgements there were strong pressures against the independence and objectivity promulgated in the literature on management consultancy. The study highlights the problems of 'speaking truth to power'. The authority and dynamics of the client-consultant relationship meant that consultants were heavily dependent on their clients for the success of particular contracts and for continued success in the central government consultancy market. A traditional function of the civil service grapevine is to assess and communicate reputation (Heclo and Wildavsky, 1981). It was well able to extend that into appraisal of management consultants.

It was generally agreed that the key to a productive client- consultant relationship was to identify where the power lay in the client organisation. While consultants differed as to how far they should tailor their advice to the preferences of the senior civil servants who held the power in departments, all recognised that recommendations had at some level to be acceptable to those civil servants if they were to be implemented. Some consultants placed ultimate confidence in the rigour of their analysis; others felt that negotiation was the key factor. Their attitudes were partly linked with the nature of their expertise and the assignments for which they were commissioned.

In the client-consultant relationship, evaluation is firmly linked to existing power relationships. It is most plausibly understood as convincing as much, if not more, by persuasion, argument and negotiation as by analysis (cf House, 1980). The main dynamic that emerges here is that between senior civil servants and consultants. There is some evidence in the study that civil servants were persuaded that managerial perspectives had something to offer them but how deeply those perspectives penetrated is not clear. The influence of ministers is less evident in the study. We shall return to these issues in a later chapter.

Meanwhile a clear and important implication of the study, and particularly of the relationships portrayed, is that the use of consultancy strengthens central government's *a priori* judgements of issues against the influence of, for example, actors in the field. Reflexiveness with the field gives way to reflexiveness with central authority, as this form of evaluation takes hold.

Chapter Five

# The Social Services Inspectorate

The institutions discussed in the last chapter were at the boundary between the private and the public sector. We observed the encounter between the growing power of management consultants with the established power of bureaucrats responsible for policy and its impacts on evaluation in government.

This chapter stays with central government and is concerned with a government institution newly engaging with managerial perspectives. The stage is smaller and the engagement primarily internal: a not particularly powerful professional division of one government department was required in the 1980s to incorporate managerial goals and to transform itself from advisory service to inspectorate. The Social Work Service (SWS) of the then Department of Health and Social Security (DHSS) became the Social Services Inspectorate in 1985.

Like the Audit Commission, it was now asked to play a more active role in the task of controlling and changing local government through evaluation, although its mandate was more complex, and its boundaries even less clearly defined. Our study suggests that while the newly designated inspectorate worked hard to strengthen its evaluative capacities and to demonstrate its usefulness to government, local authority managers and practitioners and consumers, it did not resolve the conflicts and ambiguities in its objectives, which were intensified under the new remit.

## Origins

The SWS was created in 1971 by an amalgamation of the Children's Inspectorate of the Home Office and the Social Work Division of the DHSS to coincide with the establishment of local authority Social Services Departments (SSDs). They in turn were formed from a bringing together of local authority Children's and Welfare Departments and parts of the Health Departments.

Despite its mixed parentage the SWS' professional and advisory functions were paramount from the outset. The decision to opt for the professional mode was deliberate and understandable in the contemporary environment. There was a strong professional culture in the government of health, education and, more recently, social welfare. The rationale for the reorganisation of the health and social services in the late 1960s and early 1970s was that of division according to professional leadership. The new SSDs were expected to be professionally directed and informed by the values and knowledge of a developing social work profession (Kogan and Terry, 1970; Cooper, 1983). The mood of SWS at the time was captured by a senior respondent to this study, 'There is no need for inspections; in a year or two they will be telling us.'

The SWS was to be ' an integrated professional service' 'available to assist the Department of Health and Social Security in the social work aspect of all its functions', although it would continue to exercise some regulatory functions, defined in earlier legislation and concentrated on the inspections of residential institutions (DHSS, 1971a).

But the analogy with the medical professions was weakly based. Sources of authority and identity in the personal social services were fragmented and uncertain. The status of social work as a profession was from the beginning a matter of bitter internal dispute (see *Social Work Today*, Vol.1 No 1, 1970) and, soon, stringent external criticism.

During the 1970s, anxieties about the control of public expenditure began to mount and the failures of local government, not least in the personal social services, to overcome the problems with which they were established to deal were increasingly the subject of public attention. A greater stress on inspectorial activities in central government was advocated. Although this was at first resisted by the SWS, in 1979 it announced that it would in future include in its work programme certain activities based on the powers of inspection exercised on behalf of the Secretary of State.

In 1983, the Secretary of State issued a consultative document about the future role of SWS, proposing that it be redesignated an inspectorate for the personal social services, with extended powers of inspection and a greater emphasis on efficiency and value for money (DHSS, 1983). The implication was that the concept of a service based on a distinct profession of social work would go, even if that was not accepted in the service itself. In the same year the SWS announced the intention to include 'Efficiency

Studies' in its work programme. The national inspection of Community Homes was to be the first of these.

## The Social Service Inspectorate

In 1985, the conversion of the SWS into the Social Services Inspectorate was announced in the House of Commons in the form of an answer to a parliamentary question (PQ620/1984/85). The statement nicely encapsulated the compromise reached between the advocates of efficiency and the upholders of professionalism and between the use of powers and the use of advice that would inform the inspectorate.

The inspectorate was to 'assist local authorities to obtain value for money through the efficient and economic use of resources'. It would aim 'to help to secure the most effective use of professional and other resources, normally by identifying good practice and spreading knowledge about it.'

Inspections were to be of three main types:

- **Type 1**: those initiated by Ministers and the Department in exercise of the Secretary of State's formal powers
- **Type 2**: those undertaken outside formal powers, by agreement with the local authorities concerned and in accordance with a programme agreed by the local authority associations. They would cover issues of general concern and be conducted in a number of local authorities
- **Type 3**: those undertaken outside formal powers, but at the request of, or in agreement with, an individual authority. They would cover specific services or activities.

A steering group of representatives of the Department and of the local authority associations would be set up to agree an annual programme of the second type of inspection and 'to review from time to time the scope for future work of the Inspectorate.'

The existing staff would be supplemented by secondments from local authorities and other organisations providing expertise in management and performance measurement. But 'the Inspectorate would aim to complement not compete with the work of the Audit Commission'.

The creation of the SSI reflected, and was designed to keep pace with, what was described by a senior member of the Inspectorate (interview, 1989) as a total change of culture in the Department. The Financial Management Initiative meant that the Department accepted responsibility for seeing how the local authorities used the resources allocated them from the Exchequer. SSI recognised there was a corresponding requirement upon it to be more interventionist in its dealings with the local authorities.

## The Legal Framework

Some inspectorates (for example, Her Majesty's Inspectorate of Constabulary) were created by Act of Parliament. SSI was not. Its existence and functions are dependent on the administrative decision of the Secretary of State. Formally, he has done no more than devolve some of his statutory powers and duties onto a group of professional staff employed as civil servants in the Department of Health (separated from the Department of Social Security in 1988). His powers of inspection are contained in a number of Acts of Parliament concerned with services of different kinds or for different groups, in particular children with placements of any kind in local authority care and in private foster care, people with learning difficulties, with mental illness, and with physical disabilities and elderly people in need of care. They extend, in some cases, to inspection of private and voluntary agency provision, mainly of residential care.

The purposes of inspection under statutory powers include registration and renewal of registration, mainly of voluntary provision (eg Children Act, 1989) but also of secure units in community homes for children; compliance with the law and regulations governing the restriction of children's liberty (Children Act, 1989; Secure Accommodation Regulations, 1983 and 1986); maintenance of standards and the protection of vulnerable groups cared for outside their families (Children Act, 1989; Boarding Out and Charge and Control Regulations, 1988; Registered Homes Act, 1984). Inspections of secure accommodation for children are the most extensively framed by law and regulations.

Statutory powers include the right of entry to premises; the right to inspect premises and on such premises to examine the treatment of children and the 'arrangements for the welfare' of 'mentally disordered' people; the right to examine records. Beyond this, the Secretary of State can refuse or withdraw registration of certain categories of provision on the advice of his inspectors. There are in addition detailed powers short of closure or refusal of registration established by convention in the working of the SSI and its predecessor bodies. Intervals between regular inspections are also established by convention, rather than law.

But the Secretary of State has more general statutory duties and powers in relation to the personal social services (PSS). Under Section 7 of the Local Authority Social Services Act, 1970, local authorities are required to carry out their functions 'under the general guidance of the Secretary of State'. One of the roles of SSI is to contribute to the formulation of personal social services policy and policy guidance at national level and to communicate them to the local authority.

## SSI's Objectives

In 1987, the SSI itself for the first time issued its own Mission Statement, which sought to encompass the objectives, values and key roles of the organisation.

Here SSI stated its strategic objectives for 1988-93. They first reiterated the duties of the SSI to 'help to develop, implement and monitor the Department's policies and to manage the Department's work; [to] assist in reviewing legislation and Departmental guidance for the personal social services.'

They established the SSI as the authoritative evaluative body for the personal social services. Under this heading the aims were to 'set, use and disseminate objective criteria for assessing quality' and 'to establish significant relationships between inputs and outputs in the PSS' (both acknowledged in the Directorate to be 'fiendishly difficult' tasks (*Interview*, 1989)). They also stated the role of the SSI as a change agent and the particular focus of the change objectives as 'improving management in the PSS: in particular by providing guidance enabling social service managers to maximise effectiveness and efficiency.' Lastly, SSI underlined its strategic responsibility for training in the PSS.

The purpose of the Mission Statement was probably as much to consolidate staff commitment to the new inspectorate's goals and identity in a period of upheaval, as to create a clear public image. It bears the marks of an organisation attempting a new resolution of the tensions inherent in it. It reflects a strong determination to hold on to its professional culture and throughout seeks a balance between continuity and change.

The inspectorate was to retain its three essential characteristics, that it was a service for Ministers and the Department, that it was a professional organisation and that it acted as an intermediary body between the Department and the local authorities and other providing agencies.

The statement confirmed the requirement on the SSI to help the Secretary of State to discharge his responsibilities towards personal social services. To this end it inspected services to promote their effectiveness and efficiency, it aimed to monitor standards and to promote the capacity of the service giving organisations 'to provide good quality services and obtain value for money.' It must implement government policy. At the same time it was a channel of information about social services and professional expertise to central government.

The functions of the SSI were most powerfully framed by its being part of government but at the same time its authority was ascribed to its professional values and expertise. High among those values were the protection of vulnerable people and the rights and worth of the individual. Professional priorities were that services were effective for individual users. At the same time they had to pursue the government goal of efficiency. These particular tensions were reconciled at the head of the SSI by the commitment in the joint statement quoted by the Secretary of State to the House of Commons to the 'most effective use of professional and other resources'.

The relationship between SSI and central government emerged strongly in the Mission Statement; that between SSI and social services departments weakly. Many people in the SSI had by this time become reconciled to the need for them to be more interventionist and direct in their dealings with the local authorities. Some SSDs were proving unable to meet the demands made on them and crises of confidence were occurring more frequently, most evidently, but not only, in London. But not all were convinced of the value of a more interventionist approach. The statement records the professional value commitment to 'achieving objectives by negotiation and consent.'

The Directorate perceived the consolidation of identity and culture round the Mission Statement, the changes in recruitment, together with the new system of incentives and sanctions in the Civil Service, as providing the essential base for a determined attempt to change the Inspectorate's image and mode of operation. The period was one of high uncertainty and turbulence in the Department, in the local authorities and in the Inspectorate and therefore one in which change was possible, provided there was a structure within which it could be managed.

It was thought that the Inspectorate must be more useful to Ministers and the Department and have more impact on the field. An influential view was that the professional social work framework was inadequate to provide that. Personal social services needed systems analysis and policy analysis, to which the inspectorate should contribute. And it had to be prepared to abandon its caution about the complexities of the central-local government relationship and to respond to crises decisively.

This meant being ready to work under intense pressure, to improvise methodology and to change direction as the pattern of events emerged. But also it entailed a clear shift from the hands off approach to a possibly risky involvement in local authority problems, such as the scandals that emerged in residential care for old people in London. The boundaries between managerial (industrial relations), professional (care practice) and political problems might be impossible to draw. The SSI would be making speedy, often well publicised and definite judgements as bases for action rather than long considered and private comments as or after events unfolded in a tradition geared to sustain equilibrium between central and local government.

A system was thus established which enabled the Inspectorate to respond at short notice to requests from politicians to investigate crises. A notable example was the SSI (1988c) study of the arrangements for child protection in Cleveland, following the publication of the Butler-Sloss Report (DHSS, 1988). This meant the diversion of nine staff over six weeks from the planned work programme.

Interviews in the field suggested that a more direct approach by SSI was by no means unwelcome, at least to managers in the SSDs. There was a felt need to reassert control over services to highly vulnerable people and to solve the acute problems of matching resources to needs in some parts of the service.

However, this robust approach to change was pursued alongside a rather different set of emphases amongst some senior staff in the inspectorate. They tended to stress the continuity retained in the midst of change. They struggled to find a new integration of the demands on the SSI that sustained their identity as a professional but multi-faceted service to government. The central strategy, as perceived by this group, was to establish a stronger linkage between professional inspection, policy development and their intermediary role between the Department and service providers. The significant change for them was that they made these activities mutually reinforcing.

The SWS had devoted approximately 25 per cent of its time to inspection work. The proportion was now to increase to 40 per cent, largely on the basis of a programme of Type 2 inspections based not on statutory powers but on a national programme of work agreed with the local authority associations. That central programme was to be firmly policy driven and so to feed into the policy development work of the inspectorate. The national programme would be carried out in selected authorities in the regions by the regional SSIs. Additionally, regions would continue to plan their own programme of work with their local authorities alongside the national programme on the understanding that that too reflected national policy interests. Thus their work would be more integrated with that of HQ and with policy development than before.

The continuing contribution of SSI to multi professional policy making in the Department was made substantially through working groups in the policy divisions. Contribution to policy development is stated as constituting approximately 30 per cent of staff time.

The third most substantial set of activities comprised policy implementation and operational contact work (15 per cent). That included the establishment of working contacts with key groups in the policy community, including the private and voluntary sectors.

Regional work following up national inspections, carrying out their own regional inspectorate programmes and their development work was part of policy implementation. Development work included disseminating tools of evaluation used by the inspectorate for adaptation and use by the local authorities. An exercise of this kind was being conducted in one region at the time of the study on developing and testing instruments for the inspection of residential care for the elderly. It resulted in the publication of *Homes Are for Living In* (SSI, 1989b).

## Organisation: Structure and Staffing

The professional staff of the SSI (approximately 100) were divided between headquarters in the DHSS and nine regions. The professional organisational structure is depicted in Figure 1.

It was designed to be part of the Departmental structure for policy development and implementation. This was changed in the 1970s from the Haldane principle of division by service. Policy divisions have since been based in client groups, so cutting across the major departmental boundaries between Health, Social Security (until 1988) and Personal Social Services. Client groups were held together in a Service Development Group under a Deputy Secretary (Kogan and Henkel, 1983; Webb and Wistow, 1987). Social Services Inspectors were attached to policy divisions as above, along with other professionals so that they could contribute to policy development and implementation for that group.

This structure essentially remained unchanged in 1985, as did the professional staff, who were imbued with the earlier 'hands off' tradition of relating to the local authorities and the professional culture of social

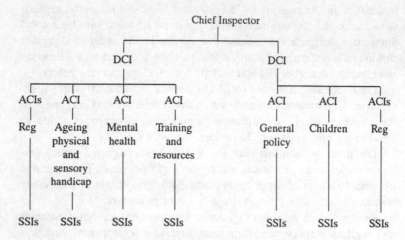

*Figure 1*

work, which was seen as having a distinct identity from, although working largely within, the statutory personal social services.

Two key posts in the management of change, those of Deputy Chief Inspector, were new appointments in 1985. One was a civil servant. Originally recruited to the department as a social scientist, he had substantial experience in the Department's management of research. The other was recruited from the field, where he was part of a new active management tradition in the personal social services.

The convention of employing people with social work qualifications was largely retained, except for the recruitment of two social researchers, to give the inspectorate a technical expertise not previously available to it. However, the newly recruited people from the field were different from most existing inspectors. They were mainly from third and fourth tier management in SSDs. Not only did they have substantial managerial experience in the local authorities post 1979 but most had more recent practice experience than had been available. They had a concept of practice framed by local authority structures and demands (*Interviews*, 1989).

The other strategies used by the SSI to fill the gaps in its staffing complement, and outlined in the ministerial statement to the House of Commons in 1985,were to employ consultants to particular inspections and, occasionally, to arrange for staff from the local authorities to be seconded to the Inspectorate for a period of time.

But for an organisation with multiple objectives and responsible to multiple groups, there was comparatively little division of labour. The main structural divisions were based on the regions and the Departmental policy divisions, providing for geographical and some professional specialisation. There was no specialisation based on the policy, management, cost and practitioner focused functions of the inspectorate.

The exception was the Training and Resources Group which housed the social scientists. This was the source of a new, policy oriented initiative by the SSI to make a substantial contribution to the Department's strategic information base. The social scientists made links with the statistics branch which led to a collaborative review of the personal social services statistics. But their biggest single project was the development of a demonstration package of key indicators for the management of local authority SSDs (SSI, 1988d).

The indicators were largely derived from existing statistics and drew on the Audit Commission's local authority profiles. They were designed for use by administrators in the Department of Health, the local authorities and the Inspectorate itself. It was hoped they could improve inspections: they could be an aid to choice of topic, provide an initial data base and take some of the data collection out of inspections themselves; they could assist in providing sampling frames or identify target authorities for inspection. They could corroborate or challenge inspection findings. In the longer term they might lead to the establishment of an expert systems base for inspections. In the meantime, the social scientists were already advising more broadly on inspection methodology. If inspections had previously been based on professional social work skills, they were now being supplemented.

## The Concept of Inspection

The transformation of the SWS into an Inspectorate in 1985 undoubtedly had a symbolic meaning. In practice, the authority and functions of inspectorates might be confused, but the notion of inspection carries with it ideas of close, critical and probably comprehensive examination, on the basis of clear standards, by an external body with enforcement powers.

The concept of close and rigorous examination is readily perceived as apposite to the evaluation of closed institutions and to practice conceived within a limited range of work or a well defined expertise. In the late 20th century it has been transposed to the evaluation of systems that are often ill bounded, in various states of change and pursuing a variety of purposes.

In SSI documents inspection is a method of work. A procedural guide was first produced for the SWS in 1984, the year after the consultative document proposing the creation of the inspectorate. It was revised in 1988. It defined inspection as 'a process in which the Inspectorate uses its skills to monitor the quality of services provided for vulnerable clients, and evaluating use of resources. It is necessarily about values and standards.' The document outlined the components of inspection: data collection, professional analysis, professional judgement and recommendations.

## Organising and Structuring Inspections

The creation of the inspectorate in 1985 brought with it a major new task: to plan the national programme of inspections. The structure for agreeing the national work programme was the Joint Steering Group whose members comprised representatives from the local authority associations, the Association of Directors of Social Services (ADSS), administrators from the Department and the SSI. It authorised an annual planned programme of Type 2 inspections with objectives, methods and a time frame built in as far as possible.

The two main types of inspection mounted under the annual national programmes from 1987 were inspections of particular services or aspects of service carried out in sample local authorities across all or some of the regions, and inspections with a broadly developmental remit.

As from 1989, the annual programme agreed in the Joint Steering Group included three main kinds of project: new projects, projects already in progress but moving into a new phase, and 'impact' projects designed to assess the impact of selected previous national inspections. Of the 29 inspections in the 1989-90 programme, four were concerned with impact. Although the general aim was that the national programme would reflect national policy priorities, SSI also tried to include at least one inspection on a low profile service.

Perhaps the most immediately noticeable contrast between the SSI national programme and the special studies of the Audit Commission was its size: 29 inspections, to which had to be added the regular Type 1 inspections and the new ad hoc Type 3 inspections.

SSI's revised guidance to inspection (SSI, 1988e) was primarily a guide to the management of inspections. It established a common framework for all SSI inspections within which tasks and accountability were clearly allocated, planning was structured within defined time limits, resources required were stated, approved and coordinated and access to agencies where inspection was to be carried out was negotiated. It made only broad statements on methodology, assuming that it would be determined in the context of individual exercises. But it envisaged inspections as based on general criteria of evaluation that would be made as explicit as possible and operated by reference to general standards. It drew attention to work already done on criteria and standards in particular contexts, but asserted that criteria would become more explicit through planning and executing of individual inspections. It also identified a general focus for inspections: services provided for specific groups of clients and staff and resources made available for their care.

Amongst Type 1 inspections, those of secure accommodation were the most strongly framed, by law, regulations and detailed specific guidance as well as the general guidance document.

Our second case study explores how those inspections were developed and changed in the early years of the new inspectorate.

The first of our studies demonstrates some of the pressures this government based evaluative body was under during the period of transformation from professional advisory service to an inspectorate with a broadened remit.

# Chapter Six

# Connoisseurial Evaluation under Pressure:
## A Case Study of the Social Services Inspectorate

The inspection described in this chapter took place when the Social Work Service (SWS) was in the process of transition to the Social Services Inspectorate (SSI). It was carried out between September, 1984 and March 1985. The national report was published in September, 1985. Reports on the participating local authorities, whose homes were inspected, were sent to those authorities at the same time. By that time the SWS had become the SSI.

The inspection was initiated as part of a new programme of work launched by the SWS under the heading of *Efficiency in the Social Services*. It provides a good example of a professional evaluation of practice in a bounded social work service: the residential care of children. But it raises particular questions about the evaluative task in a setting where policy has promoted the professionalisation of a service, which in practice continues to be delivered mainly by unqualified staff.

Residential care services for children were under political and professional scrutiny about that time. The SWS itself had recently completed a regional study in London; the House of Commons Select Committee on Social Services was examining it as part of their investigation into children in care. Local authorities were, in many cases, developing policies for the care of children focusing on alternatives to residential care. One consequence was that the young people remaining in residential care were more disturbed than had previously been the case. The demands of residential care were intensifying while its value was under question.

At the end of 1983, concern about low morale intensified in a three month period of industrial action.

## Preparation

The inspection was to be of a sample of community homes for children in England. It would be carried out under the powers contained in Section 74 of the Child Care Act, 1980. A lead manager and a lead officer for the inspection were appointed from the SWS directorate, and planning began in May, 1983. The lead officer had been part of the Children's Inspectorate in the Home Office before the establishment of the SWS, when personal social services were reorganised in 1971. The major administrative responsibility for the inspection was in her hands.

The inspection would be carried out by SWS regional teams, coordinated by a liaison officer appointed for the inspection. Principal SWS Officers of each region were consulted about the selection of local authorities and homes for inspection and methodological issues. Two months before the inspection began, a briefing seminar was held for the regional staff.

Meanwhile, interprofessional consultation within the DHSS was required with doctors, nurses and dieticians, and externally with schools HMIs. Researchers in the field were contacted for advice. Local authorities, the Association of Directors of Social Services (ADSS), professional associations and unions were kept informed.

The inspection's objectives were to visit a substantial number of community homes in England,

- 'to inform the Secretary of State and the Department ...(how).. local authorities were carrying out this part of their responsibilities, with particular reference to changes taking place in the residential sector;
- to offer an independent evaluation to providing authorities;
- to identify good practice and to stimulate discussion' (SSI, 1985).

A secondary objective was to encourage residential staff in an adverse climate of opinion and to demonstrate the demands made on them.

The focus would be on the children in the homes at the time of the inspection, why they were there, and how far their needs were being met. Inspectors would also inquire about the policy and strategy for children in care in each authority. In each authority a report of the inspector's findings would be made available to the authority's Social Services Committee and a composite national report would be published.

A total of 149 homes in 29 authorities (13 per cent of homes in the relevant categories) was included in the exercise. Originally scheduled for early 1984, it was postponed by six months because of industrial action in 1983.

Internal discussion in the Inspectorate about the design and purposes of the exercise centred on whether it should be concerned with cost effectiveness and what kind of standards should be used by inspectors.

During this period SWS itself was felt to be under scrutiny. Some thought that the SWS should demonstrate capacity to examine cost effectiveness; others considered that its expertise was in the quality of life and care in the establishments. Others again wished to avoid polarising professional purposes and cost effectiveness. Cost effectiveness could be interpreted not just narrowly by comparing unit costs but also by examining the match between children's needs and the use of resources for their care.

SWS decided against a financial analysis; the exercise would not attempt to duplicate the sort of study that would be undertaken by the Audit Commission. In the event, the focus and methods were a compromise: some inspectors were unsure about professional norms as a basis for evaluation; would they be acceptable yardsticks? Others felt a professional or 'connoisseurial' approach should be employed without apology.

Other differences of emphases were evident between those concerned to maximise consistency between inspectors' work, and so demonstrate evaluative competence, and those who felt it most important that the exercise should reflect professional thinking about quality of life and practice. One view was that the report should express professional standards; the task of measuring the performance of individual establishments against those standards belonged to the local authorities.

The law, the Community Homes Regulations 1972, policy documents and some long established, but not official, norms for staffing levels provided a framework for inspection. Inspectors were also concerned with food, buildings and clothing, as well as with the quality of relationships and the treatment of disturbed children. But hard measures of performance were not generally available to them.

The choice of the homes to be visited was negotiated between regional SWS officers and the local authorities concerned. Selection would be predominantly opportunistic and practical rather than scientific. But inspectors were required to take into account length of time since the last inspection and the value of a spread of functions, size, types of building and location among the homes. Homes where the function was changing or where there were innovative approaches should be included in the sample (SSI,1983b).

Two detailed aide-memoires were prepared for the inspecting officers to use in each authority and home: one for a discussion with authority senior managers on policy and organisation; the other for inspecting the homes themselves. They were intended to be used according to individual discretion.

Some professional practice norms were spelt out in detail. Some questions were incorporated on the advice of other professional or occupational groups; others concerned issues that had not yet been fully incorporated into general social work practice. Questions about children's racial or cultural identity featured strongly; gender issues did not. The management of children who had been physically or sexually abused was not mentioned, an example of how quickly priorities can change. Within two more years this would be a central concern.

Some of the influences on the aide-memoires were evident from DHSS files made available to the study. They included doctors, nurses, dieticians and caterers in the DHSS; material received about children from ethnic minority groups and a note drawing attention to the government's response to the House of Commons Select Committee on Children in Care. A reading list of relevant literature was compiled early on.

Forms for data collection were designed with help from the DHSS operational research service and piloted before the full inspection. They were to be completed by officers in charge of the homes before they were visited.

Data sheets on each home were intended to show the mix of children resident at the time of completion, highlighting characteristics which might explain the choice of residential care as their placement. A brief summary of staff establishments would serve as a basis for assessing the relationship between children's needs and staff resources.

Preparation for the inspection took 16 months. The SWS wanted the exercise to be as valid as possible; achieving this with the breadth of the investigation decided on was a huge task.

The inspection was an important political event for the SWS. Ministers were asserting new priorities in the department, which they wanted installed in the new inspectorate. The SWS had to be credible in the eyes of ministers. It was important that they associated themselves with the inspection. It was, for example, mentioned in Kenneth Clarke's address to the Social Services Conference in Oxford in September, 1983 (SSI, 1983a).

At the same time, the SWS stood as representative of professional standards and values in central government, as well as acting as link between central and local government. It sought cooperation from the field but had to manage pressure from, for example, Directors of Social Services to ensure the inspection recorded resource needs in the context of heavier pressures for economy and efficiency from its political masters. It invited the selected authorities to participate, although it had the power to insist. It also hoped that informing unions of the exercise would smooth its path.

## Feedback methods and audiences

There were to be two main types of written feedback: a national report and a report on each of the participant local authorities. The national report would be a collation of the individual local authority reports, which were for the use of the Social Services Director and Committee. They would decide on their dissemination. But neither they nor the individual homes would see the homes reports. A request made by the Social Care Association that they should was not, in the event, met.

After the inspections had been completed, the SSI Directorate discussed the style and thrust of the national report. One view was that it should be 'a faithful interpretation of the facts as interpreted by the best professional judgement'. It should not encourage the idea that 'a body labelled 'inspectorate' is invariably unfavourable in its criticism'. A contrasting view was that because this would be the first major report issued after the SWS was converted into an inspectorate, inspectors should 'adopt a robust approach ... we should be ready to point up the problems and difficulties that we have discovered and ... to make clear recommendations about them.'

The difference was between those who wanted to demonstrate what a report within the SWS professional tradition could produce and those who thought the new SSI should conform to the newly developing norms in the Department.

## Local authority context

One of the 29 inspections of local authorities in a shire county with a total population of over half a million was selected for this study..

In 1981 the social services department had been radically reorganised to create a reduced central management team and a decentralised operational management structure, in which residential, field, day and domiciliary services would be integrated at local level.

Fifty-five integrated patch teams were created and distributed between eleven areas. The centrally inspired reorganisation was directed through an area development programme devised and orchestrated by top management and a strong training resource. At the same time methods to monitor departmental performance were introduced, based on centralised and computerised data collection and analysis.

Between 1984 and 1985 the local authority social services committee approved a revised child care policy designed to prevent family breakdown, to return children who had had to be received into care to their own families quickly and, failing that, to provide permanent substitute homes. Residential care was to be a small scale resource; not a last resort, but sufficient only to achieve the overall policy objectives: preparing children for their long term destinations and providing longer term care itself for only a tiny minority.

By the autumn of 1984, when the inspection in this authority began, there were only six homes in the categories included in the inspection. All six were visited by the inspector. They ranged from an independence unit for four older girls to a twenty place home for young people of both sexes.

## The Regional Perspective

Two inspectors in the region were interviewed, the Assistant Chief Inspector and the person responsible for the inspection, who knew the authority well. She was also a member of a national SSI sub-group on residential care and had piloted this study in another authority.

Traditionally, the DHSS region had adopted an advisory rather than a prescriptive stance but there were mixed views among inspectors about the change of status into an inspectorate. One of our regional respondents welcomed the change. The other insisted that the advisory mode would continue to be preferred, if the prime objective was to achieve change. She implied that there might be tension between producing evaluations rigorous enough methodologically to be credible and tailored enough to individual authorities to help people change. Change was most likely to be achieved through informal methods of work. She doubted whether the new formal status of the inspectorate would increase its political power. Inspectors working in large shire counties might be relating to Directors with their own line to the DHSS and a certain amount of 'clout' with ministers.

The SWS had thought a lot about residential care but had not brought this to bear on community homes. Residential care was a sensitive area of work. If there were a crisis or scandal, it would be helpful for them to have a picture of what was going on across the country. It was a time of change; homes were closing and some experimental work was taking place. The SWS wanted a picture of practice in this context and to promote policy change in authorities so far untouched by new thinking.

The inspection was concerned with the quality of care in the homes. Both the inspectors interviewed thought it was also intended to consider whether children in the homes were rightly placed, although only one thought it had done so. The other thought this would have meant examining modes of assessment and individual files as well as discussing individual children's needs with field staff. Both thought that efficiency was on the agenda but only in a limited sense. In the words of one, the inspection was 'only playing at examining efficiency'.

Both considered the scope of the inspection excessively wide. They had no guidance about priorities and the exercise yielded far more information than it could use. The inspection of each home took at least two days. They could have given as good a picture of current practice if they had inspected fewer homes.

The inspectors thought that the clients or audiences of the inspection were multiple: the policy branch and the SSI in the DHSS, the social services departments whose homes were inspected, the public and the policy community. They were conscious throughout the inspection that they that they were there to safeguard the interests of children.

## Inspection Criteria, Methods and Procedures

The SSI at that time provided no formal training in evaluation. One respondent felt that inspectors were 'professionals dealing with professionals' and that much depended on personality and different styles of relationships. Inspectors should be knowledgeable about human relations.

Recommendations were to some extent personal, although not necessarily idiosyncratic. Inspectors had opportunities to test their judgements against those of others by joint inspection or membership of committees. At the briefing seminar, inspectors had tried to agree some common standards. But they had no model of the organisation of residential care against which to judge the authorities; criteria were largely implicit and derived from inspectors' training, knowledge and experience.

One respondent thought that criteria should be made explicit if possible and shared with those being inspected. Explicit criteria could reduce inconsistencies between reports and could form the basis of recommendations. One respondent referred to 'professional standards' but without further specification. One mentioned the importance of 'professional honesty': if inspectors observed something was wrong they should highlight it in the report.

The inspector contacted senior managers and secured agreement to the inspection from the Director. She then attended a management meeting to 'sell the inspection to them'; formally, they could not have refused. A liaison officer was appointed by the authority for the inspection.

The inspector interviewed senior managers in each division about child care policy. The inspection of the homes included an interview with the patch team manager. The team manager interviewed was asked about how he controlled, supported and managed the work of the home. He was glad to supply this information, for it was a job which he took seriously. He was disappointed that there was little reference to the team manager's role in the report. He thought it should have had a high profile.

Inspectors varied as to how they used the aide-memoire. Some gave priority to consistency and went through each question. The inspector for this authority did not: you 'can lose the heart of an inspection if you try to cover everything'. She considered child care standards and used the aide-memoire within that framework.

The inspector talked with officers in charge, staff in the homes and children. One officer-in-charge felt that her expectations of new staff were unrealistic. But the style of the inspection was appreciated; discussion and questioning of staff and children were informal, opportunistic and open-ended. Another officer-in- charge felt that the approach was not critical but inquiring; the inspector did not seek to impose a particular view of child care. The inspection was thought to be thorough. The inspector was perceived as using her own experience, together with current theoretical ideas, in a fairly ad hoc manner and that on the whole met with approval. In one home she attended a staff meeting. No other events were mentioned.

Inspectors stressed the value of observation. One felt that the detail of the aide-memoire reduced the time available for it. This was regrettable because observation was a necessary means of checking verbal statements. 'A good inspection of an establishment involves the inspector merging with the wallpaper'. It was necessary to attend to interpersonal dynamics, group dynamics, and body language to assess how a home works.

The examination of records was an essential part of the inspection and inspectors had detailed guidance about which records to cover and the criteria of good recording.

The inspector thought it important to give some immediate feedback to staff of homes and this was mentioned appreciatively by the head of one home. It was not, however, easy to provide because only at the end of an inspection was it possible to give a comparative angle on the work of homes. There was no attempt to share findings immediately with senior managers. The inspector felt it was impossible to do that 'before you have thought everything through'.

A senior manager in the authority summed up the approaches adopted to the inspection as follows: it was a professional review of the organisation and delivery of care for the children; it made qualitative judgements and observations of children in homes and took account of their views about the care they received; it examined some administrative issues that were subject to the community homes regulations; it reviewed the legal position of children in care. This manager thought it particularly important to look at the position of individual children.

## Reporting the Inspection

Reports were compiled on each authority inspected. These were collated into a national report. The report on the authority was sent to the Director so that it could be checked for factual accuracy. The Director received the final version about a year after the inspection had begun.

Inspectors were given guidance on the organisation of reports and what should be included in them. Although they were to report on residential care in the authority not in individual homes, they should include a summary assessment of the work of the homes, under specified headings. Points might be illustrated with details from the inspectors' reports on individual homes. Inspectors were also advised to comment on the authority's management, staff support and staff development as they impinged on the operation of individual homes. Finally they were asked to make recommendations. These might be grouped according to the level of the organisation where action was needed.

## The Local Report

The report reiterated the purposes of the inspection which were to provide information for the Secretary of State, the DHSS, the individual local authorities and the profession. The inspection would provide an objective evaluation for those responsible for providing residential care, an account of practice and current changes in the field, and an opportunity to promote good practice through the process of inspection and through the reports. It would also identify any serious problems requiring immediate action.

The report made 15 recommendations. After outlining the purposes and methods of the inspection it gave a brief description of the homes inspected, but no individual assessment. The findings were then reported under nine headings, but not those suggested in the guidance to inspectors.

The report began by emphasising problems created for staff when the function of the homes was unclear, in a context of a child care policy in flux. It was important for staff to know whether they were a resource for the whole county or for the local patch team and its priorities. The implications of redeploying staff needed to be taken fully into account.

The report commented on working relationships between the senior staff in the homes and the first line managers in the patch teams and on the focus and frequency of staff meetings and staff supervision. The extent of staff familiarity with and use of departmental operational instructions, community homes regulations and a fairly recently published national code of practice was noted.

The section on premises was concerned briefly with standards of decoration and maintenance. A particular point was made about good practice in the care of children in short term or transitional placements: ensuring their warmth and comfort in such circumstances could endorse their sense of being valued.

Simple tables charted the age, sex, qualifications and experience of staff. Specific staff anxieties were recorded, for example about handling violence and the sexual problems of young people; changing responsibilities in residential care were noted and existing opportunities for training discussed. Again, examples of good practice were quoted.

The age and sex distribution of the children in residential care was tabulated, together with the time they had been in care. For the most part the tables were left to speak for themselves, but they noted the high proportion of young people of 14 and over and the relatively high numbers of children who had been in care for two years or more.

The section on physical care emphasised the importance of food. Opportunities for children to help with preparing meals and shopping were discussed, together with the use of order books in shopping for clothes. Health and education were substantial items under this heading: in particular the arrangements for registration with GPs, the attention paid to health records, the quality of relationships between homes and schools and the priority given by staff to the children's education.

The report commented on the quality of recording and the organisation of children's files and drew attention to the relationship between the purpose, structure and content of different forms of record.

Planning for children was emphasised. The inspector pointed out the need for further attention to the quality and realism of planning within a well organised system. The problems were underlined by reference to the struggle staff were having to help young people in their care who were inappropriately placed.

There were few direct normative statements about what constitutes good practice. For the most part the report endorsed practice, management or policy by giving examples from one or more homes of opportunities, experiences or approaches valued by staff or children. It also gave examples of ineffective work. Thus a picture was given of good and bad practices but not of good and not so good homes. Staff and managers were left to assess their own performance against the evaluative comments.

The recommendations were short and clear. They were expressed with different degrees of urgency and insistence. They were not, however, listed in priority order.

Amongst the strongest recommendations were those on clarifying the function of homes, on health records and on the need for plans for children to be more realistic and specific.

Recommendations requiring policy decisions and senior managerial action were fairly evenly balanced with those requiring action from officers in charge. At least three recommendations had training implications. The report made no direct reference to homes' efficiency.

## Reactions in the Authority to the Report

Operational managers and those given the responsibility to structure implementation were critical of the decision not to issue reports on individual homes. The fact that good practice and problems were not identified with individual homes was a source of annoyance; staff felt they had worked hard to get something right and not been given credit for this. It also created uncertainty and speculation about which home was the subject of particular comments. A number of respondents thought inspection meant the delivery of clear judgement on those inspected. Staff of homes and their managers felt they had borne the major burden of inspection but had not had their share of its output. They had not thought about using the report as a tool for self assessment. What they wanted was direct external appraisal and validation of their work.

Otherwise there was no strong criticism of the report. It was variously described as 'useful', 'easy to read', 'quite good', and 'fairly anodyne'. The recommendations were accepted. Many were thought by managers outside homes to reinforce the general approach of the authority and to point up areas of work where authority policy was not being implemented.

Some challenged the salience of much of the report in the light of current policy. An operational manager remarked how the policy scene had changed even between the inspection and the receipt of the report. He and his colleagues tended to look to the future and wanted to develop alternatives to residential care. However, the recommendations were taken seriously and their importance to children in children's homes was recognised. Some respondents questioned whether the report demonstrated enough awareness of the kinds of children and young people living in 'ordinary' community homes in the 1980s. Most felt the report had not put forward new thinking, although one officer in charge had a different view. He thought the inspection had dealt with some issues that were emerging as important nationally at the time and whose local relevance only emerged afterwards.

There were some surprises in the report for senior managers. Examples included the continued use of order books for clothes shopping, the lack of attention to medical records and some failure to come to grips with children's educational needs.

Two senior managers thought the report highlighted broad issues for the authority, some beyond the boundaries of residential care of children. These included the authority's capacity to manage change, problems of communication and recording, the effective supervision and monitoring of professional performance, training needs and concerns about handling violence and about the importance to children of education. One thought the report would be a 'useful reference document for managers and staff'.

The inspection had some impact on the homes themselves, particularly while it was being carried out. The evidence from the three homes looked at in the research was that staff took the exercise seriously and, for the most part, appreciated it. In a home where some staff found the inspector's questions challenging, the officer in charge took the opportunity to explain why the issues were important.

But when the minutes of contemporary management meetings from one of the homes were examined, there was no evidence that the inspection stimulated discussion of practice issues or that the report provided the 'useful reference document' referred to above. Some of the issues raised were certainly being addressed in the home, but not linked with the inspection; others seemed not to be. The report was not received in this home until 16 months after the exercise and five months after the receipt of the report by the Department.

## The SSD's Response: the framework

The report was sent to the authority in September, 1985, about six months after the end of the exercise. The SSD's Management Team (DMT) obtained an initial response from its Principal Officer for child care. Her reaction was positive. She and four colleagues decided on an implementation structure. Responsibility for action on it would lie with divisional line managers. Their response would be monitored, by officers without line management responsibilities in residential care.

An amalgamated account of implementation in each division was given to the DMT in September, 1986 and immediately incorporated in a report taken by the Director to the Social Services Committee. The inspector was also invited to address the committee but was unable to do so. She had been moved to another area of work in an emergency.

The regional SSI asked for a progress report in May 1987. This was supplied by the authority in August, after the Principal Officer had received updated information from the divisions.

The staff given monitoring responsibilities consulted the officers in charge of the homes and their patch team managers about the action that should be taken in each home. They checked with them which of the recommendations applied to their homes, but did not make any independent assessment. That would have required far more time. If there had been any suggestion of seriously bad practice in the homes this would have been a major drawback.

Once arrangements for implementation were underway, the main responsibility was taken by the line managers. The 'monitor' in one division saw it as his responsibility to see that structures were in place for change where this would take time, for example in staff training. But he did not take any long term part in implementation. He and his opposite number checked on what had been done before making their amalgamated report to the DMT.

The importance of due process was thus recognised in the authority. One respondent was doubtful about the authority's commitment to the substance of the inspection. Recommendations were enjoined on homes but many required more resources or sustained implementation of policies by senior management.

However, two substantial pieces of work were initiated to follow up the recommendations. These were undertaken by a staff development officer for one of the divisions. The first was a thorough review of arrangements for health care of children in residential care. This went well beyond the actual recommendations of the inspection report to pursue an existing, but not fully realised, set of objectives. The inspection had provided the spur to strengthen the impact of a policy to which the authority was already committed. A report was made to the Departmental Management Team and accepted. It had, however, not been implemented by the time of the follow up report made to the ACI in 1987.

The second piece of work involved helping the staff of one home who were finding it difficult to meet changing demands in residential care to accept that the home should have a new function. The staff development officer described the emotional challenge to the staff involved. Another respondent emphasised the need to ensure that inspections were not sterile exercises; the response of his area was not to accept recommendations slavishly but to attempt to think through principles and apply them with discretion: for example in involving children in their own reviews.

## Implementation of the Report

In summary, this authority established a clear framework for implementing the inspection report. The framework was consistent with the general approach of the department, which was strongly committed to effective management and to monitoring and evaluating its performance. Almost all the recommendations were already departmental policy.

## Policy Recommendations

The inspection was carried out in the middle of major change in child care policy in the authority. Only one of the recommendations was concerned with new strategy to match needs and resources; two more constituted advice to review the impacts of policy change on staff in the residential units: to ensure they understood what the function of their unit was and to review the continued adequacy of staff resources when the function changed.

The authority acknowledged the need for good communication with units in a period of continuing change. The three homes on which this study concentrated reflected three modes of response by the authority. One was the site of the sustained piece of work described above. But despite the efforts of all concerned its function was still not settled by the time of our study in 1988. A second home felt its function to be quite clearly defined. The problem was that it was not adhered to in the actual placement of children. Staff felt they were bearing the burdens of failure by the authority to implement its own policies. The third home had undergone major change but had managed to keep pace with it. Staff had been involved in devising a handbook for the home incorporating policy and guidance. This had provided a framework in which several of the SSI recommendations could be dealt with.

The authority's action on the more strategic issue was made as much on its own initiative as on that of the inspectorate. By 1987, it had developed three independent living units for young people. It could claim, in its follow up report to the region, that it was targeting some of its residential provision on older age groups in care, as suggested by the inspector. But, again, it was pursuing existing policies.

## Recommendations On Practice or Systems Affecting Practice

Three of the inspector's recommendations were for training to enhance practice in residential care: training for professional supervision by senior staff in the units and training on particular aspects of practice.

Training had a high priority in this authority and the support of the heads of homes in this exercise. Progress reports, however, showed that specific responses varied. After two years the numbers of staff in units who had been on supervision courses still varied and although it was claimed in the feedback to the SSI in 1987 that supervision was a feature of all homes, this was not true at the time of our study in 1988.

In-service training on various aspects of practice was provided and many staff attended. But the inspection raised questions for some senior staff about why training was not more effective. These questions were not tackled.

In several cases the inspection highlighted systems which were in place but not working properly: arrangements for regular staff meetings; staff familiarity with operational instructions and how they could help them in their work; arrangements for the purchase of clothes for the children.

By 1987, it was reported that regular staff meetings were installed in all the homes inspected in 1984. The use of order books to buy clothes for children had been abolished and, where possible, children were encouraged to buy their own clothes. The inspection had highlighted the importance of the authority's operational instructions. Steps had been taken to see that they were fully used in induction programmes and that staff appreciated their value as tools in their day to day practice.

Ensuring the proper operation of at least the first two of these systems was on the face of it relatively simple. But the authority had been under the impression that order books had long been thrown away. And while our study in no way suggested that had not now happened, it did reveal disagreement about which homes were using them at the time of the inspection.

A recommendation that homes should more actively involve children in ordinary household tasks like shopping and cooking required a review of operational policies. Budgeting systems had to be further devolved for this to happen and this was done. It was not, however, enough for all homes to change their practice: some larger homes and short stay establishments did not.

Some recommendations meant a more substantial reappraisal of practice and beliefs underlying it. Planning for individual children was given a high profile in this inspection. The authority was enjoined to ensure that plans made at case conferences had realistic and specific goals. Full involvement of children and parents in planning was also recommended. This advice accorded well with the authority's philosophy of good management and with its increasing emphasis on consumer rights.

But complex issues of practice and management are involved here. Managers need to ensure that setting clear short term goals does not militate against trying to tackle severe problems, which may need the exercise of highly developed skills in working with young people. And it was clear from our study that managers and practitioners had varying views about participation in planning by children. Some were unequivocally in favour of it; others had anxieties about it that would have to be resolved before participation could be either real or to the benefit of children.

Other recommendations meant inter-agency collaboration. These were addressed, both in the children's homes and by local and senior managers, although some staff felt that their efforts to work with schools and not to collude with children who did not attend school had not been fully registered in the inspection. The authority's report to the committee and to the SSI recorded that homes on the whole worked well with schools. Some homes had problems with children who were suspended from schools or who needed but could not get special school placements. Some staff felt that these problems were more common than school refusals.

## Implementation Issues

The issues with which this inspection was concerned were not high in the priorities of the authority. It was aiming to develop alternatives to residential care for children. But managers recognised that the issues were important for children who were living in such care. The authority accepted the report's recommendations and established an implementation structure consistent with its commitment to clear managerial accountability and the monitoring and evaluation of performance.

In some respects the inspection highlighted the shortcomings of a hierarchical system, even where attempts are made to involve staff from various parts of the organisation in formulating policies, and even when they are implemented through a simple structure. The report showed them that some of their systems were not working and what they thought was happening in units was not.

It is unlikely that the authority was unduly surprised by this. The tasks devolved on their children's homes could not be performed well in a system designed simply to control and convey communication downwards from the top. They were mediated through relationships forged by the particular staff groups in particular settings working with particular children. Traditionally such tasks are felt to rely on the exercise of discretion within a framework of recognised principles and practice. This means having a system that is strong at the periphery as well as at the centre, a requirement recognised in this SSD structure.

The nature of residential work means that implementing change often needs a long time scale. Some of the issues raised questions of strongly contested values and interpretations of, for example, responsibility, freedom and rights; some recommendations presupposed a particular form of training and practice to which staff might not necessarily have been exposed. Some recommendations were designed to give people more confidence to tackle the problems of handling deep and troubled feelings in themselves and others. Training material might be an important means of building confidence. It is unlikely to be sufficient. (The scale of the demands on residential care staff was recognised in the Department of Health's 'Caring in Homes Initiative' launched in 1989).

The report was concerned primarily with the task of cementing policies and practice rather than developing them. The children's homes were often dealing with legacies from past mistakes and discarded practices: work that might be less exciting than that of the authority's current priority of preventing future accumulation of such legacies.

In these circumstances, deciding what is an adequate response to an inspection is hard. The inspection represented a perspective not only external to the authority but also at a tangent to its primary concerns. It took place in a climate of rapid change. It was not dismissed and the response shows that links were made between existing policies and what the report proposed. Cynics might say that enabled the authority to present itself in a good light. But if such linkages had not been made, it is hard to see how the response could have had any meaning. A more telling criticism is that only two examples came to light in our study of formal questioning by the department of those policies. And one of those came from the lowest level managers, those in the homes.

The recommendations were made separately and were treated in the authority's response as such. That meant each was attended to and the demands of accountability met. But in practice, of course, they are linked. They are to do with creating environments in which children live their lives. And there were glimpses of such links being made explicit at the level of individual unit action. One home was compiling a handbook soon after the inspection. The staff were taking an active role in identifying the function of their unit, deciding which operational instructions were particularly relevant to them, and appraising the aims of reviews and how they should work. They thus made connections between various issues that were outlined in the report, not, however, in direct response to it. They wanted, independently, to enhance their practice. That piece of work indicates what makes for effective response to changing demands but also how discrete proposals for change might be given more impact: making connections between selected items and giving them priority might have greater force than responding separately and equally to all.

Overall the authority's response might be described as thorough but contained compliance. But embedded in it are alternative possibilities. The action of the unit just described was, as it happens, independent of the inspection, which had little overt impact on its thinking. However, it also represents a potential mode of deliberate response to a summative evaluation: integrative and active, in which the evaluation is used as a catalyst for action that the unit makes its own.

A third mode was implicit in comments from two respondents in the study. They identified practice of particular homes that could serve as models for others. There was little evidence of how, or even if, others learnt from such models in this instance. However, one way of thinking about implementation in an active mode is to think of the implementing body as a learning institution. An important project for well organised hierarchical bodies like this authority is to consider what are the conditions under which groups of staff can learn not only vertically from their line managers but also horizontally or systemically from their peers and other groups including users; and what is the limit of compatibility between such structures.

## The National Report

A national report of the community homes inspection was produced in September 1985. (SSI, 1985) It was based on the regional inspectors' reports and working notes on each of the 149 homes in the inspection.

It contained information about the SSDs by which the homes were managed: their organisational structures and child care policies; arrangements for monitoring residential homes; the homes; the children living in the homes; the staff; planning for the children; daily life in the homes; arrangements for children's health care, their education, finding employment and how they were prepared for independent living; records kept in the homes.

The report provided a snapshot of 149 children's homes at a particular time during the period late 1984 and early 1985. Because it was not based on a random or stratified sample of community homes, the confidence with which generalisations could be made was limited. The quantitative analyses of the child and staff populations were of the selected homes. And although the inspectorate had an implicit point of comparison, their study of 1974/5, that was not explicitly mentioned in the report. Therefore, the report offered indicators of national trends and features of particular concern, not an authoritative account.

## Evaluating the National Report

The report can perhaps best be evaluated against its own objectives:

- to inform the Department and the Secretary of State;
- to provide an objective evaluation for local authorities;

- to identify good practice;
- to stimulate discussion.

The information provided in the report was selected and organised primarily through the perspectives of the social work profession, as represented by the inspectorate. The legal framework for the residential care of children is provided by the Community Homes Regulations, 1972. These give broad guidance on the management of homes, arrangements for medical care and safety, visits to children by family and friends, providing opportunities for religious observance and establishing control in the homes. There is thus considerable latitude for the development of practice norms.

There was discussion in the inspectorate about the function of the report. A member of the Directorate questioned whether it would be a report of a professional inspection, a research report or a guide to good practice. The planning group considered it to be an inspection report that could provide the basis of a guidance document but no such guidance document was in the event produced.

## Information

Apart from the collection of child care statistics, made through a different mechanism in the department, at this time the inspectorate had made no decisions about data bases it might keep or need. What was required of an inspection report was not yet defined but one purpose was to satisfy the Secretary of State that the local authority was providing a particular set of services efficiently.

This case study did not investigate systematically what the inspectorate itself considered to be information important for policy. And as neither the department nor the inspectorate put the report to specific use, the value of the information could not be assessed in that way. Individuals mentioned its reinforcing the general impression that the population of children's homes was now predominantly in the age group 13+; that staff were now almost without exception non-resident in the homes, a fact which appeared to be correlated with a decline in the appearance and maintenance of homes; that at a time of high unemployment the numbers of young residents in employment varied greatly, and in a way not strongly correlated with the geographical location or particular socio-economic context of the homes.

## Identifying Good Practice

The main headings under which inspectors sought to identify good practice in this report were staff development, planning for children and life in the homes.

The report made several references to the supervision and support needed to enable residential care staff to define their roles in a changing policy environment, and to give children and young people the help they needed. It gave examples of authorities who were providing needed forms of training. It also sought to identify, mainly again by example, what constituted a sense of professional identity in a residential care context.

The low proportion of staff with one of the two recognised qualifications in the homes inspected was noted with regret but there was no norm or requirement for qualification against which this could be set. Nor was there such a norm for numbers of staff. Thus the report could only note examples of homes where staffing levels were on the face of it inadequate by reference to the common sense judgement that junior staff were on duty alone in charge of groups of children and young people.

Planning for children was made a particular focus of this inspection. While the report gave no information about the quality of plans made for individual children and made no independent assessment of whether they were appropriately placed, it did attempt to identify good practice in this area in some detail. It identified, for example, the need to base planning on an understanding of children's history.

The involvement of children in planning was more generally advocated. And there were statements about the organisation of good planning. Examples of good planning were also provided.

The section on life in the homes provided some clear statements about diet, affording opportunities for contact with family and friends, activities in the home and the living environment of the home. The values underlying such statements could also be identified: normalisation, the importance of nurturing, the role of relationships in nurturing and control, individualisation, rights of minimal intervention with children's existing or newly chosen relationships and the importance of education and employment in children's lives.

However, it was noticeable that the report gave little or no definitive guidance on the principles and practice norms on which relatively new forms of provision such as those designed to prepare young people for independent living might be based. It contented itself with identifying some emerging models and stating that a range of such models was probably required.

The paucity of guidance in the sections on enhancing young people's opportunities in education and employment was striking in comparison with the section on arrangements for health care. This part of the inspection was carried out by a Senior medical officer and a nursing officer in the Department. It stood out as containing the most numerous and definitive statements of good practice in the report.

It is not possible to do more than speculate on the reasons for this. The section on health is based on the observations of two professions made for the benefit of another one. In such circumstances more explicit statements might be expected. Some of the issues are more tangible: dental care, immunisation and first aid, for example. Some concern quite controversial questions of value: for example, the degree of responsibility given to young people for their own health care, including contraception, but they were the subject of more public debate than most issues of social care for a minority of children. Medically based professions have been accorded more authority to prescribe than most. Even if professional status is ceded to residential care and social work staff, their basis of authority is an amalgamation of law, regulation and knowledge and the knowledge is rarely converted into authoritative models of care or treatment; models, principles and values are more usually seen as guides for the demands of specific situations, many of which require the negotiation of conflicting interests or perspectives.

## Stimulating discussion

It was intended that this inspection should be followed by an active programme for dissemination in the regions. In the event this hardly happened. There were two such seminars and a presentation to a meeting of Directors of Social Services. The programmes for the inspectorate became heavier with its new designation and time had not been allowed for dissemination on any scale. The Social Care Association had also originally asked to be associated in a dissemination exercise but this seems not to have off the ground either.

The authority in which this case study was undertaken did not regard the exercise as a source of discussion and there is no evidence of the use of the reports, local or national, in staff development in community homes. They were not seen as a source of new thinking. Indeed, that might be unrealistic, given the inspectorate's location in government. Too much association with innovation might be giving too many hostages to fortune. The SSI began, instead, to develop more explicit criteria of good practice.

## Conclusions

The case study provides insights into the methods and impacts of the SSI at the point of transition from the SWS. The inspection largely exemplified the work of a government based professional advisory service evaluating bounded institutional practice using well established methods of inspection. The national report provided a snapshot of provision and practice in England and identified some of the issues they were addressing; local reports offered a more detailed evaluation for local authority social services departments whose homes were part of the exercise within a familiar, if largely implicit, framework of values and theories. Instances of good practice were highlighted. But the inspection was too broadly conceived to provide at either national or local level an evaluative framework or a learning tool for particular aspects of practice; nor did it provide normative guidance for the management of residential care.

The political purposes of the exercise also largely failed. Dissemination exercises were overtaken by new demands. But anyhow, if they had been intended to heighten the profile of residential care services for children, that would have been hard to achieve on the basis of such a general review.

The new inspectorate's own political problems would not be easily solved. Residential care was an important test bed for the definition of effective evaluative practice in the personal social services. Policy development since the late 1960s had been directed to professionalisation of residential care but the great majority of practitioners remained unqualified.

SWS (and the SSI) were under pressure to change from a professional to a more instrumental conception of their role, on the assumptions that the prime needs of the services were for good management. Some staff thought that they should demonstrate their own effectiveness by articulating clear standards, asserting new norms of economic efficiency, hitting harder in their judgements and taking steps to ensure compliance with them. In the event, they were resisted; it was argued that instead inspectors should demonstrate the strengths and adaptability of professional evaluation. However, an alternative strategy to interpret efficiency in terms of professional objectives in the end came to nothing in this inspection. Attempts to achieve a clear focus on how effectively resources and their use matched the needs of the children in residential care were submerged in a wide ranging and largely process oriented review.

The exercise was clearly underpinned by social work values and skills. It conveyed some of the complexities of creating living environments for children deemed to need residential care and outlined some principles for planning for them. But the question of how to frame an evaluation in a field of work where values were multiple and often in tension, where knowledge for practice was uncertain, where much had to be left to individual judgement but where staff lacked professional training or identity, was not confronted. Are either the clarity and control of the managerial approach or the implicitness and flexibility of the professional or connoisseurial approach appropriate? If the new inspectorate was to sustain an evaluative function complementary to the instrumental role of the Audit Commission, how was that to be achieved?

The study highlights some of the implementation issues. Whereas in the Audit Commission special study on secondary education authorities were left in no doubt as to the salience of the exercise, SWS had chosen a subject that was low on local authorities' policy priorities and it made no effort, in the event, to raise the inspection's profile nationally. Apart from residential care staff themselves, motivation to address the matters raised by the inspection was low.

The case study authority attended to the inspection systematically and thoroughly but contained its impact and largely incorporated its response to the recommendations in its own policy agenda. Although staff recognised the need to address the organisation's learning and reflexive, developmental capacities, they did not, in the end, tackle them.

Chapter Seven

# Evaluation, Regulation and Change:
## A Case Study of the Social Services Inspectorate

This second case study describes SSI inspections of secure accommodation in community homes for children and young people. Although these exercises are often considered the most straightforward examples of inspection carried out by the SSI, inspectors bring with them a number of objectives and strategies that are not easy to reconcile: regulation and change, comprehensive and focused evaluation and coercion and collaboration or encouragement. They are also attempting to promote a multiplicity of values that are more or less difficult to assess and install. These problems are the product of both history and contemporary policy.

We have noted that Rhodes (1981) identified two major forms of inspectorate in British government: enforcement, designed to ensure compliance with statutory requirements, and efficiency, to secure, maintain or improve standards of performance. Inspections of secure accommodation are concerned with both compliance with the law and regulations and maintaining and improving standards of performance.

Rhodes also noted how professionals employed as inspectors tended to shift the emphasis of their work from regulation to development and change and from coercive and legalistic to collaborative and persuasive approaches to their work. The SWS staff had been no exception. But the inspections described in the case study took place at a time when the inspectorate was establishing itself, was being required to reconcile a managerial perspective with its professional identity, and under pressure to reverse the trends. It was also endeavouring to apply more rigorous standardisation in its evaluations.

These pressures and conflicts constitute strong themes in the case study, as it explores the objectives, methods, outputs and impacts of secure accommodation inspections and examines the concepts of evaluation entailed in them.

Secure units were inspected annually. The study was based on inspections carried out in two local authorities, a shire county and a metropolitan district, in one of the nine regions of the SSI and examined inspections of the establishments from the beginning of 1986 to the end of 1988. The evidence was drawn from interviews of inspectors and those inspected, documents and the observation of two inspections.

## Secure Accommodation

Secure accommodation consisted of secure units provided within Community Homes with Education (CHEs) or Observation and Assessment (O & A) Centres. CHEs, O & A Centres and their secure units were normally managed by local authority social services departments. But some functions were carried by the education and by technical services departments.

Secure accommodation was a minute resource: the SSI *Guidance for Local Authorities* on secure accommodation (1986) records that 'at the end of 1985 there was a total of 48 local authority secure units ... Units ranged in size from 2 beds to 36 beds but the majority fell within the 5-8 bed range'. Many local authorities had no secure units; most had only one or two. There was no authoritative view on how much such accommodation was needed; some believed it was not needed at all. Its purpose and use were being reviewed in the Department of Health at the time of the study. An SSI analysis showed that there was wide variation in rates of usage between individual local authorities; some authorities used secure accommodation very rarely.

It was established in the 1960s following disturbances in a then Approved School. The rationale was that the treatment of children in Approved Schools was being undermined by the presence in them of a small disruptive and disturbed element. If they could be removed and provided with specialised help within a secure environment, both they and other children might benefit.

The law limited powers to restrict children's liberty in this way. They could be detained for more than 72 hours only by the order of a court and for clearly defined reasons, mainly the protection of the children themselves or of other people. Courts could make secure accommodation orders only in respect of certain categories of children and where a local authority had requested them to do so. Children placed in secure accommodation would normally be in the care of a local authority or remanded to care by a court or made the subject of a place of safety order. Otherwise they were most likely to have been found guilty of a grave crime and sentenced under section 53 of the Children and Young Persons Act, 1933.

There were a few large establishments, mostly in the North of England, in which children could stay for periods of up to three years. The more widespread network of smaller units normally expected to accommodate children for periods of up to three months, but it was not unusual to find periods of residence of up to a year.

Secure accommodation was therefore an exceptional form of provision and isolated in a number of ways. Many local authorities failed to integrate it into their managerial structures or their provision and policies for children. Units were usually housed in large CHEs which might themselves not be effectively managed by their local authority. Some of these CHEs had long histories. They were originally independent organisations who, as Approved Schools before the implementation of the Children and Young Persons Act, 1969, had direct relationships with the Home Office. Their ethos and leadership were sometimes those of education rather than social work. Their heads had often established power and status, which eluded heads of other residential establishments.

Staff in secure units could themselves be metaphorically locked in to that form of provision and cut off from the field of residential social work or child care. There were financial disincentives for teaching staff to leave for mainstream teaching jobs. Other categories of staff might not have an occupational identity outside their CHE, and so be highly dependent on powerful heads. A high proportion were unqualified and their opportunities for professional or broader based training were more limited than those of other staff in residential care. Geographical isolation in some cases exacerbated their professional and managerial isolation.

Local authorities had varied success in tackling these managerial, professional and policy problems. But the requirements of the Inspectorate to keep secure accommodation under close scrutiny, coupled with the fact that units were directly dependent on central government for capital expenditure, reinforced the tendency of secure units to by-pass LAs and to see SSIs as advisers, brokers for resources and as the authority to which they were accountable.

## The Local Authorities

The problems outlined were relevant to both the local authorities in this case study. But their individual histories were also important. The shire county had set up a relatively large number of secure units as resources for its CHEs. In addition, it inherited an exceptionally large 'controlled' CHE, which was a regional, if not a national, resource and was still partly managed by a trust. Its site included a small secure unit attached to the O & A Centre and a large secure long stay establishment, the majority of whose residents were there under section 53 of the Children's and Young Persons Act, 1933.

The county managed the whole complex (along with some other residential establishments) centrally. It was under an Assistant Director, who had other quite different responsibilities. The CHE was weakly linked to the authority's structure for child care policy. The officer in the SSD with responsibility for monitoring quality of the care and the environment of the CHE, together with staffing and conditions of service, was not a member of the child care policy group. Responsibility for plant was carried by a separate department. Structures for the implementation of policy in the CHE were thus fragmented and relatively weak.

The recent history of the metropolitan district was marked by political and financial difficulties and the management of the SSD had suffered from depletion and discontinuity. In these circumstances, the Inspectorate had played a more than usually active role in supporting and advising the department. As the most acute problems receded, senior managers and politicians took a new look at the department. Structurally, the O & A centres to which the secure units were attached were formally linked with residential and, less directly, child care policies in the department.

In both of the authorities the structure, however, separated residential work from fieldwork and from the work of the courts section. The managerial focus was thus the running of the institutions rather than use of those institutions by the LA and the courts. However, this issue was increasingly important to the Inspectorate. They wanted to know why and how children were admitted to secure units, whether they needed to be there at all and, if so, for how long. Responsibility for safeguarding children's rights extended well beyond the boundaries of the institution.

## Framework of Secure Accommodation Inspections

Local authorities wishing to provide secure accommodation in CHEs must have it approved by the Secretary of State. The powers of the

Secretary of State in this area were delegated to the SSI and exercised through inspections. This practice, like most of the powers of the Secretary of State over the administration of secure units, was established by convention, not by law.

The powers were formidable. Units could be closed on the recommendation of inspectors. Limits could be imposed on the length of time children could be held or on the number of children accommodated at any one time. These powers could be exercised if units broke the law but also if they failed to observe unit-specific conditions of approval or inspectors found 'serious deficiencies in practice' (SSI, 1986).

The law, supplemented by the Secure Accommodation Regulations (1983 and 1986), defined when courts could order a child or young person to be accommodated in a secure unit, and for how long. It also stipulated that the child's need to be so accommodated must be kept under regular review and it regulated restriction of the child's liberty within the unit. The Community Homes Regulations, 1972 which set out the conditions governing residential care included secure accommodation in their remit.

Maximum periods for approval of units were laid down by the Secretary of State on the advice of the SSI. Units were approved for up to three years. But there were three types of inspection: *initial*, before a unit could be opened; *approval*: these happened at least every three years, but more often in the case of units approved for shorter periods of time; and *interim*. Units were subject to annual interim inspections, less comprehensive than those for approval.

Inspections were strongly framed, not only by the law and the regulations, but also by detailed guidance to inspectors about the conduct of inspections and guidance on secure accommodation issued by SSI to the local authorities.

The most recent of these was the inspection 'pack' produced by a DHSS working party in 1987. It was also the most comprehensive and contained cross references to the guidance to local authorities and to the Secure Accommodation Regulations. It identified documentary information to be required of the units in advance of the inspection. Inspectors were expected to analyse that information and use it in the inspection.

The pack included a detailed aide memoire, organised under six headings, which also provided a suggested framework for inspection reports.

The aide memoire comprised 128 questions. It was not a check list. It assumed that inspectors would exercise discretion in its use. While, therefore, it was introduced to enhance the standardisation of inspections and to inject more order into reports, so making them more susceptible to comparative analysis by the Department of Health or SSI HQ, it did not constitute a definitive framework of criteria.

However, core elements of the inspection were identified and an analysis of these reveals some priority ordering of values, underlying assumptions about practice and the function of law, regulations and guidance in structuring inspections.

Within the core, major emphasis was given to law, regulations and policy decisions designed to safeguard children's rights not to have their liberty restricted except under explicit and controlled conditions. Linked values given prominence were rights to information and individual dignity and integrity, for example in the regulation of body searches.

Importance attached to generally recognised good social work practice was equally evident in, for example, the requirements to review methods and quality of assessment, to ensure that individual treatment plans were made and implemented, and to check arrangements for professional support and supervision. Similarly the balance between control and the security of the environment and the quality of care was stressed. Values of individualisation and social and cultural identity were prominent, alongside health, education and safety.

The importance of systematic recording as a means of monitoring standards and compliance with the law and good practice was made clear. The value of efficiency figured in neither the inspection pack nor in the guidance to local authorities.

Observation and other ways of evaluating practice were mentioned but more emphasis was placed on ensuring that there were effective managerial arrangements and clear policy statements. Many of the core elements of the inspection required inspectors to analyse specified data and monitor records, although inspectors themselves saw interviews with key staff as essential in establishing the quality of professional practice.

The inspection pack, in effect, went some way towards providing a clear evaluative framework, but within the limits inevitably imposed by recognising the importance of individual discretion in professional evaluation.

All local authorities had copies of the inspection pack and the guidance for local authorities on secure accommodation issued by the SSI in 1986. This covered broadly the same subjects as the inspection pack but under different headings. It brought together the relevant law and regulations and SSI views on professional practice. It was, however, more obviously incrementally constructed from 'long experience' than the pack produced by a small working party established with a clear task.

## Purposes of Inspections

Within the elaborate framework described, nowhere were the purposes of inspections defined, beyond the requirement to make recommendations about approval; nor were the duties of inspectors specified in so many words. The study will suggest that in practice the balance between inspectors' responsibilities to inform central government, to provide tools for management of units by local authorities and to effect change themselves was uncertain.

Four inspectors from the region in which this study was undertaken summarised the purposes of inspection of secure accommodation as follows: to see whether the law was being observed and policy implemented; to give formal approval for units to be established or to continue; to check on the quality of care and the welfare of a vulnerable group of children; to look at the organisation and policies of secure units.

On the face of it the prime purpose of inspections of secure units was to provide the Secretary of State with a comprehensive picture from which to decide approval. The scope of the guidance issued for inspectors reinforced this interpretation, even if the need for focus was acknowledged. But it also suggested some shift of emphasis towards policies on the usage of secure accommodation.

The new emphasis on standardisation of inspections pointed to a need for a national perspective and a comparative analysis of performance. Again that might facilitate policy development by central government or stronger central government control over units through more frequent use of sanctions. Central government's right to intervene in this aspect of local authority management was established in law.

The issue of responsibility was less clear. It could be argued that the more comprehensive and regular the inspections, the greater acceptance there was by central government that responsibility for what happened in units was shared. Department convention tended to reinforce that view. Although, formally, local authorities were expected to apply to the Secretary of State for approval and its renewal, in practice the initiative for arranging inspections was always taken by the Department and the inspectorate. And while inspection reports were sent to Directors of Social Services, it was nowhere made clear whether they were seen as tools of local authority management. The guidance for inspectors contained no discussion of their relationship or responsibilities *vis à vis* local authorities.

Further evidence of the purpose of inspections must be sought in the practice and perceptions of inspectors. All the inspectors observed in the study saw themselves as change agents. In constructing their reports they were trying to find ways to initiate, support and, sometimes, participate in achieving change. In some cases, they encouraged local authority managers or unit staff or both together to make their own policies, within guidelines or regulations. Elsewhere, in the absence of effective local authority management, they paid more attention to points of change in the units themselves.

In adopting this approach they were acting in the tradition of the Social Work Service, in which evaluation and change were seen as integrally related.

But they were also embodying the general attitude in inspectorates noted by Rhodes (*op. cit.*). Inspectors tended to work collaboratively, partly on the grounds of effectiveness and partly from preference.

## Planning and Organising Inspections

The time absorbed by secure accommodation inspections each year was out of all proportion to the number of units in the country and the children accommodated in them. All inspections entailed some advance planning, but this was most important for the approval inspections. Formal notification, together with the request for the advance information specified in the inspection pack, was given six weeks ahead of the event. Inspectors were expected to analyse the data beforehand to illuminate patterns of occupancy and to assess these against formal function. The inspector in the research region who had chief responsibility for secure accommodation inspections had developed simple computer programmes to facilitate these tasks.

One purpose of such analyses was to enable inspectors to determine the focus of inspections. For example, an inspector had analysed the numbers of readmissions to a unit, together with admissions for periods of less than 72 hours (for which no statutory order was required). This had enabled him to structure the inspection round the issues of proper use and of children's rights against restriction of their liberty. He had then examined individual files in order to refine the analysis and demonstrate the basis of his concern.

Inspectors most commonly used the previous report and the authority's response to it to determine the focus of an inspection. They normally informed the authority of any predetermined emphasis for the inspection, sometimes identifying how that would affect their approach: for example, it might determine the principle on which individual files were selected for close examination. Inspectors often invited the unit or the authority to propose topics in advance and it was normal practice at the initial meeting of an inspection to ask authority and unit representatives to highlight any significant issues that had arisen since the last inspection.

Schools HMIs were usually invited to join approval inspections. Sometimes medical or nursing colleagues from the Department of Health were also recruited. In the approval inspection observed a dietician from the Department was included, because of long standing concern about catering in the establishment.

In the part of the country selected for the research, a banding system for the approval inspections of regional secure accommodation had been started. Inspectors from three regions carried these out jointly. The purposes were to enhance standardisation of inspections and to maximise objectivity. Inspectors got to know 'their' units well: not only did they inspect them annually but they frequently acted as advisers and brokers for resources for them. They could be more familiar figures to unit staff than their managers in the local authority. For these reasons inspectors valued the help of colleagues at the time of the inspection.

Approval inspections were normally preceded by at least one planning meeting for the inspectors and colleagues. The responsible SSI used the planning meeting observed for this study to brief colleagues on the current local policy context, the issues he had identified as requiring scrutiny and how he proposed to address them. It gave the HMIs the opportunity to raise issues of their own, although they seemed to accept that SSI would take the lead. SSI also distributed some preliminary analysis of the advance information submitted by the establishment.

## Preparation by Units

Of the two authorities in the study, one sent the SSI a detailed account of actions taken on receipt of inspection reports and the inspection observed in this authority was strongly structured by this document. The other authority paid less attention to such formal feedback and the approval inspection observed was undertaken without reference to this document, received only just before the inspection began.

Units had two main positions on preparation for inspections. The unit which valued inspections most highly also made most preparation for them. The head and the staff separately prepared written material on developments in policy and practice since the last inspection and on current concerns which they wished to discuss. The respondents from the other units considered the main purpose of inspections to be to ensure compliance with the law and the maintenance of national standards. Most thought that they should not prepare so that the inspectors saw them as they normally operated. Some felt inspections should be unannounced. However, they did admit to some 'tightening up' and to checking that their records were in order.

## Standardisation and Evaluative Criteria

Standardisation of inspections has been seen by many as an important instrument of change in the inspectorate since 1985. The inspectors observed in this study did not dissociate themselves from it; one, indeed, was strongly identified with it.

Attitudes towards standardisation and the use of hard data varied. For some these objectives were not incompatible with their established way of working, but they entailed an adjustment to their practice. Most inspectors relied heavily on the relationship they developed with the authorities under their aegis, based on professional values, knowledge and authority, combined with the authority of government. They preferred to work through reinforcement of existing good practice and motivation for change. Their models of change were based either on concepts of internalised values and of normative reeducation (Bennis, Benne and Chin, 1970) or on exploiting social pressures within a work group.

In some cases, where there was particularly strong resistance to change, inspectors found it useful to have hard evidence of discrepancy between actual practice and assigned functions. They might then work on a model of change based on notions of rational persuasion or in some cases coercion. Facts had their own authority or could be used to confront.

Some criteria, such as compliance with the law, are relatively easy to standardise. Adherence to the law and regulations was an important component of the SSI guidance on these inspections. However, even here absolute standardisation was not a declared aim. The core elements of inspection did not include scrutiny of all the regulations, nor was any particular form or subject of data analysis mandatory.

While inspectors were unanimous that they must ascertain that the rights of children to have their liberty restricted only within strict legal limits were upheld, there were differences of view among them about the relationship between restriction of liberty and human rights. Some felt that locking up children was by definition an infringement of rights; others felt that children's rights could be safeguarded in such a context, and that some children's needs could best be met in that way.

Strenuous attempts had been made to devise an inspection pro forma that ensured coverage of the main lines of policy. But the substance of that policy was imbued with professional and administrative values; it had developed over a period in which emphases on, for example, rights had shifted; its implementation was often a matter of judgement.

For example, no formula was offered for assessing a requirement at the heart of secure accommodation policy: balancing security (meaning safety *and* control) and quality of life in designing premises and regimes for units. Nor was it likely to be: inspectors were expected to make judgements according to a range of factors, such as particular populations of particular units, the quality of staff and the models of care on which units were based. In practice inspectors moved between the concepts of quality of life and quality of care in assessing this key issue. Quality of care was concerned with input, specifically of professional practice. Quality of life was a more output- oriented notion, and on the whole less used than quality of care.

A number of organising principles or criteria were mentioned as framing inspectors' evaluations of the quality of care or life in units: human rights to, for example, liberty, dignity and individuality; the importance of young people developing responsibility for their own lives. Mention was also made of principles of good child care practice; good primary care; racial and cultural identity; healthy living; a sense of community.

Inspectors recognised a wide range of models of care for children in residential settings and there was no detectable attempt to establish an ideal. However, the evidence from this study was that models based on behaviourist psychology were discouraged.

In one of the inspections observed, individualised treatment plans were made one of the main issues. This was an important feature of various types of inspection and was included in the inspection pro forma for secure accommodation. It thus represented an attempt to articulate particular priorities of practice. It was associated with beliefs in the importance of grounding intervention in sound assessment, but not with any particular theory of intervention. Practice norms linked with it in the inspection observed included giving children planned help rather than simply holding them in a safe place; life story techniques in helping children to come to terms with what had happened to them and what they had done; mobility programmes for children in secure accommodation to prepare them for the demands of returning to an open environment; the assumption that local authority care meant acting *in loco parentis*. Inspectors also stressed the need to integrate the contributions made to children's lives by care staff, teachers, psychologists and field social workers.

The main line of inquiry concerned how systematic work with the children was. Inspectors were not looking for a particular set of applied theories. But they were evaluating the substance and quality of engagement with the children. And although professional standards and values were not well articulated, inspectors thought there was a strong measure of agreement about them within the inspectorate.

All the inspectors interviewed used the law and regulations governing community homes and secure accommodation as sources of evaluative criteria. The *SSI Guidance for Local Authorities on Secure Accommodation*, 1986, the SSI's inspection pack (1987), *Home Life* (Avebury, 1984) and the DHSS' design guide for secure units (DHSS, 1979) were also important basic documents, although no one mentioned them all explicitly. The social work experience and training of all inspectors influenced them in their work, but to different degrees. One person referred predominantly to his own experience in answer to a question about evaluative criteria; another rated professional principles, research and concepts of human rights as most important sources of reference for him. Three of the four inspectors observed in action were visibly influenced in their judgements and in what they were looking for by theories and values of professional social work practice. The dominant perspective for the fourth was managerial.

## Methods of Inspection

The account is based on the observation of two forms of inspection: *approval* and *interim*. The approval inspection of an institution for boys was 'banded' and conducted by a group of inspectors all from different regions, who had ,however,worked as a team on three previous inspections of secure units.

The interim inspection of an establishment for girls was conducted by the inspector normally responsible for liaison and oversight with that unit. A strong working relationship had developed between the Principal in charge of the establishment and the inspector. Latterly relationships between the establishment and the SSD management had been significantly strengthened. Interviews in the authority and with the inspector suggested that inspections were based on substantial mutual respect between the three parties. Observation largely supported that interpretation.

The approval inspection was led by the inspector responsible for oversight of the establishment, who knew the establishment and the staff well. He was also seen by SSI as having particular expertise in the field of secure accommodation. However, there were significant differences of view between him and the principal of the establishment about management style, objectives and priorities. Relationships between the establishment and the SSD were weak.

Each inspection was based largely on the same methods: meetings with staff; individual interviews with staff; inspection of buildings; observation; unstructured conversations with the young people resident; examination of unit and individual records. But naturally the approval inspection, which lasted for five days, contained far more elaborate and prolonged encounters than did the interim inspection (one and a half days).

A relatively strong structure was imposed on the approval inspection. SSIs determined to centre on the extent and quality of individualised treatment planning and implementation in the establishment. Concern about the management and practice of one of the units would be examined through this perspective. Records would be a key means of pursuing that concern. Inspectors asked for individual files that staff thought would display a range of work, relatively successful and relatively unsuccessful or posing particular problems. Inspectors chose to interview staff who had been most involved with the young people concerned. They hoped this would enable them to examine staff practice and its specific impact on children. They did not systematically interview the children themselves.

Some prior analysis of unit statistics was made for this inspection but it was not observed to have significant impact on the conduct of the inspection. Unusually, neither was the inspection framed by the authority's response to the previous report. This was mainly because none was received before the inspection began.

By contrast, the LA response to the previous report was a major point of focus for the interim inspection. The first meeting attended by SSD management as well as the Principal of the institution was based entirely on it.

In each of the inspections an attempt was made to ensure balance between structure and openness to new issues, but structure was given more attention in the approval inspection. That inspection was marked by tension between the requirement for reasonably comprehensive coverage and the aim to pursue chosen issues in some depth so as to initiate a process of change: a tall order for a five day exercise.

At the beginning and the end of both inspections, inspectors met senior staff from the local authority as well as from the establishment. The styles of the respective meetings were quite different, a difference largely explained by the status of the inspection, the disparity of size between the units and the number of people involved. But it was also a function of the intended impacts of the two events. The interim inspection was set up by the inspector as a collaborative event and staff had plenty of opportunity to comment at the final meeting. The aim was to encourage a unit which had for the first time been given approval for three years at the previous inspection. By contrast, the final meeting of the approval inspection was heavily structured. The inspectors wanted to get some major themes across to their audience, with the minimum of intervention from them.

The examination of records played a relatively minor role in the interim inspection. It was almost entirely concerned with ensuring that the law and the regulations had been adhered to. Nevertheless all admissions of less than 72 hours were closely scrutinised and staff were questioned about the circumstances.

The approval inspection demonstrated the range of purposes that examination and analysis of records can serve. Inspectors used records to determine the quality of practice with individual children and to help them assess the nature of the regimes maintained in the units. They looked for records of individual treatment plans on the children's files; they checked whether those plans had been implemented, and, if not, why not; they wanted to know how far care staff, teachers, psychologists and field social workers combined to contribute to care plans. They considered how far programmes aimed to help young people begin to adapt again to the world outside security; how often staff had to resort to sanctions and what those sanctions were. Their concern here went beyond ensuring that units complied with the law.

Individual interviews with senior members of staff and with staff closely concerned with the children whose files were selected formed a major part of the approval inspection. There were no group meetings, apart from the initial and final events. Inspectors did not try to standardise their individual interviews with people occupying similar roles, but key interviews were conducted in pairs or by all three. Individual approaches shared some features. Inspectors used interviews to get as accurate a picture as possible of staff roles and procedures; and to check impressions gained from observation or from other staff. They used them to put proposals for change to staff. Interviews were tools for development as well as for gaining evidence and understanding; they were also used to test strategies for achieving institutional change.

Within these common approaches there were individual styles and emphases. One inspector, strongly oriented to improving management through getting across a few simple precepts, demonstrated these in his encounters with staff. Another aimed to give staff confidence in themselves, not simply by giving praise but also by telling them why he thought what they had done was important. He demonstrated his own style of practice in his encounters with staff. The style of another inspector was more inquisitorial. And he did not hesitate to confront in order to get a message across.

Observation was an essential part of all inspections of secure accommodation: of specific and significant events, such as case conferences and admissions; of routines, such as getting the children up and bedtimes, mealtimes and assembly; of unstructured time and of organised activity. Events such as case conferences could be assessed against some standard expectations. But in observing what happened on units inspectors were trying to assess less tangible phenomena such as the quality of relationships, the importance attached to individual dignity and the opportunity for young people to express their individuality. An inspector spoke of some things being a matter of 'feel'. Another said he saw a boy's remark that 'he was not respected for what he was' corroborated by an observed encounter between the boy and a member of staff.

Inspectors tended to combine observation with talking informally to the young people and to more junior members of staff. Conversations with young people themselves tended to figure least in inspectors' accounts of what they do and how their judgements are formed.

The methods employed were for the most part common to all inspectors interviewed. But individual inspectors put their own stamp on them and subsumed them to a variety of purpose. They acted as professionals working within a prescribed framework.

## Methods of Inspection: Views of Those Inspected

Most of those interviewed in the local authorities thought inspections were done well. They were thorough. Inspectors checked records meticulously and picked up breaches of regulations or failure to follow guidance. They spent substantial time on the units, observing practice and talking to staff and children. They examined furniture and fittings carefully. The robust approach of one inspector, who tested the security of fittings by attempting to wrench them off walls, was mentioned without resentment. Inspectors' knowledge about security was appreciated, as was their willingness to share information about the furnishing of other units and about changes in practice. Widely disparate individual inspectorial styles seemed to be approved, suggesting that relationships with inspectors worked well. Only one unit expressed doubts about whether a snapshot of the unit gained through a short intensive visit gave a good picture of how it worked. This unit felt its approach to secure accommodation was not fully understood, because it was not seen in the context of the whole establishment. It also considered too much weight could be placed on statistics for similar reasons. They could too easily be interpreted within a particular set of assumptions and so be self fulfilling prophecies.

For the most part exchanges between inspectors and staff were felt to be useful and honest. Inspections undoubtedly caused anxiety. Although this was little admitted to in interviews, it was evident on the observed inspections.

## Reaching Judgements

Inspectors in the approval inspection used informal exchange of ideas and impressions to help them make sense of what they observed, pull out the main issues and make judgements. In the feedback they concentrated mainly on treatment planning, the effectiveness of review procedures and the quality of work with individual children. The judgements were about both the standard of work achieved and how far management in the establishment and the LA provided adequate policies, resources, training and support for such work.

Inspectors were inhibited in forming clear judgements by contradictions in their role and in the functions of secure accommodation itself: the requirements to ensure safety and security and to promote quality of life. Inspectors found themselves in a quandary. They strongly advocated that relationships of trust between staff and boys were more effective in maintaining security than building design or physical safeguards against risks. But they were also concerned at the relaxed attitudes towards arrangements for boys allowed out of the unit, at the risks of absconding and at the availability of potential weapons afforded by a highly imaginative garden created in the grounds. They resolved the puzzle by requiring the unit to make a more conscious appraisal of risk.

The detailed checklist against which they were working - as this was a full inspection - also cut across the need to concentrate judgement on key issues rather than to evaluate every dimension of the establishment.

If the organisation of the inspection and the structured encounters provided the main frame for judgement, inspectors also drew on observation of interactions, unstructured conversations and participation in events like meals. For the most part, they used them to corroborate other perceptions. For example, an observed routine in which children had toothpaste doled out direct onto their proffered brushes heightened concern about an over- regimented and depersonalising approach.

The banding system undoubtedly enlarged the perspectives brought to bear on the inspection of a unit. The 'home' inspector in the observed inspection commented on how valuable it was to have two pairs of fresh eyes looking at a unit, which had enormously improved its work since he had known it. The other two inspectors pointed out shortcomings which he might have underplayed. Individual inspectors highlighted distinct aspects of problems (management, procedures affecting children's rights, and quality of practice and relationships). These were then brought together to form more rounded judgements.

Inspectors were partly testing already identified hypotheses and partly responding to new issues and making judgements on them. For example, on this inspection senior staff in the establishment ascribed the main management problems of a unit to the shortcomings of a particular member of staff. Inspectors listened to them, questioned them and talked to the person concerned. In the end they did not accept the diagnosis offered but saw the problem as stemming primarily from the system and ethos of management in the whole establishment.

Some conclusions were reached early in the week. For example, inspectors agreed by the end of the second day that there were significant numbers of able people in this establishment whose gifts were being underused. On the fourth day a related conclusion was formulated: the establishment lacked direction on critical aspects of its work, objectives, policies and resource needs; at the same time staff were subject to rigorous control of behavioural norms.

Opportunities to share hypotheses, possible solutions and strategies were structured into the programme, notably in the daily end of the day meetings between SSIs and the HMIs and in the planning sessions for the feedback meeting. The feedbacks by the dietician and by an HMI to psychologists also helped to focus judgements.

There were definite changes of mood during the week. Inspectors shifted between wanting to confront and deciding to sustain a more enabling approach.

The strategy adopted for the final feedback meeting to the establishment set specific demands and time limits for action and attempted to avoid demoralising staff by focusing on management problems, in the local authority as much as in the establishment itself. However, there were differences of emphasis in the team and the researcher felt that if she had not been there there might have been more open disagreement leading to a process of more open negotiation.

## Feedback

A formal feedback meeting was held at the end of an inspection to convey the main substance of the report. The meeting was normally attended by managers from the local authority and senior staff in the establishment. In a small unit, more junior staff might also attend. Specialist advisers to the inspection might give a separate feedback to those particularly concerned in the establishment with that area of work. The main purpose of the meeting was to convey judgements; discussion was allowed according to the discretion of the inspector.

Inspectors had an impressive array of powers, which they rarely used. One way to compose the report would be to make a synoptic appraisal of the options available. This did not happen.

The feedback was effectively based on three models:

*managerialist*: set a few clear, short term targets; carry out an early and specific review and apply sanctions if the targets are not reached. (In this instance, the last part of the formula was not in fact included. Inspectors did not decide what they would do if the targets were not reached.) Underlying this model is an assumption that clear instructions, with the threat of sanctions, will produce action;

*catalyst*: give positive reinforcement and link it with clear advice, the rationale for which is explained. This model assumes that people will be motivated to change or given strength to do so, if they are rewarded for what they do well with praise, particularly if that comes from a body seen as having power to influence the system in which they work. The movement towards change comes at least partly from inside the action system.

*natural justice*: if the first two models are essentially linked with change objectives, the natural justice model is a reminder that inspections' prime formal purpose is regulation: institutions are being given licence to operate. Inspections must therefore be comprehensive and all the main conclusions fed back. They are the basis of critical decisions and recipients of the decisions have the right to know on what they are based.

Inspectors in the observed inspection wanted to structure their feedback round a small number of key themes to maximise the possibility of change. They wanted to highlight their central concerns and link them to the levels in the organisation that could affect them and the nature of the tasks that they would entail. But in the event the structure and content of the feedback were determined only in part by that objective. Although the inspectors had deliberately not based the inspection on the last report and the response to it, they did review action taken on it in first part of the feedback meeting. They also felt constrained to use the inspection guidance to make sure they had not omitted anything that was relevant to the units. This was in part dictated by the need not to overlook significant safety factors. The requirement to be comprehensive in an inspection undertaken for the purposes of approval asserted itself. In consequence the feedback meeting lost some impact.

This inspection, in contrast with its original intentions, targeted many of its judgements on the local authority. Inspectors intended to have a separate feedback session with the LA managers alone. In their immediate feedback they stressed local authority responsibility to provide a stable policy environment for the establishment, to ensure there was a clear role for the establishment within the framework of the authority's child care policy and to link the establishment to the resources of the authority.

Most of the rest of the inspection and its feedback were aimed at managers in the establishment. If practice was to improve, managers must manage.

### Interim Inspection Feedback

This provided some clear contrasts. The interim inspection aimed to review action taken on the previous report; to monitor work since the last inspection; to encourage staff. Feedback was structured round the six sections of the inspection pro forma. It gave positive reinforcement; it identified issues that needed action, for example unit practice on body searches. It encouraged discussion of emerging problems (AIDS) and new directions (organisation of staffing; developing the mobility programme). The inspection was intended to be a catalyst for further change and to identify ways in which the inspector could best fulfil that catalyst role. But she was trying to do so through supporting the authority in taking on a more active management role.

This might suggest support for the proposals under discussion in the SSI and the Department of Health to distinguish more clearly between the functions of the interim and the approval inspections: interim inspections might be geared to advice and development and approval inspections to summative evaluation and requirements for change.

## Reports

The detailed observation of the inspections reported above were placed in the context of a larger range of examples to be found in secondary sources. 14 reports of inspections in all were analysed: all those available on four secure units in the county (10 reports) and two units in the city (four reports) in the period 1986 to the end of 1988.

Draft reports on inspections were sent to the agency responsible for the secure accommodation inspected for comment on matters of fact. Reports with recommendations on approval were then sent by the lead inspector to the Children's division of the Department of Health for decision. Final reports which must not be released before the Secretary of State's decision was conveyed to the local authority were sent to the Director of Social Services, with copies for the Social Services Committee Chairman and for the LEA in appropriate cases. Two copies of the final report were sent to the Policy SSI at Alexander Fleming House, one of which was for the Children's Division. Final reports were normally documents of public access.

## Structure of Reports

The SSI guidance on inspections (1988e) aimed to make reports more standardised. It had variable impact on the structure of the reports examined for this study. The reports examined on county units from 1987 onwards were all structured according to the prescribed outline. Those on the metropolitan district showed little evidence of change until 1988.

The guidance did not give clear instructions about whether or how reports should record action taken on the recommendations of previous inspections. The metropolitan district reports examined reviewed that action systematically; the county reports tended to give an overview of progress since the last inspection. Although the working party simplified the main structure of the report, some important things remained obscure. Some reports identified the focus of the inspection; some did not. All reports contained a brief section summarising the key issues highlighted by the inspection but not always in the same place. Some reports contained separate sections for action by the unit itself and action by the local authority. For the most part, however, responsibility for implementation was not detailed in the report.

It was rare for reports to contain any timetable for action and there was no systematic method of highlighting recommendations which must be implemented. There was a bewildering variety of formulae indicating degrees of prescription and urgency. In short, the reports did not provide the kind of framework that would be expected of an inspectorial approach to evaluation. Their authority was not clear and there was no strict monitoring of action.

The 1987 guidelines asked for simple statistical analyses of particular features of the child population of units. This would facilitate scrutiny of patterns of use of secure accommodation in individual authorities and in the national arrangements for dealing with children and young people in trouble. Inspectors varied in the attention they paid to such analyses and in the connections they made between them and other findings of the inspection. In some cases they were a powerful means of highlighting issues of both policy and practice.

## Content of Reports

The reports examined all referred to the major issues identified by the 1987 guidance as the core of inspections. They reported on the population of the units, compliance by authorities and establishments with the law, regulations and guidance and paid particular attention to whether children were legally held in the units. They identified in detail repairs, alterations and additions to the fabric required for security, safety and the quality of the living environment. They gave an account of, and made recommendations about, the care, treatment and control of the children and young people resident in the units, and addressed the central issue of the balance to be struck between security and quality of life or quality of care. They considered organisation, management and staffing and reported on their examination of records.

## Buildings

All those interviewed for the study, inspectors and authority staff alike, thought the attention paid to buildings should diminish. However, buildings were a major preoccupation of almost all the reports read and caused substantial dissatisfaction and conflict. Three of the six units in the study had periods of closure because of building problems or requirements during 1986-1988; one of these was actually closed when the researcher visited the establishment.

Reports contained evidence of failure to repair buildings, to undertake alterations to create more space, to repair or install needed items of equipment, furniture and fittings, sometimes over periods of years. They also showed wide variation, within as well as between authorities, in the attention paid to fabric and the standards achieved. However, there was no evidence that inspectors of the Department of Health had set time limits for action on authorities who appeared negligent on these issues nor that any unit had had approval withdrawn in the period of the study.

In one of the authorities finance was obviously a critical factor. In the other that was less true. But there were still serious problems. In part they arose from differences of opinion between the authority and the SSI about the right balance between physical security and quality of environment. The authority deliberately resisted some of the recommended alterations, in particular to replace glass with polycarbonate in the units. They also delayed installing alarm systems in some of their establishments, in one instance for four years. This was partly because they put a low priority on them, but also because of difficulties with Department of Health procedures and communication. On a number of such issues this authority argued that if relationships and management in the units were satisfactory, the kind of precautions recommended were unnecessary. Moreover, in some cases they might make the trouble they were designed to prevent more likely: the balance of trust and confidence would be disturbed. They considered that some of the guidance for the equipment of secure units was based on other regions' problems and irrelevant to their own authority.

The issue of the balance to be struck between security and quality of life was, as we have seen, at the heart of inspections of secure accommodation. The inspectorate was thought to have gradually relaxed its concerns about security; even if some respondents in this study felt they had not gone far enough, in many cases they encouraged staff to see security as dependent more on the quality of relationships in establishments than on the design and robustness of the fabric. They aimed to support staff in putting such beliefs, reflected also in the Community Homes Regulations, 1972, into practice, even if, at times, they drew the limits more tightly than the staff of units would want.

There were other reasons for the preoccupation with fabric. Some buildings had major structural problems. It was also clear that the goal posts were moving all the time. New solutions to security problems were constantly being discovered but also, as ideas about the balance between security and quality of life changed, it was realised that technology did not have all the answers. For example, an alarm system that maintained almost constant surveillance of young people in their rooms was soon pronounced obsolete. It was felt to constitute an unacceptable invasion of privacy. Inspectors recognised that degrees of hazard constituted by buildings and equipment could not be assessed without reference to unit regimes and levels of staffing They saw that quality of life was inseparable from quality of environment: comfort, colour, design, space etc. There were entirely liberal reasons for paying attention to buildings.

But if there was ample room for legitimate value conflict between authorities and the inspectorate about buildings and good reason for holding the spotlight on them, some problems could not so easily be explained away. The background to inspections in the metropolitan district was one of financial constraint and crisis. Inspectors took that into account in their work, but reports catalogued how failure to act on recommendations had led to serious deterioration in security and, in one case, an unacceptable living environment. There came a point when they told the authority that it must take a grip on the consequences for children of its own problems and review its priorities.

In the other authority, too, instances were found of 'unacceptable delay' in dealing with repairs and adaptations. In this authority, property was the responsibility of another department, Property Services. Links with that department had to be made from a relatively low level in the SSD or by managers with other more pressing responsibilities. At the same time Property Services felt that the Department of Health failed to provide a clear and up to date system of requirements. The management arrangements in the authority were not sufficiently integrated to deal effectively with the range of problems that arose.

## Values and Style

Inspectors wished to establish conditions in secure accommodation that would endorse social work norms. Reports highlighted the need for qualified staff, training in general social work practice, some more specialised knowledge, professional supervision and planned staff development. Another common theme was the need to have systems for regular review and critical appraisal of plans for individual children.

Within this common set of objectives there were variations among the reports. Some concentrated on values of normalisation and individual identity that are firmly embedded in professional practice literature. Others focused their thinking around concepts of rights: of liberty, of privacy and personal integrity. Or they might be concerned with rights to information, to unrestricted contact with family and friends and to redress through complaints procedures.

For the most part, reports reflected a summative style of evaluation. While there was plenty of exchange between inspectors and unit staff, the majority of reports set out judgements in a fairly straightforward way. In a few cases, however, inspectors carried a more interactive style into the reports.

Most reports contained praise and encouragement to staff, particularly the staff of the units themselves, for changes they had initiated. Several reports sharply criticised delay by the local authority in attending to recommendations on fabric and in establishing satisfactory monitoring arrangements. But at the same time unit staff were praised for their achievements in creating an attractive environment, in working towards greater mobility and variety of activity for children, and, in particular, for attempts to set in motion individualised treatment programmes for children and effective supervision and support for staff. Where they felt there was a real possibility of instilling social work practice into units, they tried to foster that through encouragement, rather than through any kind of threat or sanction.

## Authority of the Inspectorate

All those interviewed in the authorities and establishments thought that an external authoritative review was important, if not essential. No one considered that local authorities could take over inspections of secure accommodation. Local authorities would be inspecting themselves and that was not an adequate safeguard for children.

Most regarded the inspections as a mixture of inspection and advice. Inspectors evaluated against the law, regulations, and explicit administrative and professional guidance. They had the power to compel compliance, against the sanction of closure, even if they did not explicitly invoke it. 'In a conflict, the SSI always wins.' However, most respondents distinguished between recommendations that had to be implemented and those that were advice. One thought that inspections were more like a shared review; the staff did not feel they were being 'policed'.

The degree and nature of authority given to the SSI varied. Some institutions considered SSI to carry a combination of legal and professional authority. In the unit exhibiting this attitude most strongly, staff took the inspector's report as the framework of their objectives for the next year. A strong sense of mutual trust was established.

At least two institutions considered themselves to be experts in the field of secure accommodation. Such institutions could sometimes persuade inspectors that they should continue practice over which there was disagreement. Otherwise an institution might comply unwillingly in cases of serious conflict but remain convinced that they were in the right and their work was misunderstood. In such cases, inspections were seen as necessary, but as cutting across an established philosophy. They were not seen as learning opportunities.

Sometimes inspectors were seen as sources of defined expertise or information. They had a good knowledge of the law or a wealth of information about security devices and safe furniture and fittings. Institutions might use these without necessarily conceding inspectors' authority to challenge fundamentally their values or practice.

## Impacts and Implementation of Reports

Reports were examined to see how often recommendations were recorded as having been met or not, although, as has been noted, there was no systematic record of implementation.

Reports showed that conflicts with one authority about safety requirements remained unresolved over a period of four years or more. In this same authority an interim report noted nine safety concerns that had not been dealt with since the previous inspection. They included failure to install an alarm system or to provide lockable storage for cutlery, a glass wall kettle vulnerable to dangerous use and screws to power points and electric sockets that could be interfered with.

Inspectors in the other authority reporting on a unit that had just reopened after closure noted nine items in the building that either still had not been attended to since the previous inspection or had caused problems more recently. The report reminded the authority of its responsibilities to maintain the building in an acceptable condition. 'The Social Services

Committee has a responsibility to ensure that the state of the premises is never again allowed to deteriorate to the level it reached in ----.' 'It should not be necessary for a member of the DHSS Inspectorate to spell out, at every inspection, details of repairs required.' In the same authority repeated reminders were given of the statutory requirement to install review systems to monitor the continuing need for each child to remain in security.

There was evidence, too, of long running failures to change institutionalising practices, in particular in the purchase of clothing for children.

Need for major changes in staffing and philosophy at one unit had been identified at least as far back as 1984. By 1988 they were slowly being introduced. One residential social worker had been appointed by 1987, after recommendations for a shift in care staffing from teaching to social work. But by the end of 1988 that appointment had been dropped in favour of an administrative post.

Recommendations for introducing individualised care and treatment plans for children, a major theme of inspectors' reports, were also slow to be implemented. One unit had drawn up plans for implementation just before an inspection. By the time of the next inspection no further progress had been made. Other units had gone further but failed to establish recording systems for such planning, thus rendering it vulnerable to inconsistent application or to neglect.

Training was an important part of the inspectorate's strategies for change. But staff in the units remained substantially unqualified. A note by the inspectors that the role of a deputy head in a large unit was incompatible with his responsibilities for managing training for the whole establishment was recorded in three inspection reports. At the fourth inspection it was found still to have been ignored.

Inspectors saw professional supervision of staff as an essential prerequisite of effective care and intervention in the case of deeply troubled children. In none of the units was it firmly established. The use of records, not only for accountability, but also as tools of good practice, was little appreciated, despite emphasis on this in reports.

Reports, then, provided substantial evidence of failure to implement recommendations about fabric, regimes, staffing and professional practice. This is not to say that no changes were recorded in units. Reports also spoke of staff's willingness to review beliefs and develop new approaches to practice. Anxieties about over relaxed attitudes to security in two units were allayed at the subsequent inspections; another unit was commended for reviewing a conservative approach to mobility and making change. Perhaps the clearest examples of change were found in attitudes to control and sanctions. Use of single separation declined in at least three of the units in the study. The use of very short stay admissions to security, which did not need a court order, was reduced.

Interviews with staff confirmed that inspections made them more conscious of the law and more conscientious in complying with the law, regulations and guidelines on security. But, for the most part, inspectors' influence on practice was gradual and percolative. They were often aiming to encourage quite profound changes of belief.

## Factors Affecting Impact

Both departments in the study felt that inspection was a collaborative exercise, based on mutual respect and concepts of professional peer review, as well as the legal authority of the inspectorate. But one unit and one department seemed to have been increasingly responsive to inspections during the last three years.

The SSD management had taken a firmer grip on their responsibilities for secure accommodation and saw the inspectorate as an ally in enabling them to do so. They continued to be anxious about how far they would succeed. However, they did not see the answer as being that the inspector should wield the power to close the units. They wanted help in determining clear policies and standards but felt they should then exercise their authority to implement them. Whether in the end they would be able to muster that authority remained uncertain.

Congruence of values between the inspector and those inspected was crucial to their perception that a collaborative approach worked best. The same was true of the relationship of the inspectorate with the unit. The senior manager in the establishment was no less powerful than others who maintained a stance more independent of the inspectorate. But she saw her power as enhanced by working with the inspector. They had broadly shared aims and could pursue these more effectively in collaboration. If plenty remained to be done in this unit, it was clear that major changes had been achieved in the previous four years.

But what happened where there was no strong congruence of values and objectives? Theoretically inspectors of secure accommodation have immense power. They can impose a huge range of requirements, backed up by sanctions of closure or severe limits on operation. They choose not to. Why?

A reason advanced by some inspectors was that they feared the impacts of such an approach on the children and young people at present housed in secure units. It would, they thought, inevitably lead to many more closures, some of which would be permanent. In consequence, some children would be placed in custody; others would be sent home or to placements which neither wanted them nor were equipped to deal with them. Certainly, one of the units in the study was closed while the research was being undertaken and that had encouraged some people in the belief that it would be better not to reopen it. It was argued that closure had made the redeployment of staff to open units possible and so increased their capacity to care for disturbed and difficult children.

However, that argument was advanced in a vacuum of knowledge of need. It contained the presumption that secure accommodation was primarily to accommodate children who would otherwise be in open community homes but who for various reasons could not be contained there. But many children in secure units were remanded there by the courts, because open placements were thought to be unsuitable for them. The pressure on units to take many more such children was acute in some areas. Inspectors might well be justified in their fears.

Inspectors' reluctance to impose requirements might derive partly from professional culture. Social workers in their practice prefer to use persuasion and psychological reinforcement in promoting change.

But whatever the inspectors' beliefs, it could be argued that the problems facing local authorities in the administration of secure accommodation were largely outside their control. There was a massive shortfall in the numbers of qualified staff in residential care and many of the reforms advocated by the inspectorate depended on recruiting such staff. Moreover, authorities must rigorously determine their priorities in allocating scarce resources, be they human or financial. Secure accommodation was very expensive and catered for a minute proportion of local authority responsibilities. Local authorities had no duty to provide it. If pushed too hard to do things for which they have inadequate resources they might be tempted to withdraw from provision.

All these arguments had to be weighed before decisions were made to close units. And, of course, such decisions were ultimately those of the Department of Health. There might be occasions when inspectors' recommendations for closure were overridden by the Department either because of the knock-on effects upon provision across the country or because of national policy implications.

Another set of problems arose from the remit of social service inspections. Their only stated purpose was to advise the Secretary of State on whether he should approve secure accommodation. Neither the local authorities nor the units themselves were defined as the clients of inspections. Frequently, inspectors did not make it clear whether their comments were primarily for the managing authorities or for managers in the units. And there was no laid down procedure for reviewing the units with the local authorities. Inspections took place within the units and attention was almost wholly on unit staff. Reports were sent to the Directors of Social Services but inspectors did not necessarily discuss them with local authority management or members.

This mattered for a number of reasons. Local authorities were not convinced that the problem of secure accommodation belonged to them, rather than to the courts or the juvenile justice system. Some regarded it as a form of provision largely cut off from the rest of their work. Contemporary child care policy was to reduce residential care provision and to divert as many young people as possible from residential care or custody. Maintaining facilities to lock children up, although not incompatible with such policies, was unlikely to be high priority.

Local authorities were not much encouraged to extend their responsibilities for children and young people in trouble in the 1980s. They were subjected to severe criticism for their handling of them following the implementation of the Children and Young Person's Act 1969 and parts of the Criminal Justice Act, 1982 were designed primarily to limit their discretion in dealing with them.

The management problems of secure accommodation were far from straightforward. Units were traditionally established as part of large CHEs. We have seen that many continued to be run by Heads who had a great deal of autonomy before they were incorporated into the local authority system and held onto their power. Many units were, effectively, not managed by local authorities. Several participants in the study spoke of local authorities simply performing a liaison and low level monitoring function in their contact with them. If the units were then criticised by inspectors, local authorities had little choice but to support them, if they were not to admit they had taken no positive action to control them.

In such circumstances, inspectors might feel they had little chance of affecting the management of secure units, without confronting Directors of Social Services: making local authorities much more central to the inspection process.

## Conclusion

The case study shows the SSI in an area of work where it had delegated legal duties and authority. The evaluative task was strongly framed by law and statutory regulations and the SSI worked hard to standardise inspections. But ambiguities and conflicts remained, some inherent and some the product of evaluative tradition, professional identity and policy context.

The SSI was expected to evaluate the detailed practice of a total institution as it affected individuals. That inevitably meant exercising discretion within the legal framework and judging the balance to be struck between competing imperatives. But ambiguities also arose because the SSI, in the tradition of professional inspectorates, did not confine itself to regulation. Inspectors wanted to act as agents of change. They were caught between the need to be comprehensive in their evaluation, if they were to fulfil the regulatory task, and the need to focus and determine priorities if they were to cause change.

SSI's uncertainty on these issues was particularly acute in secure accommodation inspections. This provision was often not fully incorporated into the SSD management structure. It was directly dependent on central government for many of its resources and inspectors were often the brokers for these resources. These factors affected their own and others' perception of their role and the division of responsibilities between them and the local authorities. They were often on the edge of managing as well as inspecting secure accommodation.

The substantial formal powers of the SSI and their relative impotence to cause change, even on apparently straightforward dimensions of practice, afforded a striking paradox. The analysis suggests that SSI's professional identity made it more sympathetic to self generated change, more reliant on shared values with those subject to inspection and more at home with a conception of itself as a catalyst. But it also questions what could be expected of an evaluative institution in this context. Power to compel local authority action was inevitably limited, without a quite radical review of the policy field.

## SSI's Broader Context

SSI's predecessor body, the SWS, was already managing multiple objectives and identities. It was a part of government, it represented the profession of social work in government, and it was a channel of interpretation between central and local government. The new SSI's role in implementing government policy was more strongly emphasised, its identity with social work, as distinct from personal social services, was weakened and it was required to pursue instrumental values alongside substantive professional values. As the emphasis on management in local authorities increased, a new duality emerged between the SSI as the developer of evaluative frameworks, criteria and instruments for use by local authorities in evaluation and performance review, and as direct evaluator. The White Paper on community care (Department of Health, 1989) tipped the balance towards the indirect role when it proposed local authority inspection units and a new role for the SSI as overseer of local authority plans for community care.

The case studies suggest that the new SSI largely eschewed the criteria of economy and efficiency. But the secure accommodation study revealed some movement towards managerial conceptions of change and how to achieve good practice. The SSI was under some pressure from within its ranks and from SSDs to loosen its overwhelmingly professional commitment. One reason for this can be deduced from both the case studies. Both demonstrated the complexity of values and practice implicit in inspectors' conceptions of residential care for children, the gap between those conceptions and what they found in the field and the attenuation of values at the point of implementation. Their work was predicated on the professionalisation of residential care, a prospect as remote in the 1980s as it had been in the 1960s. The professional social work model of effectiveness was quite different from managerialist philosophies: it concentrated on input and process more than outcome and emphasised the human as well as financial costs of giving effective help to vulnerable, damaged or deviant groups of people.

Social work's conception of change was gradualist. Its capacity to cause major change was unproven. We shall describe in Chapters Nine and Ten how the SSI confronted the challenge to combine a professional identity with demands from the field, as well as from government, to help improve the management of the personal social services.

Chapter Eight

# The Health Advisory Service:
## A Professional Advisory Service and the Managerial Imperative*

The account of the Health Advisory Service is based on eight case studies covering the period 1982-1988, when devolution to district management was accompanied by strenuous attempts to tighten central control of the economy, efficiency and effectiveness of the NHS. The line of accountability was, once more, to be clarified and at every level, accountability was to be concentrated into the role of the general manager. The dominance and autonomy of professionals, particularly doctors, were to be challenged and pluralist values and influence attenuated.

It was to be expected, therefore, that we should find a service whose identity was grounded in the values of professional judgement, advice and support under increasing pressure as it worked its way through those years. However, some of the tensions and ambiguities of the HAS extended back to its roots.

The origins of the Health Advisory Service (HAS) lie in the creation of the Hospital Advisory Service in 1969 'to monitor and improve the quality of care received by the elderly, mentally handicapped and mentally ill in long stay hospitals' (Henkel et al, 1989).

The Hospital Advisory Service was born out of a political response to a scandal about conditions and care in a long stay hospital. The then Secretary of State for Social Services, Richard Crossman, responded eagerly to a recommendation from the committee of inquiry (Howe,

---

* This chapter is largely dependent on data collected for a study of the Health Advisory Service funded by the DHSS and the King Edward's Hospital Fund for London and published as M. Henkel, M. Kogan, T. Packwood, T. Whitaker, P. Youll (1989), *The Health Advisory Service: an Evaluation*, King Edward's Hospital Fund for London.

1969) for an inspectorate. His conception of what was required was an organisation independent of the administration of the NHS that would act as his 'eyes and ears'. It was to be an instrument of control, to safeguard ministers politically against civil service reticence in exposing the internal shortcomings of NHS management of hospital services for a particularly vulnerable group of chronically ill patients. What emerged was an advisory service that was as much for professionals working in the service as for ministers, although it was independent and it did report directly to the Secretary of State. Its initial terms of reference were to help improve the management of patient care 'by constructive criticism and propagating good practices and new ideas' (Watkin, 1978).

In 1976, the scope of the service was at the same time narrowed and broadened. Concern about the failure to implement the White Paper *Better Services for the Mentally Handicapped* (1971) prompted another Labour Secretary of State to create a new body, the National Development Team, to advise on the development of services for this group in England (although, confusingly, not in Wales). As a result, the HAS shed its responsibilities for people with a mental handicap. But its remit was extended to include community services for the elderly and mentally ill, including those provided by local authority social services departments and voluntary organisations. At this point it was renamed the Health Advisory Service and it began to work in partnership with the Social Work Service of the DHSS. Together, they were to form 'joint multi-disciplinary teams' to review 'in a comprehensive way the complementary services provided in an area by the health service and by the social services departments of the local authorities' (DHSS, 1976).

These changes reflected some major developments in health policy. A key objective of the 1974 reorganisation of the NHS had been to achieve greater integration of the hospital, community and primary health services. At the same time, consensus management of the NHS by multi-professional teams was installed, together with a new emphasis on service coordination and, soon, on joint planning and joint finance between health and local authorities. By the mid-1970s, the combination of demographic change, economic crisis and increasing pressure on hospitals from acute illness had brought a new urgency to the demand to implement community care policies.

In 1986, the responsibilities of the HAS were extended once more to monitor and help promote services for another group with a high contemporary political profile, drug misusers. The Drug Advisory Service was created to operate under its auspices.

But by the beginning of the 1980s, the changing assumptions about public sector services resulted in changes in the NHS that had more profound implications for the HAS. Consensus management by professionals was replaced by general management following the Griffiths Report in 1983 and performance indicators were introduced as part of the new emphases on economy, efficiency and effectiveness. The role of a multi-professional advisory service committed to achieving improvement by persuasion inevitably came under scrutiny as the era of managerial control dawned. An indicator of the shift in approach was the decision to publish HAS reports, a practice established in 1985: a move towards combining a discreet, professional educative approach with one invoking the media and public interest and power.

## HAS Objectives

In its early years the HAS concentrated on the detail of service provision. It had been created to monitor and improve patient care. As its remit was extended, it widened its focus to service policy, planning and management, without abandoning its concern with the point of service delivery.

Its functions as outlined in a DHSS circular of 1984 (HC(84)16) were to 'maintain and improve the standards of management and organisation of patient care services, mainly those for the elderly and mentally ill'. HAS also had a remit in respect of the care of children in long term hospital care.

These functions were primarily carried out through visits to services by HAS teams who were to 'provide an objective assessment' and ' to advise those concerned on how to build constructively on what they have by concentration on:

- methods of management and patient care organisation;
- interdisciplinary cooperation;
- education and training of all staff;
- cooperation between agencies, especially in planning;
- mobilisation of the necessary resources.'

HAS had more general responsibilities to keep the government aware of the impacts of service provision, problems in making that provision and needs for policy change. It was also to identify and disseminate good practices.

But the central task, as outlined in official documents, was, as a professional body, to provide peer review and advice for the particular

needs of individual authorities. It was to be a catalyst for improvement
and change. This emphasis was strongly reinforced by the Director at the
time of our study, although HAS' origins were not forgotten. Many team
members and health and social services staff felt that HAS also acted as
a necessary watchdog or safeguard against unacceptable standards. The
new Director appointed in 1989 endorsed this view, as the future of the
HAS came under scrutiny.

During the 1980s the HAS directorate was aware of 'a growing
demand for definitive statements of the necessary components and functions' of services for elderly and mentally ill people (HAS, 1987) and its
publications, *The Rising Tide* (1983) and *Bridges over Troubled Waters*
(1985), were intended to go some way to meet that demand in the case of
elderly mentally infirm people and mentally ill adolescents respectively.
But it made no pretensions to establishing national standards and criteria.
That would have flown in the face of its conception of the most effective
way to evaluate and promote development of services.

## HAS Organisation

HAS worked on a modest budget of approximately £1 million per annum
and a minimal permanent staff: a Director, seconded from the NHS, an
administrator, seconded from the DHSS and a handful of executive and
clerical staff. Directors serve for periods of three to five years. To date
they have all been doctors drawn alternately from psychiatry and geriatric
medicine.

Although the functions of HAS have evolved in response to broader
policy change, the personality of individual Directors has been highly
influential upon the direction, style and public face of the service (Day,
Klein and Tipping, 1988; Henkel et al, 1989).

The main task of the HAS was carried out through visits to the mental
health services and services for elderly people in each district health
authority in England and Wales. These visits were made by multi-professional visiting teams of, usually, between four and six. The teams were
drawn from a pool of between 200 and 300 selected individuals, psychiatrists, geriatricians, health service general managers or retired administrators, nurse managers, therapist managers, and social services managers
with social work experience. Many of these were retired. HAS aimed to
have not more than 20% retired members on each team but normally had
to be content with 50%. There was no formal incentive either for individual staff or their employers to supply members to HAS teams. Nor was

the kudos sufficient to draw enough high status or high flying people in the health and social services away from increasingly demanding jobs.

The Director selected members drawn from the NHS. Potential members were identified through the networks of the professional colleges, through advertisement in professional journals and often recommendations of HAS teams themselves made in the course of their visits. There was an informal selection process, now somewhat tightened by inviting prospective members to seminars and appraising them.

The SSI was responsible for the selection of social services members, who were appointed temporary inspectors and answerable to the regional Assistant Chief Inspector of the region where the visit was taking place. They were thus institutionally linked to the DHSS in a way that their NHS counterparts were not and carried a status not wholly compatible with the independence of the HAS. They were interviewed and participated in a minimal orientation programme which involved meetings with permanent staff and visits to regional offices. But, as with the NHS visitors, the real test was performance on the first visit.

While in theory teams were selected on a 'horses for courses' principle, in practice selection was more likely to be a matter of availability. The problems of selection threatened to undermine the model of peer review on which HAS worked. This essentially depends on members having generally acknowledged professional authority and on their capacity to respond to the needs of widely differing services and areas.

At the time of the study, visits were organised to services for the two main client groups separately. This meant that, on average, services would receive a full visit once every ten years and a follow up visit to monitor progress between two and three years after the full visit. Most visits each year were organised on a rotatory basis, although HAS was moving to a more problem oriented selection. For example, the 25 per cent of districts with the highest average length of patient stay were likely to have their visits brought forward. Visits might be grouped to cover successively all the health authorities co-terminous with a county social services department or all authorities affected by the closure of a particular hospital. Sometimes, a district health authority would request a visit, to help them with specific problems or proposals for change.

There were several problems about the pattern of visiting. Ten year intervals between full visits meant that the role that HAS could play as adviser or inspector was marginalised. Follow up visits after a period of two to three years were unsatisfactory as a monitoring device but neither could they realistically take on an advisory function. In a time of rapid change, the preoccupations of the previous HAS visit were likely to have been overtaken. Also the separation of visits to mental health services and to those for the elderly could mean that evaluation of services for the elderly mental infirm was neglected or uncoordinated.

In 1989, the HAS began an experiment to combine the full visits to both services and at the same time to halve the interval between them, by cutting out follow up visits altogether.

## HAS visits

### Preparation

HAS informed authorities a year in advance that a visit would take place. Three months before the visit was due they confirmed the precise date, sent a provisional programme and the names of the visiting team. They communicated direct with health authorities but it was for the SSI to inform social services departments.

Full visits normally lasted two weeks with an additional week at HAS headquarters for the team to write the report. Follow up visits, including the writing of the report, were completed within one week.

The practical arrangements for visits were primarily in the hands of the district health authority (DHA) but there was little evidence of a coordinated strategic use of the preparation period either within or between health and social services authorities. The exceptions in the study were in an authority where the HAS had been invited to visit to help strategic planning (though even here there was no coordinated approach to the visit between the DHA and the social services department (SSD)) and in an area where there was a crisis of relationships between health and social services to which senior staff of the health authority hoped the HAS visit would find a solution. Otherwise, any preparatory work undertaken was likely to be carried out within disciplines and on the initiative of individual managers or consultants.

Members varied in how far they sought to control the programme, and how much activity they tried to fit in, although all added some events to the standard outline circulated in advance.

HAS required the DHA to send information prior to the visit but the SSI had the responsibility of obtaining information from the SSD. Delivery of information from SSDs was erratic: it might not be supplied before the visit at all or conveyed only to the SSI team member.

The HAS also tried to ensure that maximum advance publicity was given the visit in the DHA to encourage staff members at any level of the service to contact them if they wished to do so.

However, the HAS did not tightly structure the information made available in advance of visits and although RHAs and DHA management sent some data on demographic and service trends, needs, resources, policies and planning, it was neither on a uniform pattern nor, usually, collated specifically for the visit. Other information or concerns were conveyed by professional heads of services as and if they thought fit.

The Community Health Councils (CHCs) in our study displayed the most consistently active and focused approach. Usually they had prepared a written statement of the main issues which they wished to put to the team before meeting them in person.

Perhaps because of the lack of structure and coordination of preparatory data, most team members saw the HAS Director's briefing as a key source of information. The Director visited the authority to meet officers of the DHA and the SSD following the three month notification of each visit. From this meeting he produced an outline of the main issues for the team. There was universal praise for these briefings from team members interviewed for our study, although also some variation in the extent to which teams explicitly used the items identified to frame their work. Some teams resisted any notion that their priorities should be predetermined.

The approaches described to preparation for the visit highlight some important tensions in the nature and purposes of HAS visits and in perceptions of how responsibilities for the success of HAS visits should be allocated between the HAS Directorate, the teams and the authorities.

If the purpose of HAS visits was overwhelmingly to provide advice on the planning, organisation and development of services, of which the authorities were to take maximum advantage, clear, coordinated and focused information and predetermined planning of the visits was required. But that might remove opportunities for initiative, flexibility and fresh judgement on the part of teams and underestimate the value of their interaction with staff.

Moreover, if teams' most basic responsibility was to act as watchdogs for standards of service to vulnerable groups, many would argue that they must bring to bear their own professional judgement without too much predetermined focus or framing originating internally and from the top of the organisations. Their evaluation, in this case, needed to be as comprehensive as possible and open to the perceptions of staff whose voices were not normally heard.

The origins of the HAS, which were of extirpating scandals that had for too long remained hidden in closed organisations, the importance of professional judgement and discretion to the running of the services, as well as to their evaluation, the ultimately highly individualistic nature of

HAS' organisation and the paucity of its resources all militated against a strongly structured approach to its work. And if there was ambiguity in its early terms of reference between advice and inspection, that had been compounded by the widening of its remit and the greatly increased complexities of the services with which it was concerned. Eventually questions were bound to be raised as to whether HAS had an overload of demands and tensions.

## The Process of the Visit

The main components of the visit had changed little since 1976: they included meetings with health and social services authority members together with senior staff, single and multi-disciplinary meetings, meetings with operational staff, visits to service sites and meetings with community representatives. Services incorporated included hospital in patient and outpatient services, primary care, community based day, residential and domiciliary services provided by the health and local authorities and, sometimes, voluntary organisations. Priority for site visits was given to in-patient hospital provision and residential care. Additional meetings and site visits were set up on the initiative of team members and at the request of staff in the authorities.

Teams did not meet until the first day of the visit, when they came together on site. Teams used this first meeting, the only event of the first day, to allocate tasks, in particular how they would cover the various aspects of the visit and who would take responsibility for the different components of the report. HAS took care to ensure that there was always at least one member with substantial experience of visits who could convey and maintain conventions. Generally, leadership tended to fall to the administrator or consultant on the team, although in some it rotated according to the membership of the meetings. Most teams designated someone to coordinate the writing of the report.

The Memorandum of Guidance to team members laid strong emphasis on the importance of modelling multi-disciplinary working. But little attention was paid by team members or by the HAS itself to the conditions for multi-disciplinary collaboration or team building.

Members felt that usually teams quickly established effective working relationships based on mutual respect for each others' professional background. However, individual disciplines and individual working styles almost inevitably dominated in the impression they made on authorities.

The integration of SSI members into the teams posed particular problems. The HAS directorate was aware of their potential isolation and specifically reminded teams that 'the SSI member should never be left to visit social services staff or facilities alone' (HAS, 1987). Although, from our observation, teams normally adhered to this injunction, the evidence from interviews was that teams often found it difficult to absorb the SSI members. The most serious problem identified was that SSI members were reluctant to criticise SSDs. Occasionally, and this occurred on one of our observed visits, they seemed compelled into the role of advocate or defender of the social services. The structural factors outlined above almost certainly contributed to the problem. Differences of culture, professional identity and conceptualisation of need might also be important. SSI members are inevitably oriented towards the development and maintenance of community services. At the same time they might be less sympathetic to developments initiated by health professionals, particularly doctors.

Coverage of tasks by the HAS teams and allocation of roles were discipline based. 'The rationale for this was that credibility and authority were seen to reside in the competence and status of the individual professional: team credibility derived from the calibre of its members rather than from its performance as a team' (Henkel et al, 1989).

Authority staff tended to place highest expectations on encounters with the team member of their own profession. It was here that the greatest satisfaction, but also the greatest disappointments, were experienced.

HAS has been criticised on the grounds that teams promoted certain models of service, policies and approaches as a matter of dogma rather than responding to the different circumstances and histories of authorities. (*Bulletin of the Royal College of Psychiatrists*, 1986). We were struck by the variation between teams as to the focus of the visit and the number and balance of recommendations. Except that it was rare for teams to make many substantial recommendations at a strategic level, there was little consistency between teams as to the relative emphasis placed on different functional areas or on the various professional and practice issues. Community care policies and practice figured more strongly in more recent reports but otherwise the factors affecting team orientations seemed to be combinations of the authority context and ' the professional background, interests, experience and personal authority of individual members' (Henkel et al., 1989).

Styles and methods of work varied within as well as between teams. Some members relied primarily on observation and listening, others actively cross-checked views and information and pointed out inconsistencies of perception and approach within and between the DHA and the SSD.

Teams had a variety of concerns. They wanted evidence on which to base assessments of the services; they needed to gain understanding as a basis of advice they might offer; they aimed to elicit ideas about issues and possible solutions from staff and to encourage staff, particularly where morale was low or conditions poor. They also wanted to sound out their own developing ideas.

The quality of evidence was a cause of concern among both team members and critics of HAS in our study. In one study visit the team was unable satisfactorily to verify a key set of figures, crucial to the task set for the visit by the health authority, which had in this instance invited assistance from HAS. (They wanted advice on the model of service to adopt and on strategic planning.) Elsewhere, we observed teams trying to verify statements of need and criticism between groups or to establish the prevalence of particular perceptions or concerns. Some used site visits partly to check statements made in meetings. It is probably significant that a team in which there were, unusually, serious internal conflicts could not incorporate some issues in their report because they had insufficient and irreconcilable evidence. They had been disabled in using each other as sources of verification.

Critics of the HAS interviewed in the study linked quality of evidence with the structuring of visits. Sometimes it was felt that teams had no clearly defined structure or purpose in their investigation and in consequence picked up arbitrary evidence or evidence biased towards people 'with axes to grind' (cf *Bulletin of the Royal College of Psychiatrists*, 1986).

Again what was reflected was tension between purposes and method. Teams were expected to investigate and to encourage; and to be responsive as well as active. An advisory process had to depend partly on exploration. Teams needed to discover how staff perceived their problems and what solutions they had formulated or half formulated. They also had to test how far the views of various groups were compatible and how effective the support for them was likely to be. That required systematic coverage and inquiry. But teams were also encouraged to assume that crucial information and keys to problem solving might be found anywhere in the organisation, not only amongst professional leaders, planners and managers. In that case opportunistic inquiry might be more successful than clear and planned structure.

Coverage of sites, services and local staff posed problems for all teams, partly because time was limited and partly because there was little predetermined focus for visits. Teams normally used the programme of formal meetings, multi- and uni-disciplinary and multi-level, as the main vehicle for obtaining views and comments. This was supplemented by selected site visits where the team relied significantly on the authorities to identify relevant wards or establishments. Individual meetings, usually with senior staff, managers and consultants, were often set up during the visit.

The coverage of SSD services varied but tended to reflect an assumption that the emphasis of an HAS visit was on health services. SSD provision was looked at to the extent that it interfaced with or impinged on health services.

Multi-disciplinary, inter-agency and multi-level meetings often posed problems for staff, who felt inhibited about expressing frank opinions or criticisms in such contexts, particularly where relations were strained. Team members were aware of this kind of self-censoring but felt they could spot signs of internal or inter-agency tensions in these forums. Many members had more positive expectations and experiences. They raised multi- disciplinary and inter-agency issues and felt they were stimulating communication between units, professions and agencies. There were cases where this seemed to have resulted in increased or new cooperative activity following the visit, at both operational and planning level, but there were certainly resistances to this kind of shift. Staff derive power, influence and identity from their professional group which could be threatened by integrated approaches to service provision.

Uni-disciplinary meetings tended to have a different flavour. Local staff were more likely to be given or to take the initiative. Sometimes powerful groups, such as consultants or senior managers, made strong bids to influence the team. A group of consultants tried to dictate their recommendations to the team in one observed instance. On another occasion, an SSI team member meeting alone with a group of SSD middle managers attempted to identify their perspective and subsequently to interpret it to his team colleagues and critical DHA members. More generally, individual team members spent time in working through problems and possible solutions with their own professional groups. It is at this level that staff expect to benefit most from the visit and members expect to have most to offer.

Members' approaches to site visits were influenced partly by individual style, partly by disciplinary methods of work and values. For example, one Social Services Inspector team member aimed to look at the daily pattern of life for the patient and to assess the quality of life experienced on a ward or in an old persons' home. A nurse focused on nursing practice and organisation. A physiotherapist checked that the physical environment and facilities were of an acceptable standard. Teams sometimes arranged second visits at different times of the day (and night) to make further assessments of working arrangements and the ambience of the ward or home.

Members took the opportunity to talk to staff at various levels on site visits but few spoke to patients. On the whole team members valued site visits and felt they obtained a reasonably accurate picture of the most important features. Authority staff were not so sure. They criticised the brevity of visits, the apparent arbitrariness of interaction and also sometimes the professional acuity and authority of the team. Some staff felt they were themselves more progressive and more rigorous in their criticism than their visitors.

## Feedback and Reports: Framing Advice and Delivering Judgement

Teams were required to give authorities formal verbal feedback at the conclusion of the visit, as well as to produce a report for publication and distribution to the authorities and the Secretary of State. The formal feedback meeting included DHA and social services committee members, senior managers and other key staff of the health and social services authorities.

Teams met daily during the visit to check and discuss their experiences and developing ideas. Members shared their perceptions of their individual disciplinary areas with their colleagues and there were instances of challenge within the team to individuals' criteria and appraisals. For the most part, however, members were constrained by professional convention from pressing such challenges. And the strongly discipline based allocation of responsibilities for components of the report meant that the forces against interdisciplinary integration of feedback were powerful.

HAS hoped that teams' advice would, as far as possible, be formulated collaboratively with staff in the meetings that constituted the core of the visit. Teams varied widely in how far they achieved this. They were, of course, dependent on the responsiveness of authorities, but this in turn was affected by the style of individual members and the models of evaluation and change they brought with them. Although most team members interviewed for the study saw HAS as an advisory service, not an inspectorate, they meant by this a number of different things: that HAS had no coercive power or sanctions; that its role was actively educative (introducing staff to new ideas and disseminating good practice) or even corrective: 'sometimes authorities have to be told they are wrong' (interview); that evaluation was formative and interactive: HAS was a catalyst for change that would come primarily from self reflection and raised consciousness of the implications of current approaches. In this model, teams could enable and encourage; they could not teach or impose.

They sometimes met with changing or conflicting expectations in authorities, particularly with the advent of general management and performance indicators. Managers wanted clear assessments of their services, precise advice about costs and benefits of different practices and methods and firm messages about what changes were needed and where. Professionals tended to emphasise the importance of enhancing professional morale, recognising the pressures of resource constraints and lending weight to claims for increased resources.

It was not surprising that teams did not always agree on how strongly to frame their criticisms and advice. Most, however, managed to reach agreement and worked hard to resolve internal conflicts over major issues. In one of the visits in the study this did not happen and the team had to refer a major disagreement to the Director after the completion of their fieldwork.

There was usually an informal meeting with senior managers of the health and social services authorities towards the end of the visit, to prevent surprise and errors of fact at the formal feedback session in which the team presented their main conclusions and advice. At the time of the study, formal feedback precluded any possibility of discussion, although correction of factual error was again welcomed. The HAS directorate has since built in a short period for discussion of issues and the Director and the Deputy Director attend as observers.

Of all the stages in the visit, the feedback session provoked the keenest anxiety amongst teams and the most criticism from those visited. It also often made the strongest mark. As the format and style were overwhelmingly those of a summative evaluation, many staff were left with the impression that the visit had been predominantly an inspection. Moreover, because the presentation was strongly discipline based, with each team member making his or her own presentation, many people experienced it as fragmented, rather than offering a model of multi-disciplinary collaboration, as the HAS directorate hoped.

The aim of leaving authorities with clear advice that would motivate and facilitate action was not easily achieved. Audiences sometimes heard different things and took away different messages. Visits had covered an extensive range of issues. The task of presenting findings lucidly and acceptably from a concentrated visit, with participants from a range of organisations and groups with different agendas, expectations and perceptions, was formidable.

At the time of the study, the problem was the more serious, since authorities received nothing in writing from HAS for about two months. Teams completed their draft report in a week's work immediately following the visit. But it had then to be edited and checked by the Directorate for style, presentation and organisation and to eliminate any emotive or overtly political statements, ambiguities or typographical errors. After that it was cleared with the regional SSI office before being sent to the authorities for correction of factual error.

Corrections by authorities deemed valid were incorporated. The final report was then prepared by HAS headquarters for printing by the Department of Health. It was usually published about five months after the visit. The DHA and the SSD concerned decided on the precise date of publication and arranged press releases.

There was general dissatisfaction at the length of time it took to produce the report. After this research was completed, a mini-computer was installed at HAS and the draft report should now be sent to authorities only a week after the end of the visit. Publication should then follow three months later.

## The Response to HAS Reports

The HAS itself asked for a report from authorities six months after the receipt of the report of the visit and, at the time of our study, carried out a follow up visit between two and three years after the main visit. Follow up visits were carried out over a period of five days by small teams of two or three members; sometimes they were conducted single-handedly by an administrator member of the original team. They were intended only to discover how authorities had dealt with the HAS advice and whether their responses had led to improvements. Authorities' expectations after a period of that length were rather different. They were more likely to want the follow up team to address issues of current concern.

HAS reports evoked some action at regional level: by officers of the RHA, who were represented at the final feedback meeting of the main visit, and by the Regional SSI. Information from HAS reports was used by regional officers in monitoring the progress of DHAs, but as one among many monitoring devices. Regional officers sometimes took up aspects of the report with their professional counterpart in the district. Indeed, regions seemed to be increasing their use of HAS. At least one region had set up a procedure whereby its districts provided it with an implementation programme and a note of any disagreements with the advice. But although the HAS evaluation might provide some background material for District Reviews, it was not likely to be used explicitly by regions in that process. Interestingly, SSD respondents saw HAS reports as being more explicitly and unambiguously taken up with them by their SSI.

Apart from this rather minimal external framework, responsibility for action on HAS reports was left largely in the hands of authority managers. They managed the press release on the report and they made initial recommendations to their authorities on the action required, although copies of the report were made available to members and members might set up their own mechanisms for overseeing further action.

For the most part, authorities viewed HAS visits and reports as forms of liberal summative evaluation, rather than as collaborative or formative evaluative exercises. Their mode from the preparation period through the visit itself and afterwards was largely reactive, despite some attempts by particular groups to engage or even co-opt the HAS team to resolve particular problems or advance a particular cause. Even an authority which had invited HAS to visit, in the end did not treat it as a collaborative exercise, since the approach of the team was not what they expected or wanted. The format of feedback meetings and of the reports themselves reinforced the impression of a summative evaluation.

Because authorities viewed the work of HAS in this light, they often resented the fact that reports repeated back to them information and judgements which they had themselves conveyed to the team. They felt that reports told them little that they had not already worked out for themselves. This was not so inappropriate if the exercise was viewed by all participants as formative and advisory, as the HAS memoranda intended. But as it was on the whole viewed quite differently, it caused considerable resentment, particularly in the period since HAS reports have been published. Staff who had openly conveyed anxieties about their service to the teams felt betrayed when their own judgements appeared in reports as if they were those of the team and not already incorporated in the authorities' own planning and management strategies.

The variety of response structures and processes in the authorities underlined the discrete nature of the recommendations and the pluralistic nature of the services concerned, at least for much of the period covered by our study. The impact of general management was only slowly becoming evident. There was no general pattern. While severe criticism of services likely to provoke public scandal, staff anger or plummeting morale galvanised senior managers into prompt action, otherwise HAS reports were taken up in a range of forums based on unit management, professional groupings, institutions, community based teams in health and social services, inter-agency operational or strategic management and authority committees.

HAS visits and reports thus stimulated discussions at a number of points in the organisations. If they supported a local interest or cause they would be quickly taken up by the relevant group or, in some cases, individual. But recommendations that were to have lasting impact were likely to require absorption over time and, often, substantial negotiation to overcome resistances to changed patterns of work and allocation of resources.

As a general rule, HAS reports were given most attention by the less prominent service professions, such as nursing, the therapies and clinical psychology. However, SSD staff did not, on the whole, regard them as impinging directly on them, unless they occupied key liaison roles with the health services.

The HAS retained a primary identity with the health services. The importance of community care for both the main client groups, elderly and mentally ill people, was increasingly emphasised in policy documents. But the structural, political and cultural obstacles to the greater integration between the health and social services contribution to HAS that had to be achieved if HAS commitment to community care was to carry conviction persisted. SSI was struggling to assert its role in central government with limited resources. Some of the structural arrangements for HAS which reinforced the separation of social from health services can be seen as part of its determination to establish and maintain its own professional and institutional identity. But they, if anything, worked to reinforce the marginalisation of social work and social care in HAS and did nothing to challenge its medical hegemony.

## HAS: Implementation and Impact

HAS is a professional advisory service whose mandate covered services for people designated as priority groups in policy documents since the mid-1970s but whose command over resources continues to be relatively weak. The remit has greatly expanded since the creation of the predecessor body, the Hospital Advisory Service, in 1969 to include advising on policy and planning strategies as well as monitoring, evaluating and helping to improve the management of patient care. It now extends across a number of important boundaries: between health services with their direct line of management from central government and social services governed by local authorities; between institutional and community care; between professional and managerial cultures and priorities.

While its coverage is, in some senses, comprehensive, extending to all health and local authorities in England and Wales and including all aspects of health services for old people and people with mental illness, its resources are meagre and the cycle of its activities elongated. Even under the experimental programme initiated in 1989, it requires intensive activity and response from authorities only once in five years. And it operates on a small patch of the large canvass of the health and social services.

The ambiguities evident at the time of the creation of its predecessor body in 1969, between safeguarding acceptable standards of care for vulnerable groups and an advisory and developmental mandate, remain.

As a multi-disciplinary professional service it is in tune with the conception of a service with multiple sources of influence and multiple sites of decision making: a pluralist rather than a hierarchical structure: a conception that was giving way to managerialist assumptions in the course of our study.

It is hardly surprising that respondents from all disciplines and agencies in our study were pessimistic in their expectations of HAS as an agent of change. However, its evaluations were taken seriously, at least in the health services. At minimum, HAS focused attention on the services being evaluated and reports provided a useful source of reference. Many saw visits as useful in stimulating individuals or disciplinary groups to take stock of their own work. Some thought them more influential: in clarifying different viewpoints and indicating gaps in provision and possibilities for redirection.

It was widely agreed that HAS visits raised questions about the balance of resources allocated to services for groups requiring long term provision as against acute medical services. More tangible outcomes of HAS visits included allocation of additional resources to a service, changes or increases in staff allocations and better connections, more immediately at the operational level, between parts of one authority or between health and social services.

It was possible in seven of the eight case studies to make rough quantitative assessments of the acceptance and implementation of HAS recommendations by reference to authorities' own reports of progress. According to these, over 50 per cent of recommendations were either already implemented, or intended to be implemented when circumstances allowed, within six months of their visits (The range across the seven studies was from 52 per cent to 92 per cent).

HAS evaluations had some impact but these figures tell us little about their significance. Closer examination shows that recommendations implemented quickly were to remedy glaring faults and were uncontentious or required few resources or were directed to individual or group attitudes or behaviour. They did not require radical reallocation of priorities, resources or new patterns of service or collaboration.

Advice with larger implications was for the most part diffused among a range of groups. In only one of our authorities did general management take a decisive lead in the implementation of the HAS report. This report was in general line with the authorities' policies and commanded wide consensus. But even here, action was hampered by the opposition of a key professional group, the consultants, as well as by resource difficulties.

HAS was not seen as providing an integrated or systematic lead towards change. Teams did not succeed in engaging authorities at that level, partly because of the deficiencies in the structuring and preparation of visits, partly because they did not normally carry the degree of professional authority with those visited that would have been required and partly because of the pluralist nature of health and social services organisation. Their reports read as a series of discrete recommendations rather than as a more integrated collation of advice. Where they attempted more fundamental appraisal of authorities, they met strong resistance. In at least two of our study authorities some attenuation of resistance was discernible over time, but then the influence of HAS became increasingly difficult to disentangle from other forces.

In one instance powerful groups in an authority endeavoured to co-opt the HAS team to resolve an intractable problem in their own terms. This was not successful. Groups who saw HAS as one of a number of sources of percolative influence or as providing added impetus for changes already mooted in the organisation were more realistic in their expectations.

But in the dawning era of general management, managers looked increasingly to external evaluation to provide clear criteria and measures against which their own and others' performance could be assessed. HAS did not provide them. As noted in Chapter Ten, it worked largely on the basis of implicit and personal values and standards, internalised by individual team members, although major value dissonance was avoided by the professional network based selection of teams. Meanwhile, professionals under pressure from managerialism might expect to look for support from the HAS as a professional advisory service. They did not necessarily find it. Either HAS teams were not seen by them as sufficiently professionally authoritative or they might find the HAS advocating policies cutting across their convictions and practice. HAS ran the risk of pleasing neither managers or powerful professionals.

Chapter Nine

# Evaluative Models, Methods and Knowledge

Chapters Two to Eight have presented detailed accounts of four types of UK evaluative institutions at work in the 1980s. These accounts were set in the context of the radical objectives of the Conservative government returned to power in 1979. Chapter One showed that public sector evaluation, albeit itself reformed, was to facilitate the achievements of those objectives: reduced pluralism and the centralisation of policy norms and political power; the installation in the public sector of a technical-rational form of managerialism characterised by the promotion of economy, efficiency and effectiveness; the reduction of professional influence and the promotion of market values and mechanisms.

The case studies highlight a number of themes relevant to the relationship between government purposes and evaluation. These last four chapters of the book will develop them in a comparative analysis of the four evaluative institutions.

The findings challenge government claims that political evaluation can be neatly divorced from instrumental or professional evaluation. They highlight the multiple objectives of evaluative institutions, the complex pressures upon them and the uncertain relationships between their authority, independence and impacts. They describe encounters between professional, managerial and bureaucratic cultures in the course of evaluative practice. Issues of knowledge traditions, values, evaluative methods, authority and power constantly recur and diminish any lingering hope that evaluation is an objective activity.

Accordingly, in embarking on a comparative analysis of our selected institutions, we shall examine continuities and change in the knowledge traditions within which each one worked, the influence these had on the models and methods of evaluation they adopted, the values they endorsed, and their authority and impact in the relevant policy communities. We consider how far there was convergence between the institutions on these dimensions, how internally coherent were their modes of operation and how consistent with the dominant objectives and values of government.

## Theories of Knowledge and Evaluative Institutions

Chapter One showed how the general direction of evaluation theory had moved from a positivist epistemology, which assumed it was possible to achieve authoritative generalisable knowledge on the basis of empirical observation and measurement, towards hermeneutic and constructivist theories, which challenged such concepts as objective reality and endorsed multiple forms of knowledge. Within the positivist perspective, the task of evaluators is to determine under what conditions desired values are realised and to observe and measure them in what is being evaluated. Their judgements are thus value free. Constructivists claim that evaluative practice is necessarily partial, restricted in scope, shaped by theory and imbued with values. Evaluators purvey argument rather than value free and conclusive analysis.

Government, however, took a positivist approach to evaluation. It assumed that complexities of provision could be broken down and definitively assessed on measurable indicators of performance. It also exemplified a particular form of the 'scientisation' of politics, depicted in a substantial body of literature on twentieth century politics beginning with Weber (Habermas, 1971; for a succinct account of this set of theories, see Hawkesworth, 1988). But while in Habermas' technocratic model of politics it is the scientists and the technical experts who conceal their power, affecting to be only the servants of politicians, in this case the position was reversed. Government presented their choices as ultimately technical. The facts of the contemporary world demanded that the solutions of market liberalism were adopted. But the force of their moral commitment to the values underlying it was incontrovertible. Here was a case of the politicians rather than the technical experts 'camouflaging what is really as political as ever with the logic of reality' (Habermas, 1971).

The government's analysis of the political and economic context reinforced an increasingly dominant trend in developed societies: to perceive the manager as superseding the professional as the force required to continue the successful rationalisation of twentieth century society. What was needed in an increasingly resource conscious world was not simply to entrust parts of it to self regulating groups accorded power in those fields in exchange for specialist knowledge but to ensure that scarce resources were used with maximum effectiveness, not only to produce goods and make profit, but in all forms of human endeavour. The problems of complexity would be solved by quantitative technology and management skills.

The next chapter considers how far that trend was reflected in the values endorsed by the institutions in the study; but first its implications for the knowledge base of evaluative institutions are examined. How far were positivist and technocratic assumptions shared by the institutions? What forms of knowledge did they deploy and what kinds of evaluative models resulted from that? Could the trends in their practice be linked to the political objectives of reducing pluralism and centralising power?

## Theories of Knowledge in Evaluative Institutions

The institutions in our study apparently differed sharply between the positivist and technocratic assumptions of the Audit Commission and the deployment of management consultants in advising government, and the professional and incipiently constructivist approaches of SSI and the HAS. In practice, their work was all based on a pragmatic mix of knowledge theories.

Technocratic assumptions are inherent in an approach to management which stresses that it must work according to the logic of its environment. They are evident in the forms of argument repeatedly used by the Audit Commission that there is a definitive way of understanding the political and economic context and that certain solutions follow logically from that; that all organisations, whatever their ideology and whatever ends they wish to pursue, must respect the logic of, for example, shortage of resources and demographic change and that it leads to single solutions or, at most, restricted alternatives. But the Commission's arguments were both deductive and inductive.

They made substantial use of managerial and professional networks in the fields they investigated and tried to ensure that their reports were either based on an approach to problem solving already in use by recognised leaders in those fields or that they would be acceptable to them.

Consultants were engaged by government departments within a division of labour based on a distinction between technical expertise and policy values. But we have seen how that distinction could be broken down and consultants' advice structured by political feasibility and departmental preferences.

The SSI and the HAS came from a different starting point. They assumed that effective practice was value led rather than dictated by the 'logic of reality'; and that evaluation must incorporate professional values. The HAS expected to provide objective evaluation but to base its work, as far as possible, on authorities' own models of service, definition of problems and approaches to solutions. Their range would be limited by the existence of a broad professional consensus and the self regulating devices of peer review.

Sustaining professional norms and standards rested on the recruitment to peer review bodies of those of high reputation within their own discipline and, in the case of HAS, with proven records of interdisciplinary collaborative approaches.

Such peer review models reflect important beliefs about the professional and reflective judgement of specific, often individual, needs and circumstances. As articulated by, for example, Schon (1983), professions are open systems, whose members shape, respond to and learn from the demands of their environments and communication with their peers. Practitioners make intelligent judgements informed by tacit or internalised knowledge, values and standards. They need to do so because they are dealing with varied human needs in part defined by varied conditions and circumstances.

Both HAS evaluations and SSI inspections were, in part, designed as advisory and developmental processes, geared to understand and appraise belief systems, visions of service, attitudes and relationships: a form of inquiry that might therefore illuminate multiple worlds and the perceptions and desires of different stakeholders within the assumptions of a hermeneutic epistemology where there is no one truth.

But for both bodies, that was only one aspect of what were ambiguous functions. Both also aimed to inspect, to discover the truth about what was happening in a service or institution, 'objective reality'. Both saw themselves as reaching objective judgements about fact and value, based as far as possible on evidence: they checked conflicting accounts of, for example, events or allocations of resources and tried to reach their own conclusions; they also made qualitative judgements.

They took seriously, and incorporated, the perceptions of service users, patients and many different kinds of employees but with a mix of purposes: to find the truth, to see that less powerful groups were given a voice, as service needs, resources and achievements were discussed and, particularly in the case of the HAS, to help groups with different, and sometimes conflicting perceptions, to a better mutual understanding. They worked partly on common sense assumptions that it was possible to reach the truth about facts and partly on professional assumptions that they brought professional authority to their judgements.

Thus, although their approach often contained the seeds of a herme- neutic theory, they believed in the authority of specialist knowledge.

But that was nothing new. The shifts in evaluative theory that rejected concepts such as objectivity, saw evaluation as inevitably partisan, mak- ing choices as to which stakeholders they should regard as primary, and engaged in argument and negotiation (Guba and Lincoln, 1989) rather than authoritative judgement, had never penetrated public institutional evaluation in the UK.

## The Search for More Differentiated Expertise

In none of the organisations was evaluation itself regarded as a form of specialism or expertise. Otherwise, they differed on a number of counts: the flexibility of their workforce, the degree of specialisation, the extent to which they had access to public and private sector experience, and the types of expertise on which they drew.

Access to multiple and discrete sources of advice was increasingly in demand in the private and the public sectors in the 1980s. The combina- tion of economic imperatives, new technologies and fast moving institu- tional change highlighted the advantages of reducing permanent specialist advisory staff numbers in favour of the flexibility of second- ments and consultancies (Peet, 1988).

Among our institutions, the SSI had the least room for such strategies, although, as its remit had broadened in recognition of the complexity of the personal social services, it needed new types of expertise. It had a small budget for short term secondments and *ad hoc* consultancies. They were normally contracted with other parts of the public sector, local authorities or academic bodies, as distinct from the private sector.

While the HAS could, in theory, recruit 'horses for courses', the pool of team members was too small and the demands on members' time too great for them to ensure any fine tuning in the composition of HAS visiting teams. The relatively rigid multi-professional formula for mem- bership combined with the huge scope of visits precluded any substantial specialisation beyond professional discipline and broad categories of experience.

The Audit Commission had an entirely new form of governance and, as noted earlier, a new superstructure strongly rooted in the tradition of private sector management consultancy deployed in the public sector. Its special studies directorate deployed two kinds of specialist expertise. The core capacity was that of quantitative analysis, based on statistics, economics and operational research. Flexibility was provided by secondments of academics and others with specialist knowledge of the particular field of studies being addressed and periodic input from 'the great and the good' in relevant services.

However, as was the case in the other statutory institutions in the study, the Commission's main workforce was ill adapted to the changes impinging on it in the 1980s. Auditors were trained in procedures geared to financial regulation rather than resource or organisational management; their knowledge base was authoritative but within tightly defined limits. At least in its early years, the Commission was undertaking local 'value for money' audits with substantially the same type of expertise (that of accountancy) as had been deployed on the much narrower functions carried out by its predecessor body. Seventy per cent of its local auditors were employed by the District Audit Service but Tomkins suggests that the quality of auditing resources in private sector firms was little different from those available in the DAS. Moreover, the new demand on auditors to certify an opinion on local authority accounts meant that firms, which tended to split 'value for money' from regularity audit, spent more of their available time on the latter than previously (Tomkins, 1986).

The quality of value for money auditing in the private sector firms was an issue for the Commission (Audit Commission, 1987c). It was sometimes linked with the question whether sufficient senior staff time was allocated to such assignments.

The Commission's reports also indicated determination to raise graduate recruitment to the District Audit Service and, in line with the comments made by DAS respondents to our study, 'to upgrade management and presentational skills' among existing staff (Audit Commission, 1988d). By 1988, the DAS was also investing in specialist leadership for value for money projects in its regional offices.

Social services inspectors were social workers recruited to the civil service from a personal service profession with low levels of specialisation, trained to promote loosely defined practice and service norms and adapted to an era that assumed a profession-centred service and liberal, collaborative relationships between central and local government. Their knowledge base was generally perceived as uncertain and internally conflicting; and its susceptibility to ideological influence and interpretation unconcealed. Their skills were directed to understanding and mediating between values, beliefs and relationships.

Professional inspectors recruited after 1985 were in some respects different from their predecessors. Their conceptions of social work had been substantially shaped by experience in local authority social services departments where needs were increasingly perceived in managerial terms. However, these recruits were more likely to have come from middle management than to have had comprehensive or strategic management experience, so that their status, authority and capacity still might not meet the expectations of top managers in social services departments endeavouring to resolve complex managerial problems.

The multi-professional teams working under the auspices of the HAS were geared to the 1970s conceptions of NHS management by professional consensus and its underlying values of professional freedom and organisational pluralism, which had largely failed to stimulate effective, integrated models of management or practice. Inevitably the level at which the members of HAS teams could communicate with each other was that of values and implicit norms, rather than of technical detail or precise standards.

Organisations like consultancy firms and the directorates of the Audit Commission with more built-in flexibility and specialisation, to say nothing of resources far more substantial than most other evaluative bodies, could provide for the increasingly differentiated needs of organisations. As the use of consultants grew, consultancy firms were developing a strong public sector base in their organisations. They varied as to the degree and kind of specialisation they pursued.

Accountancy firms which had broadened into consultancy with the expansion of value for money auditing tended to have strong technical expertise in information technology and data processing, as well as in accounting. Traditional management consultants characteristically combined top level strategy advice with more specialist expertise in, for example, finance. They employed large numbers of Masters of Business Administration but some also demanded successful management experience of their recruits. Some firms specialised in human resource or personnel consultancy. But the most common feature of consultancies commissioned by civil servants was the range of quantitative and technical expertise at their disposal.

Technical expertise, particularly if it could produce quantitative measures and standards for generalist managers or bureaucrats, was highly valued. That was not to say that it necessarily carried wide authority. It could be contained not only by powerful civil servants but also by local government officials. It could be used to legitimise managerial or bureaucratic preferences. And much of it was subject to fashion, a trend exacerbated by market conscious consultancy firms.

The institutions held different attitudes towards the role of context or field specific research as a potentially independent source of knowledge. It was not generally part of consultants' repertoire; while the HAS explicitly eschewed a research-based in favour of an experience-based approach.

The Audit Commission special studies teams did see research as a resource, although they varied as to the extent to which they used it. It is likely that as the Commission focuses more on effectiveness, research will become more important to it. An Audit Commission special studies manager regarded research as an important resource, partly for him but also for the local authorities. He thought one of the Commission's roles was to be a channel to practitioners for useful and reputable research. His selection was largely dependent on recommendation from his network and therefore likely to endorse prevailing wisdom but he did subject it to the scrutiny of his teams.

At the time of the study, the SSI was probably the most interested of our institutions in developing its use of research material and techniques. It had not forged strong links with the Department of Health's research management branch (although that might have changed with the movement in 1989 of one of its deputy chief inspectors to head that branch). However, it did appoint two social scientists as inspectors to strengthen its analytic expertise. They were both grounded in the positivist tradition of research favoured both by the Department of Health (Kogan and Henkel, 1983) and by the dominant research tradition in social work and the personal social services in the UK (Goldberg, 1981, 1982, 1984). This tradition emphasises the importance of generalisability as a goal for social work research and the cumulative nature of research: its ambition to develop conceptual and theoretical frameworks within which needs can be more precisely differentiated and apparently conflicting perspectives reconciled (Davies and Knapp, 1981). The research commissioned by the SSI (1989e) on consumer research in residential care of the elderly appeared to be based on similar assumptions.

As far as the SSI was concerned the employment of researchers was linked to its changing perceptions of its role: contributing to the Department's capacity for policy analysis; and making its evaluation more systematic, authoritative and useful to managers. This evokes the issue of quantification, and its importance compared with qualitative inquiry in all four of the institutions.

## The Use of Quantitative Methods

The evaluative methods of the HAS and the SSI, as described, were predominantly qualitative, although there were differences between team members. These methods evolved from the intensive examination of practice within bounded institutions such as hospitals and residential homes. They were geared to evaluating the professional work process, the interfaces between receivers and providers, individual needs, responses and associated personal planning. Professionals tried to adapt them to cope with evaluating systems of care and intervention, their planning, coordination and management and the policy and resource frameworks within which they work. But not surprisingly, the effort did not wholly succeed in tasks such as the assessment of flows of demand and supply, distribution of services, strategic planning and information systems.

HAS visiting teams were provided with some quantitative data before the start of the visit and inspectors were required to collect such data in preparation for inspections. The data might be used to help visitors and inspectors identify issues or matters for further investigation and determine the focus of their on-site work. And some of that work might include the collection of further quantitative data, checking information, particularly in the case of conflicts of perception among either those being evaluated or the evaluators themselves, and establishing patterns of service. However, quantitative analysis and advice normally played only a small part in feedback and reports. They were usually confined to recommendations for increase or decrease in numbers of staff or beds.

How far have either HAS or SSI introduced different or more diverse methods and, if they have, does this mean a change in their priorities?

There were some signs of change, particularly in the SSI. While HAS used some national performance indicators as a means of identifying national trends and helping HAS teams to locate the performance of individual authorities in a comparative context, SSI went further.

Quantitative analysis was beginning to find a place in inspections themselves. The inspections of home care included comparative analyses of staff resources, costs, intensity and cover of service, expected and actual delivery of service for the inspected authorities (eg, SSI, 1989c). A relatively simple computer programme had been developed to enable inspectors to analyse admissions to secure accommodation and so monitor more effectively whether the law on the restriction of children's liberty was being complied with in the spirit as well as in the letter.

At the time of writing, these developments were not incorporated into a systematic policy change in the inspectorate. The secure accommodation review of inspection methodology had taken place without reference to the Training and Resources group of which the social scientists were part. Where inquiry on costs was included in inspections, it was not always fully integrated and the level of sophistication in the collection and analysis of such information varied widely. The majority of inspections continued to be based overwhelmingly on qualitative data.

However, there was evidence that more varied methods of inquiry were being used in inspections and that there was a trend towards a more systematic approach that would make comparative analysis over time and between services and authorities more possible.

At least in some instances the SSI was attempting to identify criteria that could be used both in future inspections and by local authorities in their own monitoring and evaluative work, which SSI was encouraging them to develop.

In the Short Term Care inspection (1987a), an attempt was made to distill a wide ranging evaluative inquiry into a few key criteria. These were in fact four key characteristics or dimensions of short term care that could act as focal points of interrogation by external or internal evaluators. And they were not systematically linked with specific values or sets of values. But the exercise was important partly because short term care was a relatively newly recognised form of provision and had not previously been the subject of inspection. And the dimensions were not just raised as issues, as had been the case in the Community Homes inspection report when it discussed units for independent living. They were proposed as dimensions which must be considered and on which decisions must be made if there is to be good quality of provision in this form of care.

In some cases, fieldwork for inspections was preceded by the administration of precoded questionnaires, the analysis of which formed part of the inspection report.

Experiments were being made in producing rating scales for some forms of institution (Family Centres and Youth Treatment Centres) and, in the case of one inspection, a group of researchers developed performance indicators for one dimension of residential care of old people (SSI, 1989a).

Thus the impact of the social scientists on the social work based inspectors was emerging in the outputs of inspections. Social scientists were by this time running short courses on quantitative and qualitative research methods in the inspectorate, as well as advising on particular inspections. They stated that their objective was not to convert inspectors into researchers; rather to make them ready to use research expertise. In their view quantitative and qualitative methods and research and professional expertise were complementary. All were needed for evaluating services.

The social scientists were shifting the emphases in the inspectorate from intensive and particular inquiry to extensive and generalisable analysis. They were incorporating or reinforcing norms of consistency and comparability into inspections, based on positivist norms of scientific rigour and precision, for example about the separation of fact and value in investigation and judgement. But they argued that this would provide stronger bases and frameworks for professional evaluation.

Social work theory and methodology retained a strong role in inspections but, as we have remarked, it was an uncertain source of authority. The case studies suggested that many (not all) senior operational staff in the field tended to play down its value either because it was not at the leading edge of practice, or because it represented a different theoretical framework from that used by those evaluated or because it represented a political threat, (eg the replacement of teaching expertise by that of social work in secure accommodation). In these cases, staff focused on the technical or legal knowledge possessed by inspectors. Junior staff tended to appraise the knowledge of inspectors partly against such technical criteria and partly against its basis in experience.

Meanwhile some senior managers (again not all) concerned with the overall output of their organisations tended to want clear performance targets and evaluative criteria which they could readily test themselves. Changes in SSI towards managerial priorities did not come simply from government.

The key responsibilities of the Audit Commission were to monitor and improve local authority management of financial and other resources, the probity of their accounting practices, and the economy, efficiency and effectiveness with which they acquire and use their resources.

There was thus a premium on quantitative information and methods of inquiry and analysis. In this study they have been considered primarily in the context of the special studies and, to a lesser extent, management practice directorates.

The early special studies focused on issues of economy and efficiency and on areas of local authority work where these could be most easily and demonstrably measured or calculated. From the beginning, a key output of the local value for money projects was the calculation of savings or opportunities for 'value improvement' that local authorities could make in the selected fields of inquiry.

Even when the Commission shifted its emphasis towards effectiveness, these calculations remained as critical benchmarks of improvement in authorities' performance.

Special studies reports made major use of financial and demographic statistics. Reports were concerned with the reliability and predictive capacity of authorities' quantitative information, with relative budgets, costs, patterns of expenditure and the relationship between inputs and outputs.

Quantitative analysts were essential members of special studies teams. These formed the permanent staff of the Commission and it was they who built up the Commission's own expertise. Quantitative analysis was never just contextual; it was central to the studies. The teams were built round exchange and argument between their perspective and that of specialists in the field under investigation, who were brought in for specific studies.

An important feature of the analytic expertise is modelling. Models are tools of explanation, presentation and problem solving. The construction and testing of models are familiar and valued components of analysts' approach. A particular feature of the studies used for the research was the use of modelling to analyse alternative uses of resources and to promote thinking about opportunity costs.

The function of modelling was a significant point of contrast between management consultants and the Audit Commission on the one hand and HAS and SSI on the other. It is arguably a point at which the power of technology can dictate. Quantitative models provide options that are clearly defined and grounded in hard data. While it is true that HAS's and SSI's political roles inhibited them for different reasons from prescribing, their practitioners might still, if they were trained in this mould, be ready to present clear alternative models of service. It is probably significant that (with one exception) only doctors on HAS teams displayed some propensity to prescribe such models.

Presentational skills linked with analytic techniques were a particularly important tool for the Commission, making resource analysis accessible to a wide audience of managers in local authorities as well as to members. The use of models and flow charts in reports lent increased authority and impact. SSI and HAS were aware of this but had not taken action. Constraints were, arguably, as much technical as budgetary.

Consultants used by central government had a similar range of quantitative techniques of analysis and civil servants involved in commissioning consultants laid strong emphasis on such skills. Consultants themselves, while recognising their importance as tools of systematic inquiry, often drew attention to other forms of expertise that they brought to projects: theories of management and strategic planning. They identified their role as sometimes to help civil servants perceive issues and problems as managerial. Some felt it important to negotiate the terms of consultancies so that they could influence how they were framed. Alternative framing might make a more fundamental contribution to departments.

## Evaluative Models and Institutions

To what extent did the evaluative institutions convert a widening range of expertise into coherent and authoritative evaluative models?

The broad distinction (Scriven, 1980) between summative and formative evaluation provides a useful framework for addressing this question. In summative evaluation the evaluative body is expected to reach conclusive and objective judgements which it delivers to the clients or subjects of the evaluation. The evaluators do not involve themselves in the processes of change. Impartiality, externality and authority of expertise are important in this model. Some would see the model as accommodating different degrees of prescription and distinguish between a liberal summative and prescriptive summative mode. Others would maintain that summative evaluation is inevitably a form of argument (House, 1980). In formative evaluation, the evaluative body collaborates with the client to promote self evaluation, development and learning. Evaluative criteria and objectives for change may be determined collaboratively or by negotiation with clients. Evaluators may be regarded as catalysts for change or more fully integrated into the process.

The Audit Commission could be categorised as working in a prescriptive summative mode. It devotes expertise to constructing models within which problems can be addressed and presenting arguments for their adoption. Its approach is focused, geared to problem solving rather than simple problem identification and it has created a structure for the achievement of change, although it makes a clear distinction between auditors' responsibilities and those of local authorities. It tends to develop programmes of work over time that build on or make further use of frameworks it has established in particular fields. Its work is characterised by use of hard data, quantitative framing and analysis leading to relatively elaborated solutions, (see Mitroff and Kilman, 1978, for differentiation in scientific styles). Its approach is structured by criteria established in law, supplemented by empirically established criteria for individual projects. Research specific to the field may be incorporated into the development of evaluative criteria and methods and proposals for change.

These features emphasising coherence and generalisability assume a relatively stable environment, in which key values, objectives, structures and methods are set at the top of organisations and mediated down through them. They are likely to be useful to managers seeking to impose more rationality, although it is less certain whether they can be adapted to the more turbulent entrepreneurial environment envisaged in the Commission's own recent management papers.

Management consultants worked in more than one mode. While their evaluations were largely liberal summative, in some cases briefs were defined through negotiation and in others consultants were incorporated in the process of change. Their work thus took on some features of formative evaluation.

Projects in the liberal summative mode were more likely to be based on hard quantitative knowledge, framed by financial management tasks or problems. The commissioning departments bounded the scope of the advice that would flow from assignments, highlighting their technical and specialised value.

Assignments in the formative mode involved theories or techniques developed within a concept of generic management expertise. Here the consultants' work might overlap with the generalist orientation of the civil servants and their influence on policy become more extensive.

Assignments were geared to problem solving, as well as problem identification, and had to be focused, either by the brief or by the consultants themselves.

There were critical differences between consultants in the determination of evaluative criteria and appropriate solutions, some emphasising the objective tests provided by their analytic framework, some seeing criteria as more a matter of negotiation. Evaluation was, however, project specific and geared to advice rather than systematic, cross departmental monitoring.

SSI also worked in mixed evaluative modes, reflecting its struggle to combine a professional identity with usefulness to services in need of better management. In the past much of its work had been in a formative evaluative mode. Now the prescriptive- summative mode became dominant. Inspections became more focused towards problem solving, not just problem identification, even if the analysis was not often converted into prescriptive models of service.

The inspectorate attempted to make evaluative criteria more specific and to establish generalisable frameworks of evaluation. However, incorporating social science expertise into a connoisseurial evaluative tradition was bound to make it hard to achieve a coherent approach.

Social work knowledge still predominated in inspections, although its authority was uncertain. Social services managers tended to welcome SSI's adoption of some hard, quantitative analysis. SSI's attitude to quantitative methods and knowledge was that they could help focus its more intensive inspection work, while providing an input to its more managerially oriented exercises. However, such an approach was likely to emphasise managerial problems and solutions. Professional inspection methods relied heavily on conceptions of change derived from a reflexive model of professional practice. The studies showed that model to have severe implementation problems and to depend on extending rather than reducing professional culture in social service departments.

HAS evaluative processes were formative. In theory at least, teams' starting point for evaluation was the local scene: local values, objectives, policies and plans and it was geared to producing local solutions to local problems. Teams were to act as catalysts for a process of change. But they brought their own professional criteria to their work. And there was a second and often equally important agenda: the protection of vulnerable people against harmful or unduly restrictive practice.

HAS teams' evaluative mode was therefore mixed. Its output was liberal summative. It also had conflicts similar to those of the SSI between comprehensive inspection geared to problem identification and more focused work geared to problem solving.

Its knowledge base was predominantly qualitative and there was not the technical base from which to develop complex models of service. The approach was that of the reflective practitioner, drawing on personal experience and internalised models in preference to the generalised knowledge derived from research. Again such knowledge was often perceived in the field as strongly contestable and, in some cases, imbued with particular policy preferences. If its formative evaluative mode made it, in principle, adaptive to change, its restricted sources of expertise prevented it from exploiting it in that way. It also entertained different assumptions from the SSI or the Audit Commission about the organisational structures for control. HAS methodology is predicated on the influence on services of a range of professionals, with varied organisational relationships to those services. It also appears to be more open to the views of multiple stakeholders: junior as well as senior professional staff, community health councils, interest groups, voluntary organisations, patients and relatives. However, its collaborative work is predominantly with senior professionals and ultimately its evaluation is more strongly shaped by their perspectives and their needs.

## Performance Indicators and Political Purposes

So far in this chapter the discussion has focused on the different knowledge bases of evaluation and how they linked with different evaluative modes. Links between evaluative practice and political objectives, those of the evaluative bodies themselves and those of government, will now be considered.

A comparison of the SSI's indicators project with that of the Audit Commission is instructive on a number of dimensions. It demonstrates at the same time the changing character of the SSI and the continuing difference between the political purposes and identities of the two institutions; it shows how indicators, the epitome of hard, technical measurement, may have ambiguous political functions.

Government policies for control and change in the NHS and higher education were predicated partly on the development of reliable indicators of performance. Throughout the 1980s the performance indicators industry mushroomed in the public sector (Cave et al., 1990). But while originally intended to give central government an overview of local performance, which might then be used for policy and resource allocation decisions, they came to be seen as equally key tools for local management. The Commission, in line with its independent political status, chose to concentrate on the latter function. SSI has ridden both horses.

The Commission's work on indicators was divided between the special studies directorate and the management practice directorate. The latter aimed to provide comprehensive guidance to local authorities on performance indicators as part of a broader concern with performance review; performance review was in its turn conceived as a key component of management. The special studies directorate both drew on its work and developed their own indicators, which were then fed into the performance review material. However, a member of that directorate perceived a difference in the two approaches. Special studies teams, dealing with the variety of local authority services in detail, felt that developing indicators was often a 'messy' business; their management practice colleagues, viewing services from a loftier perch, emphasised the need to be as precise as possible.

The SSI produced a demonstration package of its own key indicators on local authority social services which were to be tools for local authority management and a data base for the Department of Health and the Inspectorate. SSI was a governmental body and was showing that it could develop systems within and for government. It was advantageous for it to strengthen the linkage between the collection of statistics, the development of indicators and the needs of the SSDs and the inspectorate. The Departmental infrastructure for its strategic planning role had long been perceived as weak (House of Commons, 1980). The inspectorate may have considered it advisable to see that personal social services got a good foothold in any improvements that were made.

While the Commission saw itself as developing performance indicators, SSI stressed that their package contained none. It was 'a quantitative account of PSS resource use and PSS service users in each local authority area' set in the context of demographic statistics and some indicators of need. They gave 'information on the extent, level and cover of PSS provision' (SSI, 1988d). In particular there were no policy and no outcome indicators, although the importance of clear and coherent policies was stressed.

The Commission on the other hand tried to extend its coverage to effectiveness and outcome and it did have some policy indicators. In practice, it presented very few outcome or impact indicators for the PSS and much of the policy related material identified issues rather than giving hard measures.

Both bodies stressed the interrogative function of the indicators for authorities themselves. The Commission, despite its larger ambitions, presented a range of disclaimers, designed to preempt criticism - in the context of advocating performance review as a means of strengthening the effectiveness of local government, not making it more accessible to external control or imposing on it uniform policies, structures and practice. Few indicators could ever be regarded as providing absolute measures of performance, individual measures should never form the basis for conclusions about comparative performance with other authorities and authorities should beware of allowing indicators of input and efficiency to drive out those of quality which might not be quantifiable (Audit Commission, 1986b).

In the light of the more recent policy emphasis reflected in both the Commission and the SSI on consumers, it is interesting that all their indicators were authority or service related. None followed the line suggested by Barnes et al (1988) that indicators of performance should as far as possible be user based, showing, for example, what combination, amount and intensity of service are received by individuals.

Even if the Commission handbooks and the SSI guidance were primarily documents of persuasion rather than explication, their own experience of evaluation and their attempts to develop indicators have negated assumptions that performance indicators could provide uncomplicated short cuts to useful evaluative judgements. Both bodies emphasised their indicative rather than their evaluative functions.

The discussion suggests, too, how intertwined are political and managerial uses of evaluation. Both bodies recognised the value of indicators to policy makers and managers. But they developed and used them to support their own political purposes as well. This activity displayed the Commission and the SSI in competition with each other rather than performing distinct functions based on distinct expertise. It would have been more rational for the SSI to have left the development of service indicators to the Audit Commission, particularly since its staffing establishment had not been increased. However, there were strong political reasons for it to use some of its precious resources for that purpose, in addition to the undoubted strategic need for a better database for the personal social services.

Conversely, the SSI might have had a useful input into the Audit Commission's work on effectiveness indicators. But at the time of the study there had been no collaboration on these issues.

## Generalisable Evaluation: A Force for Centralisation?

The analysis of the development of performance indicators by the Audit Commission and the SSI shows how the two bodies related differently to central and local government. It does not support the idea that they unequivocally reinforced trends towards greater centralisation. The last part of the chapter considers whether attempts to generalise and standardise evaluation were part of a drive for greater central government control.

Of the institutions in the study, the Audit Commission was most clearly committed to providing national models of performance. Special studies involved all local authorities and the aims were to establish criteria against which all would be assessed and to ensure consistent application of these by local auditors.

In carrying out its aims, it was inevitably influenced by government policies. It took major policies as 'givens' in the policy environment. It saw one of its tasks as facilitating local authorities to achieve maximally efficient and effective management within that environment. But it did not act simply as an instrument of government. For example, its special studies teams identified the most promising approaches to problem solving by intensive networking, team discussion and argument, and the use of research. The purpose was to develop universal models and argument for their adoption, but to ensure that, as far as possible, they could be seen to derive from existing work.

The SSI felt under pressure to establish knowledge and methods of inquiry for the development and maintenance of national standards. Its Mission Statement affirmed its responsibilities to develop evaluative methodology, and by 1989 it was well on its way to doing so. The aims of inspection were becoming clearer: programmes were geared more strongly to replicating inspections in different parts of the country, applying evaluative and management tools developed in earlier exercises, helping local authorities to implement recommendations and introducing new dimensions of evaluation. In areas of work where there was substantial consensus, SSI was beginning to reinforce national standards of service.

But if SSI at the centre was setting standards more clearly, it was also working towards delegating inspection tasks in some types of work (aspects of secure accommodation and residential care) to local authorities themselves.

At the same time, the SSI had tightened the links between inspections and implementing and developing government policies. SSI regions' time was now taken up largely by inspections that were part of the national programme. And while the field were consulted on its contents, it was generally felt that SSI was more closely tied to government policy than was the Audit Commission. Moreover, the introduction of inspections specially instigated by ministers or local authorities to inquire into crises or problems constituted a marked shift towards an interventionist role for SSI.

If both the Audit Commission and the SSI emphasised generalised evaluation, the opposite was true of the use of consultants and the HAS. However, the implications for centralisation were different in these two latter cases. The case study on consultants showed that responsibilities for policy evaluation were being shared with the private sector, but equally that the civil servants had strong control over the consultants' access to central government commissions and their implementation. The corresponding reduction of input from those in the field tended to concentrate power at the centre.

The HAS aimed to evaluate all the health and local authorities providing services in the relevant categories but not to make precise comparisons between them. It stood as purveyor of good practice but as a resource to be tapped primarily on the initiative of authorities. That resource was not converted into a national framework of evaluative criteria, standards and measurement. Its intention, albeit not always achieved, remained to provide a customised resource for those working in the field, through interactive visitation in which the values of those visited remained more important than *a priori* assumptions of good practice.

Such beliefs are consonant with the notion of diffused leadership in the development of new norms. They are also integrally linked with a professional model for planning and managing services to clients in which administrators provide the infrastructure for services: the model on which the NHS worked until 1974.

The discussion of the knowledge preferences of evaluative bodies has concluded by examining their role in increasing centralisation. Throughout the chapter, a demonstrable link has been established between the types of knowledge used and the authority and power to which each of our institutions has aspired. Other factors are important - the compatibility of political beliefs with the government of the day, or the salience of the policy fields under review - but our study also shows that when knowledge is bounded within hard technical formats it both generates and succeeds in gaining more authority. Where it preserves openness and permeability, perhaps at expense of clarity and economy of thought, it may sustain the support of practitioners whilst losing power within the political and managerial systems.

Chapter Ten

# A Changed Order of Values?

The main questions for this chapter are whether there is evidence of a changed order of values in bodies whose task is evaluation in the public sector and whether that can usefully be analysed in terms of a shift from a professional to a managerial culture. First the nature and place of values in managerial and professional traditions are analysed. The study institutions are then compared in the light of these analyses, to determine how far there has been convergence between them and how coherent and robust are their respective positions. Evidence will be sought mainly from the outputs of the bodies concerned and the procedures by which they establish evaluative criteria.

## Two Concepts of Management

'Management ... deals with action and application; and its test is its results. That makes it a technology. But management also deals with people, their values, their growth and development - and this makes it a humanity. So does its concern with, and impact on, social structure and the community' (Drucker, 1989).

The quotation represents a recent attempt to do two things: first, to integrate two traditions of management, management as technology or rationalistic management and management as human relations or the harnessing of human potential and motivation; and second, to counter the claim that management is essentially amoral, manipulative and exploitative of human relationships or cut off from what gives meaning to human lives (MacIntyre, 1981).

It was noted in Chapter One that government policies in the early 1980s reflected a rationalistic and instrumental conception of management. Good management requires setting and adhering to clear objectives and developing policies, structures, strategies and techniques consistent with those objectives. The manager is a technician applying theories, methods or tools derived from management science. The task of management is to make it possible to implement policies economically, efficiently and effectively, to measure performance against objectives and to learn from that. Outcome criteria are preferred to those of process. Management is instrumental to realising the values and goals set by others.

This, broadly, reflects the Weberian tradition of a clear division of labour between value free management and value committed politicians. This conception of management is one reason why MacIntyre selects the manager as one of the 'characters' of Western society in the twentieth century. To him the manager epitomises the hollow triumph of emotivist moral theory. Questions of morality have, in this theory, become simply questions of arbitrary preference and the language of morality is no longer appropriate to the dominant belief system. The preparedness of management to present itself as offering only skills and knowledge with which to implement the values and goals required of it is a logical part of such an interpretation of morality.

During the 1980s, theories of management in which values have a more central role became influential in the USA and Britain (*Administrative Science Quarterly* Sept. 1983; *Organizational Dynamics*, Autumn, 1983; *Journal of Management Studies*, May, 1986). The management of organisations was to be built round a few key values, a vision, a mission, even an ideology (Brunnson, 1985). A primary task of managers was to establish and nurture an organisational culture, in which values, motivation and style were reinforced by strong relationships between management and staff. To that extent, writers like Peters and Waterman (1982), best sellers in Britain as well as the USA, incorporated humanistic management ideas, although they summed up their approach in the phrase 'soft is hard'; they thought that what was often characterised as irrational, intuitive and informal could be made explicit and managed: not, however, by recourse to abstract theory but by making vision or values central, simple and clearly understood by employees. Managers were for them more like craftsmen, developing and using basic precepts in response to the interplay between their vision and the demands confronting them. Linkages were human rather than logical and more loosely coupled.

Emphasis on organisational culture underscores the integrative role of management. One of the forces behind the influence of these ideas, particularly in the USA, has been the felt need to understand the secret of the success of Japanese management and to adapt its corporate culture and practices to Western organisations (Ouchi, 1980; 1981). Such developments have been seen by some as potentially a far more powerful system of control than that based on bureaucracy or the application of human relations theories (Ray, 1986).

Others see integrative management as more benign. The need for top managers to create an environment which responds to and does not simply create a dominant culture is stressed by Drucker (*op. cit.*). He also asserts the critical role of management in the exploitation of advanced knowledge. 'Modern management and modern enterprise could not exist without the knowledge base that developed societies have built. But equally it is management, and management alone, that makes effective all this knowledge and these knowledgeable people. The emergence of management has converted knowledge from social ornament and luxury into the true capital of any economy.'

Drucker nevertheless seems to suggest that managers and autonomous thinking and feeling expert employees can coexist. Peters and Waterman on the other hand seem to reinforce MacIntyre's view that management is essentially exploitative. He sees its task as being to manipulate human beings to the pursuit of desired ends. It therefore negates the essence of morality, as defined by Kant: moral behaviour is that in which people treat each other as ends not means. Moreover, the values by which organisations are driven are not compelling in themselves; they are matters of preference, chosen as consistent with the work and output to be achieved. In effect, both values and people are instrumental.

## Professionals and Values

Although there is a range of approaches to the analysis of the nature of professions and their role in society, it can be argued that in all of them there is a key role for professional values. The possession of a common code of ethics is seen as an important characteristic. In thinking about professions as a product of division of labour in society, based on notions of specialist knowledge and function, common professional values can be seen as a source of collective identity for self regulating institutions which place a premium on individual excellence and individual discretion (Larson, 1977). Analyses which concentrate on professionalism as a means by which certain occupational groups gain independence and power in society (Freidson, 1970), might see a common core of professional values as the basis of trust between society and the profession or at least as an important medium of exchange.

While it is increasingly difficult to identify characteristics that are common to all professions in an advanced society, there has traditionally been a strong emphasis on personal responsibility, individual judgement and the possibility of conflict between the professional and the organisation in which he or she works. Thus codes of ethics can provide an important justification for individual dissent from organisational policies. Professional codes give primacy to the needs of the client or adherence to professional standards over the interests or profit of the professional or their organisation.

Personal service professions tend to focus as much on the quality of the process of service as on its final outcome: the accused may not be acquitted, the sick person may not be healed but all can expect to receive high standards of practice, administered according to an ethic of non-discrimination and individualisation.

There are significant points of contrast between the profession and management as an organisational framework in these accounts. Professions are social organisations based on mutual regulation of individuals exercising personal discretion; management is designed to give authority to control and coordinate organisational performance. Resource allocation and control are central to managerial decision making; but they have traditionally been distinguished from professional decisions, in which primacy is, at least in principle, given to needs. Outcome criteria are given primacy over process among managers; but for professionals quality of process is equally, and sometimes more, highly valued.

In neither institution are values free of ambiguity. While professionals might argue that their common ethic is intrinsic in their function and essential to their identity, it also reinforces their authority and legitimacy in society. Moreover, as professions have increasingly to work in large organisations and to collaborate with each other, and as the society in which they work becomes more complex and thus more subject to conflicting conceptions of good and right, the myth of value consensus becomes harder to sustain. While most professions maintain a core of agreed values, it may often be enfolded by individual practitioners in competing ideologies or perceptions of the professional role.

Value free management has been shown to be a myth. At the least, managers make decisions about how to balance economy, efficiency and effectiveness and what priority to give any one of them by reference to other values. Value committed management gives an overtly instrumental role to values. And although managers' choices of values may not be as arbitrary as some critics suggest, they will have no force unless they are compatible with profit or organisational survival.

## Values and the Evaluative Institutions

A values analysis of the institutions can be undertaken on two main lines: the evaluative criteria that emerge as dominant in their outputs; the place accorded to values in their work in principle and in practice.

Government priorities for the public sector in this period were insistent: economy, efficiency, value for money, effectiveness or performance and accountability to the public conceived predominantly as taxpayers. They were promoted as incontestable values that were to provide the framework within which detailed and divergent policies could be developed. They were part of the instrumental, value neutral concept of management that informed such initiatives as FMI and MINIS and the formation of the efficiency unit in the civil service.

How far and how consistently were these values pursued in the institutions studied? Within what concepts of management? And how was their relationship to other values perceived?

## The Audit Commission

The identified values are central to the mandate of the Audit Commission. Its work was structured by them and the assumptions underlying them: that local authorities were working in the context of scarce resources, that they must maximise the output for any given input (even if the prediction and monitoring of that relationship are far from straightforward), and that the key to achieving that lay in the quality and style of management.

When the Commission was created in 1982, its primary purpose was seen by local authorities as to curb their expenditure. And certainly the clearest benchmark of local authority performance laid down by the Commission has been the quantification of savings to be made as a result of its nationally and locally initiated value for money studies. It announced in its major review of its work (Audit Commission, 1987d) that it had devised a more effective tracking system of the response of authorities to these targets.

This commitment to economy was reaffirmed despite the Commission's concern from the beginning not to be seen simply as a cost cutting body. At first this concern was in part political: in order to achieve results as an independent body with limited statutory powers it needed to gain the confidence of local authorities. It thus defined its purpose in focusing on economy and efficiency as to promote 'value improvement' and aimed in its early exercises to identify 'value improvements' that would not result in the reduction of services (without addressing the question whether it was possible to have 'value improvements' that did reduce services) (Audit Commission, 1986c).

It also tried to instill into local authority thinking the concept of opportunity costs. Much of the argument in the case study example is based on this notion. It is important to an organisation seeking to sustain quality objectives but at the same time to ensure that they are determined within the boundaries of resource availability. The Commission promoted the determination to manage scarce resources by the claim that 'in essence, this is a move from administration to management' (Audit Commission, 1986b). Management was a dynamic, active concept, but, apparently, administration was not.

We have seen that in 1987 there was a firm commitment by the Commission to shift the emphasis of its work towards effectiveness. It was a measure of their increased confidence that not only did they make this a priority but also they had significantly enlarged the scope of their work on this dimension. Originally they defined effectiveness as 'how well a programme or activity is achieving its established goals or other intended effects' ( Audit Commission, 1984a). As their own work began to expose the poverty of professional thinking about setting standards of effectiveness and quality and as some departments began to invite them to help them to define such standards, they abandoned the reticence about crossing professional boundaries that had inhibited their work in the case study. They put forward explicitly normative models in their study on mental handicap and tried to develop specific indicators of effectiveness in their work on performance measurement.

In effect, they began to use the professional networks established by special studies teams and the research to which they pointed them to identify general rather than authority specific policies and objectives in some ares of work. They also began to advocate and, again in the casc of the mental handicap study, to develop user studies as a means of measuring outcome.

The Commission early on acknowledged the importance of strengthening local government accountability to the electorate (Audit Commission, 1984b). It had a number of formal mechanisms to draw attention to mismanagement, irresponsibility or dishonesty, including the annual management letter to local authorities and reports in the public interest. But it interpreted its duties in this area more actively. Its policy of putting out hard hitting and widely accessible publications not only substantially increased the availability of public information on local government activity, it made sure that the issues of economy, efficiency and value for money had a high profile in public debate. It thus made a significant contribution to the redefinition of accountability in the public mind.

Thus the Commission worked hard to see that key values advocated by government constituted a consistent and visible evaluative framework for local government activity. To what extent did that framework retain coherence and incontestability?

The attempts to give more substantial and general meaning to effectiveness could have created difficulties for the Commission. It has earlier been argued that the technical connotations of 'performance' and 'effectiveness' were important to government. They were apparently free of any substantive and contentiously normative force. That work should produce results was a self evident good to which all could subscribe (Pollitt, 1986). Giving effectiveness substantive meaning certainly provided the Commission with a host of methodological problems; it also opened up the potential for conflict among a range of stakeholders that is inherent in concepts of impact, outcome and quality.

For the most part, the Commission avoided those pitfalls. First, it reinforced the notion that local authority policies were inevitably defined by central government policies and priorities. Its performance review document of 1988 produced a value framework for local authority social services that went beyond economy, efficiency and effectiveness. It did, however, remain firmly within the realm of the liberal values of choice, consumer rights, flexibility and individualisation. And it took for granted that all policies are constrained by the need to manage scarce resources. It did not engage the problem of reconciling effectiveness with economy at a general level, although it did point out in specific contexts, such as community care, that an increase in resources, at least for a limited period, might be required.

Second, where it moved into the area of effectiveness, the Commission used its networks to identify dominant professional norms that would have widespread acceptance. User views might be difficult to incorporate into a largely consensual framework. However, by 1988, the Commission was openly advocating a clear commitment by local authorities to becoming competitive enterprises and incorporating a philosophy in which service users were conceived as customers and the task of the authority was to 'keep close to' them. It was proposing that local authorities become more like private firms who had constantly to find ways of ensuring that company policies, resource limits, employee aspirations and customer perspectives were compatible. It did so within a framework of integrative, value committed management.

The 1988 document was a milestone in the development of the Commission's public persona. It can be argued that from the beginning the Commission worked in two modes that reflected different managerial traditions. At first, as government promulgated an instrumentalist, value neutral theory of management, the Commission laid more stress on the function of good management in enabling local authorities to pursue their own policies and ideologies. The Commission's role was neither to endorse nor to criticise central or local government policy; rather it was to enable local authorities 'to adapt to the changing environment in which they find themselves' (Audit Commission, 1984b).

By 1988, the government was moving more decisively to subordinating local authorities to the disciplines of the market. The environment was changing again. Rational planning and tight linkages between objectives, policies and systems were no longer going to be enough. Local authorities would have to compete in the market to sustain their role. The Commission moved from a position of taking government policies as the 'given' framework for local authority strategy to whole hearted endorsement of those policies. Local authorities were encouraged to embrace the reconceptualisation of the administration of the public sector in terms of the management of public enterprise in the market place (Audit Commission, 1988b, and 1989c).

Local education authorities who found themselves caught between the Commission's special study *Better Management of Secondary Education* (1986d) (which at least at local audit level was primarily in the rationalist technical mode) and *The Education Reform Act* (1988) (which moved the goal posts) felt that the Act had undermined the Commission's credibility. They saw that as grounded in its rational, analytic approach and its willingness to criticise government. They thought the Commission should confront the government.

It did not. Instead it in effect heightened the profile of its management practice advice where it had for some time been advocating a systemic, value driven style of management incorporated from McKinsey and Peters and Waterman (1982). It was a style geared more to the 'prospector' type of institution, 'organisations that pioneer new products and markets and seek success by providing tomorrow's product today' (Greenwood, 1987) than to the 'analyser' type.

The Commission might see itself as having at most changed gear in 1988 and as continuing its task of enabling local authorities to survive in a turbulent environment. Others might see 1988 as the point at which its value commitment became open and explicit, even if that value commitment were both to private sector style enterprise and to the continued life of local authorities.

As far as the balance of emphasis between managerial and professional values was concerned, it is true that the Commission through its special studies teams strove to incorporate dominant professional values into its work. However, these were, for the most part, mediated by those professionals who had become managers. The framework of government policies now established in, for example, education and personal social services implied strong managers interacting with stronger customers or consumers. It left open two key questions. How clearly would the voice of the professional practitioner be heard? And how strong would the customers prove to be? The answer to those questions might ultimately depend on the balance struck between two forces: those of marketing and those of civil rights of participation and redress. At present, neither has a firm hold in local government. But while marketing is a key and well understood component of private enterprise, civil rights of participation have established the most tenuous hold in our democratic tradition, and rights of redress remain unequally distributed.

## The Social Services Inspectorate

The SSI, like the Audit Commission, had economy, the efficient use of resources and value for money built in to its new mandate in 1985. That mandate incorporated a compromise between the professional priorities of the SWS and the resource management priorities which the government wished the new inspectorate to espouse and promote. The scope of the new body extended well beyond social work. At the same time, its institutional status as a professional division of the Department of Health was reaffirmed (SSI, 1987c). And values were affirmed as central to the work of inspection.

Documents and activities of the inspectorate during the five years after its creation showed the marks of compromise and ambivalence. There were undoubtedly internal differences of view about emphases, within SSI headquarters as well as between them and the regional inspectors. The SSI's own Mission Statement bears witness to these differences but also to the Directorate's aspiration to sustain a professional identity, culture and knowledge base. That there was a Mission Statement reflects the managerial language in vogue. It promoted managerialist objectives in which improving management and measuring the relationship between input and service outcome were owned as essential. However, the objectives were framed by a statement of professional values: individual worth, individual rights and responsibilities, independence, protection of vulnerable people, equality of opportunity and the achievement of objectives by negotiation.

The first case study shows that, as early as 1984, there were debates in the Directorate about how far the Community Homes inspection should take on the new efficiency values. The issue was whether the inspectorate should retain its professional identity, or whether it should demonstrate that it could adapt to resource oriented criteria and incorporate new knowledge and modes of control. Ultimately, the efficiency values had no place in either of the case study inspections and they were not mentioned in the guidelines on secure accommodation inspections.

That was not, however, the whole story. There were reasons why value priorities might not change quickly in these areas. The inspectorate had long experience in the field of residential care and had built up a broad consensus round evaluative criteria.

The SSI continued to grapple with new demands, some of which, for example cost effectiveness, required a different knowledge base, some entailed new values, grounded in different moral and political theories from those underpinning earlier practice, and some arose from the changing institutional context of social work.

As the inspectorate widened its range, an increasing number of inspections focused on the management of services and for some (such as the programme of inspections on Home Care services) the efficient management of scarce resources was a central concern.

Some inspections included an examination of service costs by economists. Three (out of a total of 29) were scheduled to do so in the 1989 programme. But reports so far reflected the concern in the Directorate that they had not found a way of integrating such cost inquiries into their thinking.

Some reports invoked the language of value for money. But scrutiny of the content revealed that costs were not closely examined, although variation between centres was identified. The report recorded frankly that 'on the basis of this inspection SSI simply cannot state which type of centre offers the best value for money' (SSI, 1988a). The problem was partly that the inspectors did not have the tools to do so.

This report also seemed to accept too easily that it should be able to identify measures of long term outcome from family centres. Again this was partly the inspectorate trying to incorporate an unfamiliar knowledge tradition, of microeconomics, and in the process failing to make distinctions between intermediate output and final output (see Davies and

Knapp, 1981) or between output and outcome. It was partly an attempt to shift attention to achievement as distinct from process. But it was also making a claim that old values could be incorporated into new language.

As yet there seems not to have been systematic debate in the SSI on the relationship between concepts of effectiveness and outcome and quality. It is noticeable that two recent exercises on residential care (SSI, 1989b; 1989d) defined quality of life in terms that gave substantial emphasis to experience in residents' lives. They conceptualised the issues in language other than that of input and output and implicitly questioned the concept of an end point in achieving quality of life. They challenged the appropriateness of external assessment as against understanding and interpretation of individual and group experience.

It could be argued that personal social services contribute to a process, that of individual lives, where measurement of outcomes needs to be used sparingly. Certainly it is possible, for example, to measure changes in dependency levels before and after the receipt of specific services. But it may be equally important to find out the meaning of those changes to the person, how he or she will manage them, and what the longer term implications of the reactions of others will be. And the question how and when to measure the outcomes of the care of young people is only partly technical. It is shot through with values. But SSI's position on these issues remained unclear.

Accountability and responsibility were more familiar managerial values for the inspectorate and social services departments than the economic values. Organisational literature that influenced SSDs in their early years (eg Rowbottom et al, 1974; 1980) and research reports on the PSS regarded these as central concepts (Goldberg and Warburton, 1978; Stevenson and Parsloe, 1978). In neither case, however, was economy or efficiency the dominant issue. The organisational literature concentrated on the need for clarity in roles, authority relationships and the boundaries of responsibility. The issue was that all should know to whom they were accountable and for what. Goldberg and Warburton were concerned about outputs and that these should be matched to expectations. Stevenson and Parsloe attempted to tackle the relationship between demands for role accountability and individual sense of professional responsibility.

The procedural guidance for inspectors required them routinely to take note of where services inspected fitted into the SSD structure and what 'the basis for accountability' was. It thus seemed to reflect the organisational literature used in the early 1970s to help determine SSD structures.

The SSI guidance showed the inspectorate to be acutely aware that its own structures and procedures would be tested against the criterion of clear accountability for the fulfilling of objectives and requirements. They thus reflected the rationalistic management assumptions entailed in the FMI but no explicit emphasis was placed on economy or cost effectiveness.

Some rationalistic management tenets were well entrenched in inspections, in particular the need for services to have clear and explicit objectives known to all staff and systems installed to meet those objectives.

A professionally based inspectorate might be expected to place strong emphasis on approaches to management designed to encourage and give space to discretion and development of professional staff.

Again, the Family Centres inspection did endorse entrepreneurial managers in an area of work experimenting with new methods. They were commended by inspectors for 'motivating staff, engendering a positive and evaluative approach to outcomes, ensuring staff have adequate training and development programmes, negotiating resources with senior managers and monitoring regularly the work and achievement of the centre'. This report was unusual in this respect and the message of its authors was itself not wholly clear. They also advocated clear direction of centre managers by senior managers, thus perhaps trying to ride two management horses.

In the case studies, dominant values were those associated with professional social work practice: individualisation, continuity of personal and social identity, normalisation, a balance of care and control that reflects the importance of these values but an implicitly greater emphasis on the quality of care than on the quality of life (although the distinctions between these were not closely attended to).

More recently, there has been a noticeable increase in a rights based approach in which users of service are identified as consumers not clients. Rights of choice have been particularly prominent. The issues surrounding race and gender in the provision and delivery of social services have been identified as important but the SSI has given little substantial lead in this controversial area, despite its commitment to equality of opportunity in the Mission Statement.

Thus the liberal tradition of social work that probably owes most to the 'new liberal' philosophy of Green, Hobhouse and others at the end of the 19th century has been merged with the market liberalism of current government policies. That philosophy emphasised that individual development depended on belonging to a society committed to altruism and community. The SSI's more recent emphasis has been on discrete individuals. Structures for the pursuit of rights, in so far as they are addressed, are those of law, complaints procedures and contracts creating possibilities for individual action and redress.

The problems for SSI in establishing a coherent value position are huge. The professional identity of social work has never been secure and challenges to it have been internal as well as external. Although the most convincing attempts to ground social work values have been in liberal traditions (see Plant, 1970 ), Kantian, utilitarian and new liberal strands of thought have coexisted along with substantial influence from socialist beliefs even in the mainstream of social workers who claim a professional identity.

Equally, it is not surprising that the changes noted in Chapter One in the identity of senior professionals in public organisations and the widespread adoption of managerial identities have particularly affected personal social services organisations. Social workers are a relatively small minority of those employed in such organisations, which draw on a variety of occupational groups, with a wide range of skills and capacities.

Finally, SSI is part of government and a government determined upon radical change and its implementation. In the light of these factors, a shift on the part of the SSI towards managerialism was inevitable. The study suggests that it has not yet decided what the nature of that managerialism should be. There are some signs that it is moving away from a narrow and static rationalist approach but that it does not have a clear alternative. Its recruits with managerial experience have as yet come predominantly from middle and operational management, not from strategic managerial positions. The pressure on social services organisations have recently been such as to emphasise the need for strong management from the top rather than styles and systems encouraging individual discretion and initiative.

The SSI has some choice between trying to hold all these together and opting for a more coherent but narrower base that might be complementary to, rather than overlapping with, the role of the Audit Commission. If it is to make a satisfactory choice it has to decide whether it has the authority and power as well as the cognitive base to sustain it. That issue will be taken further in the next chapter. In the meantime the value choices made by the HAS are considered.

## The Health Advisory Service

The HAS was, more unequivocally than SSI, a professional advisory body, although its origins also contained the seeds of conflict. Economy and efficiency had no place in its mandate. Professional evaluation of services was predominantly needs led and an underlying objective was to prevent the erosion of resource allocation to groups that were traditionally disadvantaged in the NHS economy. Certainly, HAS teams were seen by professional staff in the authorities visited as a potential source of support against inroads into their budgets. It was often hoped that their reports would demonstrate the harm being done to patients by shortage of staff and other resources. Like SSI they were concerned with the best use of professional resources, and they recognised resource constraints in their advice, but their focus was the management of care.

And while its origins were integrally connected with the impact of services on particular groups, HAS teams were in practice preoccupied with professional process values rather than outcomes: for example, the quality of nursing care and the need for interdisciplinary and interagency collaboration. Similarly, thinking about quality of service was more likely to revolve round professional leadership, team working, philosophies or models of practice and staff attitudes than structures of accountability predicated on hierarchical or linear concepts of management.

While the decision made in 1984 to publish HAS reports made its activities more accessible, this policy was by no means unanimously approved. Concepts of accountability to the public competed with professional responsibility, and sustaining staff morale in under regarded services was often felt to be more important than public knowledge of shortcomings. And nowhere was there any suggestion that it was HAS' role to make the public more aware of need for economy and cost effectiveness in the health service.

The HAS, as an independent professional advisory service showed little signs of accommodation to values of managerialism. But, by the same token, it would not itself have a strongly coherent set of values; teams were perceived as basing their work on largely personal and implicit values, grounded in experience and primarily concerned with the problems of individual patients, rather than with the running of systems.

## Consultants

The value base of consultants employed by central government is likely to be less explicit and uniform than that of the other three evaluative bodies. They come from independent private firms that need have no political or social affiliations. Their mandate is to respect and implement the policies of others rather than to insinuate their own values into policy and practice. As guns for hire, it is not for them to select the targets. But the value positions of the social and power environment in which consultancies work are bound to be contaminative, and commitment to the client must entail commitment, at least whilst the consultancy lasts, to the achievement of their goals. In the 1980s, central government goals have been strongly promulgated.

But it might be possible to go further: are there not at least some second order values implicit in consulting for central government?

Unlike the Audit Commission, consultants, perhaps because their concerns and assignments are short term, do not tackle the substantive professional core of the fields in which they operate. They remain directed towards the efficient running of systems rather than to the underlying purposes which systems might serve. But that commitment of itself entails values (Kogan, 1974); organisational values, beliefs in predictability and efficiency, rather than the professional, client based values associated with Welfare State policies would be to the fore. The fact, too, that many consultancies start from a expertise in accountancy also makes it more likely that they would more willingly endorse the current government goals of securing the three Es - economy, efficiency and effectiveness - than the pursuit of such goals as an altruistic regard for clients or holistic and redistributive social planning.

All four of case areas therefore demonstrate that the objectivity of evaluation lies primarily in disclosure of the evaluators' value base than in neutrality. Overall, there is some convergence of values, and between the Audit Commission and the SSI this has been two way. The weight of change has, however, been towards the values of managerialism in an environment informed by market liberalism.

Chapter Eleven

# The Impacts of Evaluation

## The study of impact

Evaluative bodies are expected to be more accountable and effective than in the past. Ultimately the critical questions about the institutions in this study are those of impacts and implementation. How significant were their impacts? Were there clear differences between them in the degree and kind of impact they had? If there were, could these be ascribed to particular institutional characteristics?

But the problems of finding convincing answers to such questions are notorious. Why is it so difficult to pinpoint the outcomes of evaluative activities? Partly, they are problems of definition, evidence and explanation. What counts as impact or evidence of impact? At what intervals of time should judgements on these issues be made?

A second problem is the complexity and often ambitious nature of objectives. Most of the exercises we studied were designed to evaluate sensitive work and, often, to contribute to profound changes in occupational cultures, dominant belief systems, organisational priorities and patterns of control and power. They were directed at practice and management, frequently in combination. The tasks of monitoring, regulation and change were often combined, even if not obviously compatible with each other.

Some of the changes sought required long time scales. But the longer the time scale and the greater the change, the more difficult it is to determine the key influences at work.

The metaphor of policy impact is unsatisfactory for a number of reasons. It reifies and simplifies human action in a highly complex political system. The impact metaphor derives from mechanical theories of physics. It suggests unidirectional processes in which evaluative bodies themselves rather than those evaluated cause change. It assumes that impact is directly observable and attributable.

Doubts have often been expressed about the appropriateness of linear and unidirectional conceptualisations of policy implementation (for a summary of the literature see Ham and Hill, 1984). And, as Day and Klein (1990) have pointed out, there are parallels in the literature on the impact of research on policy (eg Weiss, 1977; Rein, 1983; Kogan and Henkel, 1983).

Systems metaphors more adequately describe the consequences of evaluation. They can accommodate the intricacies and dynamics of power in the modern state. They focus attention on the complexity of change in the policy system and suggest that the management of the shape and nodal points of influence may determine the forces to which individuals and organisations are subject and the limits within which their options are constrained. But they occlude the 'reflexive monitoring of action among human actors' (Giddens, 1979); how individuals use strategies to control their environment and to exercise their power in it.

Given these complexities, there must be doubts, too, about the more obviously quantitative methods of measuring evaluative impact. Quantitative measures are indicators of response which are subject to different interpretations, of, for example, how costs are to be attributed, what the opportunity costs are and how they might be measured. As in the case studies, it is possible to count the recommendations 'accepted' by those evaluated, but what does 'acceptance' mean? Did visible procedures change and, if so, might they entail deeper changes in power relationships, organisational structures and value preferences? Were the 'acceptances' part of a larger process of 'percolative' change to which the organisations were already predisposed or were they shallow attempts to meet specific political or managerial pressures?

One of the institutions illustrates the benefits and problems of assessing evaluative achievements through quantitative indicators. Of the four, the Audit Commission has been most assiduous in setting criteria against which its work could be tested. From the beginning, when the Commission was concentrating on increasing the economy and efficiency of local authorities in its special studies, it attempted, in its Annual Reports, to review what had been achieved.

The Commission set itself explicit targets in the form of quantified 'value improvements'. It identified cash amounts of savings that could be made in the areas it had reviewed and indicated where they could be reallocated to underresourced services, such as the maintenance of schools and services for the elderly. While it disclaimed responsibility for reaching these targets - that was for local authorities themselves - it set benchmarks by which it could itself be judged.

In its 1986 review numerical targets were given but the achievements were all spelt out in terms of process. The nearest they got to outcome was a table demonstrating that 'real controllable revenue spending by local authorities outside inner London actually fell between 1981-82 and 1984-85' but no relationship was shown between the Commission's work (begun in 1983) and this statistic. Otherwise achievement was recorded in terms of 'implementation underway' (Audit Commission, 1986c).

The Annual Reports of 1987 and 1988 described an overhauled system for 'tracking' the achievements of the value for money projects more precisely. In 1987 'an annually recurring total of £490 million of value improvements has been identified as achievable in the service areas covered by the Commission to date. Around £80 million per annum of these savings have already been fulfilled.' By 1988 the claim for fulfilment had risen to £219 million out of £750 million. The figures thus show a very sharp increase not only in savings made but also in potential savings identified. This not only indicates the time required for interventions to make an impact but also suggests wide variation between auditors as to when they undertook local special study projects and how quickly they followed them up. Also, while the figures show the general pattern of savings made across authorities over several years they can give no guidance on why and how authority savings and the Commission's activity might be connected. Nor, on their own, will they indicate how these figures translate into beliefs, wider policies and practice of those responsible for public organisations.

## Conditions of Effective Implementation

The clearest forms of change observed occurred through collaboration between the evaluators and an internal individual or group with authority to act, either because they themselves had recognised a powerful need to do so or because the evaluative body had taken the issue to the top of the agenda.

Examples of such change were found in all four of the evaluative bodies but they arose from different principles and modes of action. In Chapter Nine it was suggested that the Audit Commission had developed the most tightly coupled model of practice. Their special studies were based partly on what Elmore (1981) calls 'forward mapping', which assumes that internal logic is a sufficient guarantee of successful implementation; that those at the top control the organisational and political processes and can therefore impose their own rationality on them. What we witnessed was a dialectic between the power of technical expertise and political persuasiveness.

The Commission maximised the salience of their studies through networking amongst key members of the policy community and through political and technical argument. The primary medium was the national report that preceded the local value for money studies. The audience was broad; its purpose was to see that the issue was put high on local authority agendas and that the Commission could help them to take effective action. At local level, the study suggested that the key alliance was between the auditors and chief officers or senior management groups.

The value, however, of the specific guidance was played down by the key internal figures. It was given low priority or followed unsuccessfully in the three authorities we investigated. Senior managers were reluctant to concede either technical or sapiential authority to auditors and, with occasional exceptions, tended to dismiss their advice on the grounds of professional or political naivety. Formal advice taken was shown to have had unhelpful consequences, if it did not accord with officer opinions. Although in one case the auditors had helped to secure additional resources in information technology, the boundedness of auditors' competence was underlined. And even within those bounds, some officers challenged that competence on the basis of experience of other special studies.

However, in all three authorities the exercise stimulated large scale plans for change, in two cases through substantial collaboration between senior officers and the auditors. The details of these plans were the authorities' own but all addressed the key problem identified by the Commission. The special study and the associated local audit had, at minimum, provided the occasion for them to act. And if, as their critics implied, they had proffered technical solutions to political problems, officers and members had themselves grasped the political nettles and devised their own solutions.

It is argued, therefore, that the Commission's strength and its ability to secure collaboration lay in its combination of technical modelling and political argument. In other studies, such as those on mental handicap and on highway maintenance, the balance of influence between the two was different: the technical help offered by the Commission was more important.

However, special studies required a heavy concentration of resources and had a long lead time. They, therefore, assumed a reasonably stable policy arena. Despite efforts to adjust to events as their study proceeded, in this case the Commission was ultimately unable to persuade local authorities of the continuing relevance of its approach in the face of major policy change.

Noticeably, too, the Commission concentrated on the officer-auditor alliance. Some respondents felt that if the hard political problems of implementation were to be overcome, auditors would have to strengthen their relationships with members. That, in turn, might mean auditors developing an understanding at variance with their training and ethos. The alternative was the solution pursued by the Commission elsewhere, to change the nature of the polity, to increase the managerial strength of local authorities and simplify the values being pursued.

How well did the other institutions achieve impact through collaboration, topic salience and harnessing internal authority to act? The use of consultants in central government was structured primarily by the client-consultant relationship. The identity of the client was mostly clear and consultants had no doubts as to their importance for implementation. In theory, there was also no problem about salience. Departments selected the topics on which they commissioned consultancies. However, the study showed that motivations for selection were mixed and that consultants were not always engaged to provide definitive advice but to demonstrate that several views had been taken into account or that a problem was receiving attention. An external solution might not in the end be wanted. And if it was, consultants' freedom to recommend might be restricted. There are sometimes hard choices to be made between the dictates of technical and specialist judgement and those of acceptability and political feasibility.

Consultants' influence on implementation depended on their power to persuade through the force of their analysis, the strength of other pressures on civil servants, particularly from ministers, and the degree of their need for technical or specialist expertise which they lacked themselves. Ultimately, although the civil servants held the balance of power in their relationships with consultants, the terms of exchange were quite even.

Civil servants and management consultants provided the strongest example of exchange relationships. Civil servants undoubtedly needed the help of management consultants. Their numbers had been reduced by a 'heroic' government (Kogan, 1987) which also required them to enforce changes of policy. Nor did they have the range of knowledge and skills to meet ministers' demands. They were pressed to recruit consultant help but they aimed to cede the minimum of power in so doing. They were helped in that objective by the needs of the consultants themselves who were in a competitive market, at least for the prize consultancies, and could not risk alienating the civil servants.

By 1990, changes in the workings of the policy system were occurring: negotiation between civil servants and consultants under pressure from ministers had resulted in the incorporation of external advice. This could happen because civil servants found that consultants could meet their needs and because they had sufficient power over resources and cognitive command over their territory to structure and mediate the consultants' advice.

The HAS and the SSI, although there were signs of change in both, were far less focused than the Audit Commission or consultants. The work of the HAS took place within long cycles of time and mainly by rotation. In theory their principle of starting from authorities' own preoccupations made it possible for them to identify felt need in a framework which made the active, universalist approach to topic salience taken by the Audit Commission impracticable.

At best this approach resulted in their working with authorities to speed changes already under way, to lay the foundations for redirection or to help resolve significant problems. In one of the visits studied, the HAS came into an authority at a critical point in the development of its mental health services. Its diagnosis of the problems was widely accepted in the health authority and the newly appointed unit manager was given the task of implementing the report. The combination of collaboration, salience and a person with authority to act was there and many recommendations were implemented. But it was still difficult to weigh implementation twenty months after the visit.

Such an outcome illustrates important differences between the HAS and the Audit Commission. Whereas the Commission saw local authorities as requiring a unified management structure and thought that it could effect change through an active approach, HAS philosophy was different. Its concept of change was gradualist and percolative and consistent with its belief that the NHS was, and should be, a multi-professional service and that services for the elderly and mentally ill were multi-agency. It could not easily capture at one and the same time the collaboration of managers, a range of professionals and practitioners and the many sub-organisations, whose perspectives were sometimes conflicting. Even in the new climate of general management, implementing the report in the example cited encountered obstacles from a strong professional group and delays from a local authority department unready to take up the issues.

The report was the product of a multi disciplinary team and was criticised in the same terms as many other HAS reports: recommendations and assessments of problems were too heavily qualified and they failed to identify priorities.

While, in theory, the HAS approach ensured salience, their methods were not sufficiently flexible to meet this aim, even under the most favourable circumstances. Teams tried to cover too much ground and allowed their reports to be structured by a detailed list of items on which to comment.

One of the case studies showed the SSI working within a cyclical framework, within which SSI inspectors could, unlike HAS teams, cultivate long term working relationships. The clearest example of change was the product of such a relationship, and within it, of opportunism and careful work on both sides. In an authority that went through a period of acute difficulty, the inspector and the head of a home worked together to change the philosophy and working practices of a secure unit. New managers in the department increasingly used the inspector in their bid to install stronger management of care practice. Again, the combination of felt need, staff with motivation and authority to act made effective collaboration possible.

Much of SSI's work is concerned with work at the junction between management and practice. Their methods, like those of the HAS, enabled them to reach down into organisations and get in touch with staff struggling with intractable problems on the basis of uncertain knowledge and inadequate skills. They were opportunistic in seeking out groups who might activate change but their influence could only be percolative without support from those with power inside the organisations. The case study showed how inspectors of secure accommodation sought through reinforcement to increase the internal power of those in the organisation whose practice the inspectors thought should have greater influence; however, the study gave little support for the idea that such an approach, psychological rather than structural, could produce major change.

Numerous examples of the failure on the part of both the HAS and the SSI to eradicate practices universally acknowledged to be damaging to personal dignity, let alone to secure practices that might encourage more professional work, showed the gaps they had to bridge between values and action.

However, it has already been noted in Chapter Nine that SSI was changing in a number of ways. It began to focus inspections more effectively. It started to work at higher levels of management, to formulate clearer models of practice, to be more directive in some fields and to see that their inspections were more salient to authorities. This was entirely understandable and useful: personal social services needed managerial help. But the connection between tightly coupled hierarchical management and reflective professional practice has not been made. Indeed, much organisation and recent management literature challenges any such supposition.

The community homes study indirectly illustrated the problems. It showed a department implementing an inspection through clear delegated management down the organisation. But equally clearly, it showed how failure to engage those evaluated at the level of need, motivation and value left major practice problems untouched.

## Did Compulsion Work?

The difficulty of causing change did not tempt the evaluators to resort to more coercive methods. The evaluative bodies showed no more inclination to resort to the law or other forms of compulsory power than had evaluative bodies in the past (see Chapter One).

In its struggle with a small number of local authorities over 'creative accounting', the Audit Commission supported moves to change the accounting requirements from 'dependence on law and statute' in determining 'the accounting treatment of transactions and towards an approach based more on common sense and economic substance' ... 'Only thus will the proliferation of creative accounting devices be halted' (Audit Commission, 1988d).

This followed the extension, under the Local Government Act, 1988, of the powers available to auditors to prevent illegal action by local authorities. The new powers, to take anticipatory action against authorities and to widen the conditions under which auditors could apply for judicial review, were welcomed but they, too, relied on making it possible to test actions thought to have breached principles rather than precise rules.

The Commission, even in its strictest audit mode, regarded legal action as a last and unpalatable resort. Auditors' actions against the City of Liverpool and the London Borough of Lambeth for failing in 1985 to set a rate by a reasonable date were ultimately upheld in the courts but at the expense of time and money.

The Commission was sensitive about the impact of its increased legal powers. Its 1988 Annual Report stressed that they did not mean that auditors would be expected 'to seek out matters which might be the subject of a prohibition order or application for judicial review'. Powers were to be used with discretion and only on substantial issues.

The Commission's preferred line of action, in the face of local authority intransigence, was to collaborate with other bodies, such as the Chartered Institute of Public Finance and Accountancy (CIPFA), to publicise and disseminate its thinking, as when it gave evidence to the Widdicombe Committee of Inquiry into the Conduct of Local Government. Direct formal action, such as the use of management letters, 'reports in the public interest' and prosecution had limited immediate effect when formal authority was either disregarded or seen as part of the ideology of the enemy.

The SSI, too, showed reluctance to use its formal powers of sanction. The case study on secure accommodation shows the constraints on recommending the use of sanctions to compel action by local authorities. In the observed visit, a managerialist approach, using targets for change and sanctions, competed with a preferred approach in which inspectors saw themselves as catalysts of internal change.

The formal powers of HAS were limited. The power of report to the Secretary of State was, as we have seen, limited by the political context. The power to publish reports, instituted in 1984, was not unequivocally welcomed by HAS team members. Many thought it inconsistent with the norms of professional control and a blunt instrument. It could penalise and demoralise those directly responsible for patient care, without necessarily affecting resource allocation and service delivery. And the study suggested that the local press was at best erratic and at worst indifferent in its treatment of HAS reports, even where these made fundamental challenges to health and social services management.

## A Value-based Authority

Legally based authority can be contrasted with what might be termed value based, normative or ascriptive authority. Authority in this mode depends upon a bilateral relationship: it must be acknowledged by those evaluated, as well as assumed by evaluators. It rests partly on judgement of individual behaviour and characteristics. While such concepts remain symbolically important in maintaining professional identity and influence in public life, their practical force is weak. These forms of authority rarely surfaced in our study and were less important in achieving change than were pressure, or felt need for change, on the part of those evaluated.

The case studies showed reluctance to cede to evaluators authority beyond well defined limits. A few people thought that the HAS had moral authority. It represented the welfare of patients, people in need with no recognisable political leverage. The role played by it, and by SSI, in providing independent monitoring of service providers was universally valued. But moral authority was not thought to carry with it much power.

The Audit Commission and management consultants were most commonly accorded the authority of expertise or technical authority. Their knowledge was identifiable and perceived as instrumental. Local authority officers saw it as value-neutral, although professionals nearer to practice, such as head teachers, disagreed. For the most part, the Commission had succeeded in breaking the connection in people's minds between their expertise and expenditure cuts. But it was generally felt that expertise in accountancy or in information technology should be an instrument of professional judgement and political calculation.

SSI and the HAS were accorded technical authority or indeed authority of any kind of expertise more rarely. There were exceptions: knowledge of the law and of technical safety devices in the case of Social Services inspectors; medical models of intervention in the case of HAS, but they were often rejected as inappropriate to the context, actually flawed or inferior to models favoured on the site concerned. Inspectors and HAS visitors were ceded experience-based knowledge sometimes, either their own or those of others which they could disseminate.

Over time, civil servants were broadening their conception of the usable expertise among consultants. Again the context was one of pressing need: the scope of policy change to which civil servants were expected to contribute in the late 1980s was massive and required skills and conceptions of change that were not part of the conventional civil service expertise.

But across the study, to acknowledge defined technical authority on the part of evaluators was also to reinforce a strategy of *containment*: containing evaluation to functions of legitimation or regulation. Authorities who objected to interpretations of their work by external evaluators, or who were unwilling to give priority to the issues under scrutiny, confined their response to matters of law and regulation. Or they confined acceptance of recommendations to those definable within their own policy framework.  .

Alternatively, authority of expertise might be used as political support in the case of conflicts between officers and their members or to divert opposition in the electorate to authority policies. All three authorities in the Audit Commission case study afforded examples of the exploitation of the Commission's work for political ends.

For the most part, *professional* authority was grudgingly conceded and tended to be converted into conceptions of peer review. Where conceded, it was in contexts where those evaluated faced problems which they could not resolve alone: the local authority that had experienced a period of crisis; the institution that combined high standards with a competitive resource context and a shortfall of trained staff; the professional group with relatively little power in a health authority and needing validation and external political support.

Professional or reputational authority was not enough to persuade those evaluated of the validity of the case being made. An HAS visitor with an established national reputation could not persuade his fellow professionals in the authority visited to adopt the model of service he was advocating. Indeed his attempts to do so were resented.

Professional authority was theoretically crucial to HAS' success and important to all the institutions. But all suffered in some way from personnel problems. As pressures on the NHS increased and as competing sources of evaluation and control gained strength, the authority of HAS itself was challenged. It found it harder to recruit team members of national reputation and had to rely more heavily on retired and more junior staff. SSIs were predominantly appointed from at least two levels below chief officer in local authorities. In conflicts with those evaluated, they were at a disadvantage and might find themselves confronted with officers who had more influence in the policy system than they had themselves.

Local auditors carried limited authority with officers of either their own or other professions, sometimes because of the narrowness of their training or experience, sometimes because of the level of staff used. Private firms used by the Commission and consultants used by government departments were both sometimes criticised for using staff who were too junior to understand fully the issues or to carry personal authority among senior professionals, managers and members.

The range of authority relationships, from the legal and coercive to the value-based and normative (Kogan, 1988), resulted in three main kinds of encounter between evaluative institutions and the evaluated: *conflict, containment* and *collaboration*. In the case studies explicit conflict most often occurred in the case of the HAS. It relied most heavily on professional authority and dealt with pluralist organisations, in which professional influence remained strong. Less open conflict might be disguised as containment.

*Contained compliance* was the most prevalent form of response, although in many cases, authorities combined containment and collaborative strategies. Collaboration was a rarer response, and sometimes demonstrated an authority's determination to use the evaluative body to help it achieve its own ends.

## Market Metaphors: Exchange, Persuasion and Presentation

According to Lindblom (1977), government's characteristic mode of control is authority; that of the market is exchange; while persuasion is pervasive in both. Even before the recent thrust of the public sector towards the market, explanations of control in that sector by exchange relationships were often found as persuasive as those relying on authority relationships (Blau, 1967; Ranson, 1980; Rhodes, 1981). In the current climate, as boundaries between the public and private sectors are increasingly blurred, and the language of the market becomes more compelling, exchange concepts are likely to appeal more.

Authority relationships may now be harder to distinguish from exchange relationships. Bodies may be accepted because they are helpful as much as because they are authoritative. And the lines between judgement, persuasion and marketing may be harder to detect. The techniques of presentation, the deployment of argument and the choice of language and symbol played a significant part in the acquisition of authority on the part of the Audit Commission. Arguably, these are all primarily marketing skills.

In some cases, exchange relationships can best explain the limits to the exercise of institutional authority. Inspectors of secure accommodation knew that the balance of exchange often worked against them. Government had more incentive to keep secure units open than did many local authorities. Not only could local authorities resist requirements to act, they also allowed inspectors to assume quasi management functions, so increasing their sense of responsibility for them, because they knew of the pressure on the inspectorate to keep the units going.

## The Power of Evaluators in the Policy System

The influence of evaluators might be felt at several levels, including policy review at the centre. They varied greatly in the scope of their work and therefore in the range of their potential influence and the networks they could establish in the national policy system.

Large consultancy firms work across central government departments, at central, regional and district levels in the NHS, in nationalised industries and in local authorities. Their commissions are negotiated high in all these systems. The Audit Commission spans the whole of local government and, from 1990, the NHS too. Their focus is on management and therefore their dealings necessarily include the top officials.

By comparison, inspectorates are limited to one service. SSI, in addition, is concerned with services to relatively disadvantaged groups. HAS was created to safeguard recipients of poorly resourced and politically weak services. The focus of both HAS and SSI is diffuse and traditionally directed more towards professionals and practitioners than to managers.

Evaluative bodies have affected national policy not only through the salience and competence of their evaluation but because of their ability to help shape or respond to the contemporary policy environment, though both are important.

## The Audit Commission

The Audit Commission and the SSI can be usefully contrasted in this context. The Commission was newly designed through its terms of reference, its governance, and its key appointments to implement a major component of government policy. It started with the confidence of government. The challenge was to gain credibility with local government and the professional and policy communities on whose interests it impinged.

By the time of the study the Commission had established its reputation for independence from central government. It had taken care to establish strong networks in local government and professional and policy communities and was making effective, though not uncritical, use of their thinking in its reports.

Despite its frequent disclaimers to any mandate for comment on the substantives of policy, it could claim to have influenced actual policy developments to the advantage of local government. Its work on community care provides a particularly clear example (Audit Commission, 1986e).

The Commission's report was one of a succession of initiatives culminating in the Griffiths Report (1988). The Commission's solutions were not all accepted. But some of them were. It was clearly identifiable in the 'field of forces' through which change came about, and at the macro-policy level. And it had supported resistance to the centre's attempt to reduce the role of local government in that policy area.

But, fundamentally, it saw its mission as causing change in local authorities, in accordance with government ideology. We have shown how by 1988 it was ready to take a more public stand on that. It demonstrated scope and formal authority to make that kind of impact; it also had the expertise to develop its own version of its mission and to develop strategies that would make its achievement possible.

## The Social Services Inspectorate

The SSI, unlike the Commission, started from a position of weakness with central government, an advisory body to government, on behalf of a weak profession. At the same time, it had become distanced from the workings of the personal social services, where effective management was seen as increasingly critical to the delivery of adequate services.

Government changed SSI's mandate, while retaining substantially the same workforce. The Directorate aimed to strengthen its role in central government, even if it did not speak with one voice. SSI was concerned to increase influence with ministers, with the key administrators in the Department's policy divisions, and with the social services policy community.

One element of the SSI set out to show ministers that it could be useful to them in a mode as much managerial as professional. It could act rapidly in response to political demands to investigate crises in social services departments. This gave the SSI a higher profile and shifted some power from local government.

Some members wanted to go further and to make all inspections more directive: to show that they could achieve compliance with general, well explicated standards (see Chapter Six). The strategies that prevailed were those of compromise: to shift the emphasis towards improving management without abandoning professional preoccupations.

Inspectors started from a position of relative weakness. They are almost without exception outsiders, recruited in mid-career. Career civil servants derive their strength from rigorous competitive entry and promotion systems with a high premium on excellence, from strong induction systems, an emphasis on collective policy development and mastery of complex interdepartmental connections. SSIs are recruited from a low status profession with substantial non-graduate recruitment, an uncertain knowledge base and incomplete control of admission. Their numbers are small and they are organisationally diffused in the Department.

The Department had regarded the SWS as part of its intelligence system, providing information about particular authorities, not clearly categorised but useful: answering parliamentary questions or providing information should a crisis arise in some part of the service. Or it might serve an ill-defined purpose in the monitoring or development of policy by the policy divisions.

SSI now sought to make a less subordinate contribution to policy, an intention not wholly welcomed by the policy divisions; partly because the general intelligence function was useful to them (interview, 1989) but also perhaps because it signified an attempt by SSI to change its authority in the Department.

However, there were trade-offs. Inspections would investigate issues of interest to the Department, and in a few cases each year they were targeted to collect information of use to the policy divisions: three out of 36 in the national programme for 1987 and three out of 29 in the 1989 programme.

Inspections were perceived by the SSI Directorate as part of a feedback loop system in the Department. A senior member suggested that SSI was gaining a new level of confidence from the administrators. In the past inspections had yielded a mass of unanalysed and probably unanalysable information. Inspections were still perceived predominantly as yielding professional judgements about the phenomenon under investigation at a particular time (SSI, 1988e). It was not clear how far they should be adapted to provide the basis for policy analysis. Neither the inspectors nor the policy division had systematically addressed that question by 1989.

However, SSI's investment of resources in the indicators exercise suggested that it did see itself as contributing to the information base on the personal social services and so carving out a role distinct from that of the statistics division of the Department.

The inspectorate could thus be seen as bidding to enhance its status within government, to demonstrate a broader usefulness and to gain increased influence in the policy process. It may well have become more useful; whether it increased its influence is less clear. Observers in local government considered that the Audit Commission's independent status gave it the freedom to challenge and criticise, of which the SSI was deprived.

## The HAS

By contrast with the SSI the HAS made little evident attempt to strengthen its strategic position *vis à vis* the centre. And it prized highly its independence from government and the NHS. Its power to report directly to the Secretary of State was born largely out of an idiosyncratic minister's will to assert personal control and sat uneasily with the strong professional peer review body evolved by the first director and the Department. That power was of little consequence in a period when ministers' priorities had fundamentally changed.

The HAS continued to perceive itself as essentially professional and to work through professional networks to influence practice and models of service. It used minimal resources to that end. Its independence of government was reinforced by the fact that all of its directors were doctors. It evinced a culture of professions rather than of government.

## Management Consultants

The commissioning of management consultants to evaluate and advise on policy should be seen in part as realising ministers' aspirations to reduce the role of the state, to open up government to competitive bidding from the private sector, to introduce its skills and institutionalise the concept of management itself within government.

Like the Audit Commission, management consultants had the general support of government. The challenge was to make themselves acceptable to civil servants. Many of them sought growth in their resource base to keep apace with the expanding demand from the public sector. The field was competitive: potentially the business was large and prestigious and civil servants controlled access to it.

But civil servants' power was also constrained for they needed help. They were overstretched and not able to fill all the gaps in their own expertise. Consultants had the marketing skills to ensure they maintained a high profile. They were careful to maintain contact with their commissioning departments. Some firms also had secondments in government departments, which gave them the chance to influence in a more sustained way.

## Conclusions

Granted all of the reservations about the direct impact that the evaluative groups had on central government, their strengthened role was a significant phenomenon of the 1980s in British central government. And throughout this book it has been possible to point to examples of impact made by the evaluators in the four studies.

What cannot be discerned is any systematic, predictable and sustained impact. This is partly because within our study scope they could not be fully observed. In the climate of local administration and practice, the metaphor of impact is particularly inappropriate; change is more likely to percolate than to take a more dramatic form.

Of all the forms of evaluation, traditional regularity audit is both legitimate and effective, because the norms are clear and the procedures contained by law; it is difficult to conceive of accountable government without it. By contrast, even the strongest forms of policy and practice evaluation have no such certain base. It is not surprising, therefore, that evaluative agencies with a mandate to cause change look for rational hierarchies of values and goals and organisational structures. These make it possible to evaluate by clear criteria, to expect effects to have clear causes, and inputs to lead to predictable outcomes. That optimism dominated evaluation in the late 1980s in the face of moral and practical obstinacies that see change as a product of particular commitments to individual clients.

If the uncertainties of gains from evaluation have been emphasised, that is because we believe that its role may have been misconceived. Apart from the most rigorous forms of audit and inspection that are concerned with the surveillance of standards and behaviour, evaluation is best seen as one among many sources of information, wisdom, judgment and advice.

Chapter Twelve

# Government, Evaluation and Change

This book has given an account of public evaluation in the UK in the 1980s. The final chapter summarises the findings and draws some conclusions about the role of evaluation in policy change.

In the 1960s and 1970s the trend in at least some key services had been towards professionally led, liberal and interactive evaluation (Kogan, 1988). Those evaluative preferences persisted in the work of the HAS and SWS - the precursor of the SSI.

The government of the 1980s, however, was not content to rest on the value base of the providing professions. It wanted evaluation to be an instrument of change: to help to install rationalistic management, designed to achieve economy and efficiency, in preference to management saturated with professional values and needs led policies. It wanted more effective performance from a reduced public sector.

A further policy aim was that the private market should provide services that were previously state monopolies and thus compensate for reductions in the public sector. In turn, the public sector would be expected to behave more like the market. But alongside a greater variety of providers, there would be stronger endorsement of a particular selection of values; and central government would exercise greater authority than hitherto.

In advancing these changes, the government could point to some clear deficiencies in the professionally led services, which were in any case becoming swamped in some local authorities by politicisation (Laffin and Young, 1985; Widdicombe, 1986).

Against this background, the evaluative bodies selected for study all expanded in scope during this period. Expansion in scope and a widening range of evaluative criteria were features of the SWS and the HAS before the 1980s. Their scope increased again in the 1980s, SSI more dramatically than HAS, culminating in the strategic evaluative function allocated to it in the White Paper on Community Care (Department of Health, 1989).

But the scale and speed of expansion of the Audit Commission and management consultants in government during this period were on a much larger scale, even before the Commission included the NHS in its remit.

## What the Study Says

Chapters Two and Three show how the Audit Commission established its independence and gained the confidence of local authorities, the majority of whom it had convinced that it was concerned with the quality of services, as well as with economy and efficiency. Its willingness to criticise central government was appreciated.

It had rapidly consolidated methods and established access to specialist knowledge to meet its extended audit duties. It built a reputation for penetrating analysis and began to make an impact on local authority management. It embarked, at first cautiously, on performance measurement and increasingly gained confidence in entering the exclusive province of the professionals.

It later became more adventurous in crossing the management - policy boundary, too. This coincided with the start of the Conservative government's third term of office and hardening determination to shift the public sector more decisively towards the market. The Commission embraced the changes of policy, and particularly the introduction of competition into the public sector. It abandoned its stance of value neutrality.

Some critics perceived the Audit Commission as operating in the managerialist mould set by the government when it came to power in 1979, although, in fact, it worked with more than one concept of management. In its special studies it relied on accountancy, economics or operational research based techniques to modernise the public sector while in its broader management advice asserting a more expansive approach. In this, good management embraced challenge and change and harnessed motivation and creativity. It exhorted local authority members and officers to perceive their functions as essentially those of good managers. The Commission thus contributed to a political culture in which distinctions between management and politics were eroded.

The whole of the public sector is now regarded as a growth area for consultants (Chapter Four). Central government's practice of commissioning them for policy evaluation was justified by reference to their technical skills and expertise which government departments often lacked. Consultancy enabled departments to obtain external judgements based predominantly on quantitative, financial, commercial, information and communications expertise.

They were also used for political reasons: to 'park a problem', to divert pressure for action, to legitimate a desired solution, to resolve conflicts of interest. Consultants' advice was credible partly because they came from the private sector.

Consultants depended heavily on their clients for the success of particular contracts and for continued success in the central government consultancy market. They recognised that recommendations had to be acceptable to civil servants if they were to be implemented, and although some placed ultimate confidence in the rigour of their analysis, others felt that negotiation was the key factor.

Civil servants, for their part, were persuaded that managerial perspectives had something to offer them and some began to define their work in terms of good management. However, an implication of the study is that the use of consultancy strengthens central government's *a priori* judgements of issues against the influence of actors in the field. Reflexiveness between central government and the field gives way to reflexiveness between central government and their consultants, as this form of evaluation takes hold.

The SSI case studies (Chapters Six and Seven) demonstrated a government based service using well established methods of professional inspection, although the balance between evaluation, advice, regulation and change was different in the two cases. But the inspectorate was under pressure (Chapter Five) to change from a professional to a more instrumental conception of its role, to meet the need of the services for good management. Some staff thought that it should demonstrate effectiveness by setting clear standards, asserting the norms of economic efficiency, hitting harder in its judgements and taking steps to ensure compliance. Others argued that the inspectorate should display the strengths of professional evaluation.

SSI moved decisively towards national standard setting, the development of evaluative methods and greater concern with management. It maintained the authority derived from legal powers in certain of its inspectorial functions. It showed government that it was prepared to tackle serious problems in local services by a more flexible and interventionist use of its resources. It enhanced its analytic base and made strenuous attempts to integrate its new strengths with a continuing commitment to professional goals. But in so doing it had to contend with an overload of values and demands.

The HAS' (Chapter Eight) remit had gradually expanded to include advising on policy and planning strategies as well as monitoring, evaluating and helping to improve the management of patient care. It now extended across a number of important boundaries: between health services with their direct line of management from central government and social services governed by local authorities; between institutional and community care; between professional and managerial cultures and priorities.

The ambiguities evident at the time of the creation of its predecessor body in 1969, between safeguarding acceptable standards of care for vulnerable groups and an advisory and developmental mandate, remained. However, it continued to assert its professional identity and showed little inclination to give greater priority to instrumental values. Its resources were meagre and its analytic base remained weak.

As a multi-disciplinary professional service it was in tune with the conception of a service with a pluralist rather than a hierarchical structure: a conception that was giving way to managerialist assumptions, so increasing the pressures on HAS.

In the new era of general management, managers looked increasingly to external evaluation to provide explicit measures against which performance could be assessed. HAS team members worked largely to their own implicit standards. Meanwhile, professionals under pressure from managerialism might look for support from the HAS as a professional advisory service. They did not necessarily find it and, if they did, it was unlikely to be strong enough to meet their expectations.

Chapters Nine, Ten and Eleven showed how civil servants, through their use of consultants, the Audit Commission and the SSI had expanded the range of knowledge used in evaluation and how, at the centre, the Commission and the SSI had created more generalisable evaluative frameworks and methods. The new expertise was predominantly technical. Evaluative institutions gained authority in government and the field through applying quantitative analysis, providing prescriptive models and asserting logic in policy and management. But they reinforced drives for certainty, for clear priorities and for measurement of performance.

By contrast, professional evaluation seemed to lack rigour whilst its value preferences were easily exposed; a disadvantage not suffered by those forms of evaluation which used the techniques of quantification and the more aseptic language of efficiency. Criteria such as quality of care still underlay SSI and HAS evaluation but HAS did not address the weaknesses of their existing approaches; the SSI tried to find ways of incorporating them into the new order of efficiency and outcome measures, without abandoning their own perspectives. But they underestimated that new order's intolerance of conflicting needs and multiple perspectives.

The Audit Commission and management consultants reflected and contributed to a new political culture. In so doing, they were inevitably helping to define the limits of policy options available in the public sector and at that level had substantial impact on it. They did not, however, simply impose new values; they attempted to connect with changing aims and conceptions of need in the field, where they could. But, moving away from the centre, and as they engaged with the local particularities of services, they found it necessary to collaborate and to negotiate, if they were to cause change. Day and Klein (1990) in a study carried out at the same time as this research, point out how swiftly the Audit Commission moved towards a collaborative (we are not sure about their use of the word 'consultancy') mode in local authorities. They followed the general preference of evaluative bodies to persuade and stimulate rather than to coerce. Chapter Eleven showed, however, that while evaluators did influence local action, predictable and sustained impacts were not discernible.

## General Conclusions and Policy Implications

The first conclusion is that not only has evaluation massively increased as an activity in the service of government but that its aspirations have also burgeoned. Between them the four institutions, by the end of the 1980s, had embarked on: the development of evaluative methodologies; both analysing systems and working at the practice level; monitoring standards and causing change. They performed these functions from widely different bases of authority, political mandate, knowledge base, and resources.

Our second conclusion, however, is that despite these differences the evaluative institutions, the HAS apart, tended to converge. Professionalism, evinced in peer review and connoisseurial evaluation, had to jostle with managerialism. Technical expertise, quantitative forms of analysis and the separation of instrumental from substantive values increasingly underpinned evaluative practice. Where that did not happen, evaluative institutions lost power or had difficulty in maintaining internal coherence.

Evaluators of the public sector were increasingly concerned with large systems and so included systems analysis, resource analysis and, more gradually, policy analysis in their activities. At the same time, some were also called upon to analyse impacts - how did systems deliver services and respond to individual need. All saw evaluating quality of performance as part of their remit but were aware, to varying degrees, of the complexities of that requirement.

During the 1980s evaluation or performance review increasingly came to be seen as an essential component of managerial and professional practice. This meant a shift in what was expected of evaluative institutions. Thirdly, then, they were under pressure to provide not only direct evaluation but also develop criteria and methods for use by others; the Audit Commission and SSI undertook these tasks.

Fourthly, all the evaluative bodies aimed to cause change. To do so, they needed to understand change processes and find ways to influence them at both macro and micro levels. They did this with varying degrees of success. This meant they must engage with the system and its competing interests. At the same time, if they were effectively to challenge, they must retain degrees of independence.

A further conclusion of the study is that convergence occurred, too, because evaluative institutions were in a market, competing for power. The study demonstrates that it is possible to achieve power through evaluation whilst advancing particular views of the nature and working of the public services. This has always been true of the service professionals; we found it to be equally true of those whose authority is based on technical expertise.

As a result of competition, the wholesale expansion of evaluative machinery, with its attendant costs, was not accompanied by any attempt at a rational division of labour, a conclusion also reached by Day and Klein (1990). Each of the bodies, inevitably, felt the need to acquire knowledge of substantive matters, if they lacked them, or some acquaintance with techniques, if their knowledge base was that of professional practice. As a result the boundaries tended to crumble, competition between them grew, as did attempts to colonise areas other than those of their first competence. Given the likely growth of field authority evaluative groups in both local and health authorities, there could be increased confusion and duplication of work.

This perhaps invites proposals that they should be better coordinated. Yet if convergence and coordination among evaluators are too highly prized, diversity of information and judgment will become weaker. It is the business of government to reduce interests and options to manageable proportions. It is doubtful whether they or anyone else will be best served if evaluators, whose task it is to add to information and judgment, are also in the knowledge containment game. In establishing common data bases for the evaluative bodies different interests must sustain their distinctive contribution of knowledge and value. This is all the more important at a time of political dissensus and legitimate variation in practitioner views about how to cope with social distress and needs.

The final conclusion is that objective evaluation is a myth. Evaluators bring with them values derived from occupational and disciplinary traditions, which may in turn be congruent with, or hostile to, the dominant political ideology. The study has shown repeatedly how the distinctions between technical and political argument break down. Evaluators may be part of the culture which they are assessing or they may be outsiders. They may promote the view that a particular occupational group should determine how a set of services should be delivered. Thus while their analysis might be sound within a particular tradition, the relevance of that tradition in that sphere might be contestable. These reservations apply whether the evaluation comes from those endowed with the authority of a highly regarded profession or with mastery of difficult and highly regarded analytic techniques.

The most 'technical' of the bodies, the Audit Commission, became committed to certain *a prioris* which can be fairly described as conforming to the views of the government of the day. Those values are, however, a matter of political preference, and to some extent may be vulnerable to changes in government which could bring with them a shift from emphasis on the three Es towards one on social planning and professionally led services. To some extent, the private consultancies which evince values similar to those of the Audit Commission might share the vulnerability. The HAS teams, drawn from various groups, also evinced particular policy and practice preferences. The struggles within the reformulated SSI before they shifted towards some of the preferences of their ministers have been noted.

The study has marked some of the obstacles to sustaining and developing evaluation in the public sector; it has also recorded significant achievements in overcoming them. An approach which tracks patterns of work through the twin perspectives of the authority that the new breed of evaluators wield and the knowledge they use underlines the complexity of the world they face. It also suggests that they and those who sponsor them need to be sensitive to the ways in which they use their power to inform and judge.

Appendix

# Methods Used

The methods used in the study, which was concerned with complex interactions of values, knowledge and power, were adapted to the need to penetrate the unique particularities of the four sets of evaluative institutions, and to the type of access that it was felt possible to seek. Issues of control were, therefore, restricted to ensuring, as far as possible, the integrity of the unique evidence uncovered and then subjecting it to tests of its own internal logic (how far were statements of values compatible with the evaluative objectives, styles and techniques actually employed) and their capacity for comparison with the other institutions. Unique institutions by definition constitute samples of one; but there are stocks of assumptions about governmental structures and evaluative modes against which each can be compared.

The data were collected from three main sources. Three of the bodies produce published accounts of what they intend to do, why they do it and what they have done. These accounts - fully listed in the References in this book and in Henkel et al. (1989), *The Health Advisory Service: An Evaluation* - are thus primary sources. In all four cases a substantial number of semi- structured and fully noted and recorded interviews were undertaken at the different levels of the evaluating body and of the institution being evaluated. In the case of the SSI and, even more so, of the HAS, researchers were present at key evaluative events as non-participative observers.

Two issues always arise on qualitative studies such as this. How can the researcher's observations be verified? Did the study contaminate the experience being observed? The verification took two forms. First, inconsistencies of perception not legitimately attributable to difference of individual or role bound perspectives can be weighed, albeit it crudely, if more than one account is availible, through meetings, interviews and a study of the declaratory literature. The researcher is thus then in the position of the historian weighing evidence on its inherent probability. Secondly, the researcher deliberately sets out to get statements from different perspectives.

As to contamination, where the observer or interrogator through interviews is acting contemporaneously with the evaluation being carried out it would be astonishing if none occurred. The researchers must, and did, make every effort to reduce the risk. An example of the care taken in this study comes from the evaluation of the HAS. There the team returned to the site of observed evaluations to seek information about follow-up of the HAS visitation report. The health and social service authorities were informed that this would happen early in process of securing clearance and to some extent some unavoidable contamination might have occurred if that fact remained prominent in their minds. But no reminder was given by the researchers until the last moment before they revisited for fear that anticipation of being interrogated on progress would of itself stimulate follow- up actions. Of the eight case study areas only one key role player felt the researcher's presence might have affected behaviour.

The four studies were different in kind. All could have benefited from more resources and time. In two of study areas,the process of evaluation was fully observed over some days. This was not practicable in the case of the Audit Commission or management consultants, and they have therefore to be judged largely by their declarations of intent, interviews with those evaluated and evaluators and the fruits of their labour.

The most exhaustive was the HAS study separately conducted by a team of five experienced researchers funded for a total of about350 days researcher days in all, including all access and writing up, over a period of two years. Over two years, it was not possible to take on board a complete visitation process which, with follow up, might take four years after the first series of events. Eight intensive case studies, however, enabled the team to analyse and evaluate the working of HAS at different stages of the visit process: in one case, 20 months after the HAS visit; in a second, four years after the original visit; in two more, 18 months and three years after the visits; the fifth and sixth were studies of current visits and the researchers attended almost the whole of the process over a period of two weeks, and follow-ups of the reception given the HAS reports. The seventh and the eigth case studies involved direct observation again, but of follow-up visits. Each case study was written up from full field notes, vetted by the whole team, and seen by a Steering Committee.

In addition, members of the HAS directorate, the DHSS and other analogous evaluative bodies were interviewed. In all, the research included 272 interviews for the case studies together with some weeks of direct observations of visits and meetings, and 28 interviews with members of national bodies.

The study of the SSI concerned two cases, the inspection of secure units, conducted on a regular basis, and the national inspection of community homes, a one-off national exercise.

In the first case the research was confined to inspections carried out in one of the nine SSI regions. It was chosen partly because one of the inspectors had particular expertise in this part of SSI's work. Two secure units in each of two local authorities were then chosen for the study within the region. The study reviewed inspections over a period of nearly three years to enable impact to be studied over time. In addition to conducting interviews, the researcher was given the opportunity of observing two inspections, one in each authority. This provided insights into inspection methods and interaction with the staff of the units being inspected. Other evidence was derived from documents and semi-structured interviews. All the relevant reports on the selected institutions, together with reports on some others, were made available together with national guidelines and guidance on secure accommodation issued for local authorities.

Interviews were conducted with six inspectors in all, four of whom participated in the inspections. Much more data were also derived informally from time spent on inspections with them. Careful field notes were made of all such encounters. Nine officers, one member, and 14 managerial, care, and teaching staff from the two authorities were interviewed. The latter were from four secure units and their parent establishments.

The second SSI case concerned the objectives, planning,methods, organisation and output of the national inspection. It then included one local authority through which to study retrospectively the process of inspection, the production of an individual report and the response to that report in the Social Services Department.

The methods used were documentary analysis and semi-structured interviews. Regional inspectorate files were examined together with the final national report. At the local level, the report itself and the SSD's formal responses were examined. These were set into the context of the department's child care policy. Access was also given to the minutes of the managerial meetings, over a period of four years, of one of the community homes that had participated in the inspection.

Interviews were conducted with three inspectors, one at headquarters and two in the region, one of whom carried out the inspection chosen for the study. Fifteen SSD staff were interviewed in the department and division, and from among area and patch team managers and officers in charge of two of the residential homes inspected and training and advisory staff.

At the national level, three members of the directorate of the SSI were interviewed, together with three senior inspectors and two Department of Health administrators in the Children's Division were also seen.

The main sources of data, at the national level, on the study of the Audit Commission were the Commission's own material produced for its investigation into the management of secondary education, and in particular the final report and the Audit Guide, semi-structured interviews with all of the members of the study team and nine key representatives of the relevant policy community, six of whom had been consulted before the study specification was agreed. The research traced the translation of the national study into local audit 'flavours' in three selected authorities. The aim was to explore the main instrument developed for this purpose, the Audit Guide, together with the approach and methods of local auditors in annual audit 'flavours', and to analyse implementation at this level. The authorities had widely differing characteristics. Two were audited by a private firm and the third by the District Audit Service.

Twenty nine interviews were conducted with four auditors, three chairmen of education committees, 13 local authority officers, seven heads or deputies,and two union representatives. In addition, the liason officer for the value for money audit was interviewed for each authority. Four senior staff at the Commission were interviewed. Our case study was submitted to the Commission for comment, and we should record with regret, particularly in view of their helpfulness in mounting the study, their disagreement with some of its conclusions about which we remain confident as conveying a fair account and interpretation of what we found.

The study of evaluation carried out by consultants from the private sector included semi-structured interviews of 16 consultants from 10 firms who were directly involved in studies and one senior consultant directing the public sector studies of an internationally reputed consultancy firm. There were also interviews conducted with a total of 20 civil servants within five government departments.

A major difficulty was establishing which consultancy activities could be primarily defined as evaluative. Civil service literature which offered guidance on the use of consultants was consulted. Official files enabling there to be a closer assessment of how assignments were developed and offered were not available as they were in some of our other studies.

Our research was opportunistic in the sense that we could and did push on open doors but could force none down. The SSI and HAS allowed access to files; the Audit Commission allowed free access to their staff for interview, as did many local authorities, and eased our way into the field. We cannot be certain that the disparity of access and of time put into the four studies have not affected the strength of our conclusions but feel that we fully exploited that which we did access.

# References

*Administrative Science Quarterly*, (September 1983), whole issue.

Audit Commission, (1984a), *Code of Local Government Audit Practice for England and Wales*, HMSO.

Audit Commission, (1984b), *Handbook: Economy, Efficiency and Effectiveness*, vols. II and III, HMSO.

Audit Commission, (1984c), *Impact on Local Authorities of the Block Grant Distribution System*, HMSO.

Audit Commission, (1984d), *Non-Teaching Costs in Education*, HMSO.

Audit Commission, (1985), *Capital Expenditure Controls in Local Government in England*, HMSO.

Audit Commission, (1986a), *Managing the Crisis in Council Housing*, HMSO.

Audit Commission, (1986b), *Performance Review in Local Government: a Handbook for Auditors and Local Authorities*, HMSO.

Audit Commission, (1986c), *Report and Accounts*, HMSO.

Audit Commission, (1986d), *Towards Better Management of Secondary Education*, HMSO.

Audit Commission, (1986e), *Making a Reality of Community Care*, HMSO.

Audit Commission, (1987a), *Community Care: Developing Services for People with a Mental Handicap, Occasional Paper No 4*, HMSO.

Audit Commission, (1987b), *The Management of London's Authorities: Preventing the Breakdown of Services*, Occasional Paper No 2, HMSO.

Audit Commission, (1987c), *Report and Accounts*, HMSO.

Audit Commission, (1987d), *The Way Ahead*, HMSO.

Audit Commission, (1988a), *Community Care: Developing Services for People with a Mental Handicap: Audit Guide*, HMSO.

Audit Commission, (1988b), *The Competitive Council*, Management Paper No 1, HMSO.

Audit Commission, (1988c), *Performance Review in Local Government: A Handbook for Auditors and Local Authorities*, HMSO.

Audit Commission, (1988d), *Report and Accounts*, HMSO.

Audit Commission, (1988e), *Surplus Capacity in Secondary Schools: A Progress Report*, HMSO.

Audit Commission, (1989a), *Developing Community Care for Adults with a Mental Handicap*, Occasional Paper No 9, HMSO.

Audit Commission, (1989b), *Housing the Homeless: the Local Authority Role*, HMSO.

Audit Commission, (1989c), *Preparing for Compulsory Competition*, Occasional Paper No 7, HMSO.

Avebury Report, (1984), *Home Life: A Code of Practice for Residential Care*, Centre for Policy on Ageing.

Bacon, R., and Eltis, W., (1976), *Britain's Economic Problem: Too Few Producers*, Macmillan.

Barnes, M. et al. (1988), 'Performance Measurement in Personal Social Services', *Research, Policy and Planning*, 6(2) (Special issue).

Bennis, W., Benne, K., and Chinn, R., (1969), *The Planning of Change*, Holt, Rinehart and Winston.

Billis, D., Bromley, G., Hey, A. M., and Rowbottom, R., (1980), *Organising Social Service Departments*. Heinemann.

Blau, P., (1967), *Exchange and Power in Social Life*, John Wiley.

Bourn, J. A., (1989), 'Government Accounting Standards and Ethics: the British Experience'. Paper, Seminar, *Centre for Business and Public Centre Ethics*, Cambridge, (mimeo).

Bramley, G., (1984), 'Local Government in Crisis: A Review Article', *Policy and Politics*, 12(3).

Breton, A., (1974), *The Economic Theory of Representative Government*, Macmillan.

Brittan, S., (1975), 'The Economic Contradictions of Democracy', *British Journal of Political Science*, 5(2).

Bromley, P. and Euske, K., (1986), 'The Use of Rational Systems in Bounded Rationality Organisations: A Dilemma for Financial Managers', *Financial Accountability and Management*, 2(4).

Brunnson, N., (1985), *The Irrational Organisation*, Wiley.

*Bulletin of the Royal College of Psychiatrists*, (1986).

Bush, T., Kogan, M., and Lenney, T., (1989), *Directors of Education - Facing Reform*, Jessica Kingsley Publishers.

Campbell, D., (1969), 'Reforms as Experiments', *American Psychologist*, 24.

Cave, M., Kogan M., and Smith, R., (1990), *Output and Performance Measures in Government: The State of the Art*, Jessica Kingsley Publishers.

Cawson, A., (1982), *Corporatism and Welfare*, Heinemann Educational Books.

Cockburn, C., (1977), *The Local State*, Pluto.

Cook, T., (1987), 'Postpositivist Critical Multiplism', in Shadish, W., and Reichardt, C., (ed), *Evaluation Studies Review Annual*, 12.

Cook, T., and Shadish, W., (1987), 'Program Evaluation: The Worldly Science', in Shadish, W., and Reichardt, C.(ed), *Evaluation Studies Review Annual*, 12.

Cooper, J., (1983), *The Creation of the British Personal Social Services, 1962-1974*, Heinemann.

Cope, D., (1981), *Organisation Development and Action Research in Hospitals*, Gower.

Croham Report, (1987), *Review of the University Grants Committee, Report of the Committee under the Chairmanship of Lord Croham*, Cm 81, HMSO.

Cronbach, L. J., (1982), *Designing Evaluations of Educational and Social Programs*, Jossey-Bass.

Cronbach, L. J., et al, (1980), *Towards Reform of Program Evaluation*, Jossey-Bass.

Curnock, K., and Hardiker. P., (1979), *Towards Practice Theory*, Routledge and Kegan Paul.

Davies, D., and Challis, D., (1981) in Goldberg, E., and Connelly, N., (ed), *Evaluative Research in Social Care*. Heinemann.

Davies, B., and Knapp, M., (1981), *Old People's Homes and the Production of Welfare*, Routledge and Kegan Paul.

Davies, R. U.(ed), (1986), *Watchdog's Tales: The District Audit Service - the First 138 Years*, HMSO.

Day, P., and Klein, R., (1990), *Inspecting the Inspectorates*, Joseph Rowntree Memorial Trust.

Day, P., Klein, R., and Tipping, G., (1988), *Inspecting for Quality: Services for the Elderly*, Bath Social Policy Papers, no 12.

DES, (1985), White Paper, *Better Schools*, Cmnd 9469, HMSO.

DES, (1988), Circular 7/88 *The Local Management of Schools*, HMSO.

DHSS, (1971a), Circular 22/71, *The Social Work Service of the DHSS*.

DHSS White Paper, (1971b), *Better Services for the Mentally Handicapped*, HMSO.

DHSS, (1976), HC(76)21 *Health Service Development: The Health Advisory Service*.

DHSS, (1979), *Community Homes Design Guide: A Small Secure Unit*.

DHSS, (1983), *Consultative Document on the Social Services Inspectorate*.

DHSS, (1984), HC(84)16 *Health Service Development: the Health Advisory Service*, Publication of Health Advisory Service-Social Work Service Reports.

DHSS, (1988), *Report of the Inquiry into Child Abuse in Cleveland 1987*, (Butler-Sloss Report), Cm 412, HMSO.

Department of Health, (1988), *Protecting Children: a Guide for Social Workers Undertaking a Comprehensive Assessment*, HMSO.

Department of Health, (1989), White Paper, *Caring for People: Community Care in the Next Decade and Beyond*. HMSO.

Drucker, P., (1989), *The New Realities*, Heinemann.

Dunn, W., (1982), 'Reforms as Arguments', in House, E., et al., (ed.), *Evaluation Studies Review Annual*, 7.

Elmore, R. F., (1981), in Williams, W., *Studying Implementation: Methodological and Administrative Issues.*, Chatham House.

Freidson, E., (1970), *Professional Dominance*, Atherton Press.

Fulton Report, (1968), *The Civil Service*, Report of the Committee under the Chairmanship of Lord Fulton, 1966-1968, Command 3638, HMSO.

Garrett, J., (1972), *The Management of Government*, Pelican.

Garrett, J., (1986), 'Developing State Audit in Britain.' *Public Administration*, 64, Winter.

Giddens, A., (1979), *Central Problems in Social Theory*, Macmillan.

Glass, G. V., McGaw, B., and Smith, M., (1981), *Meta-analysis in Social Research*, Sage.

Glynn, J. J., (1985), 'VFM Auditing - An International Review and Comparison', *Financial Accountability and Management*, 1(2).

Goldberg, E., and Connelly, N. (ed), (1981), *Evaluative Research in Social Care*, Heinemann.

Goldberg, E., and Connelly, N., (1982), *The Effectiveness of Social Care for the Elderly*, Heinemann.

Goldberg, E., (1984), 'Evaluation Studies: Past Experience and Future Directions', *Research, Policy and Planning*, 2(1).

Goldberg, E., and Warburton, W., (1978), *Ends and Means in Social Work*, Allen and Unwin.

Gough, I., (1979), *The Political Economy of the Welfare State*, Macmillan.

Gray, A., (1986), *Policy Management and Policy Assessment: Developments in Central Government*, RIPA.

Gray, A., and Jenkins, W., (1983), *Policy Analysis and Evaluation in British Government*, RIPA.

Gray, J., and Jesson, D., (1987), in Harrison, A. and Gretton, J., (ed), *Education and Training UK 1987*, Policy Journals.

Greenwood, R., (1983), 'Changing Patterns of Budgeting in Local Government', *Public Administration*, 61, Summer.

Greenwood, R., (1987), 'Managerial Strategies in Local Government', *Public Administration*, 65, Autumn.

Griffiths Report, (1983), *NHS Management Inquiry*, DHSS.

Griffiths Report, (1988), *Community Care: Agenda for Action.*, HMSO.

Grimwood, M., and Tomkins, C., (1986), 'Value for Money Auditing - Towards Incorporating a Naturalistic Approach', *Financial Accountability and Management*, 2(4), Winter.

Guba, E. G., and Lincoln, Y. S., (1989), *Fourth Generation Evaluation*, Sage Publications.

Habermas, J., (1971), *Toward a Rational Society*, Heinemann.

Ham, C., and Hill, M., (1984), *The Policy Process in the Modern Capitalist State*, Wheatsheaf.

Harris, R., Barker, M., Reading, P., Richards, M., and Youll, P. (eds), (1985), *Educating Social Workers*, Association of Teachers in Social Work Education.

Hartley, O., (1971), 'The Relationship between Central and Local Authorities', *Public Administration*, Winter.

Hartley, O., (1972), 'Inspectorates in British Central Government', *Public Administration*, Winter.

Hawkesworth, M., (1988), *Theoretical Issues in Policy Analysis*, Albany: State University of New York Press.

Health Advisory Service, (1983), *The Rising Tide*. NHS HAS.

Health Advisory Service, (1985), *Bridges over Troubled Waters*. NHS HAS.

Health Advisory Service, (1987), *Memorandum for Team Members*. NHS HAS.

Heclo, H., and Wildavsky, A., (1981), *The Private Government of Public Money*, 2nd edition, Macmillan.

Henkel, M., Kogan, M., Packwood, T., Whitaker, T., Youll, P., (1989), *The Health Advisory Service. An Evaluation*. King Edward's Hospital Fund for London.

Hogwood, B., and Peters, G., (1985), *The Pathology of Public Policy*, Clarendon Press.

Horrocks, P., (1986), Correspondence in *Bulletin of the Royal College of Psychiatrists*.

House, E. R., (1977), *The Logic of Evaluation*, Los Angeles: Center for the Study of Evaluation.

House, E. R., (1980), *Evaluating with Validity*, Sage.

House of Commons, (1985), Parliamentary Question 620/1984/85. Answer given by Kenneth Clarke.

House of Commons Select Committee, Education and Science, *HM Inspectorate*, (1967-68).

House of Commons Select Committee, Social Services, (1980), *The Government's White Papers on Public Expenditure: The Social Services*, Session 1979-1980, 1, HC702-1, HMSO.

Howe, G., (1969), *Report of the Committee of Inquiry into Allegations of Ill-Treatment of Patients and Other Irregularities at the Ely Hospital, Cardiff*, Cmnd 2975, HMSO.

Jarratt Report, (1985), Committee of Vice Chancellors and Principals, *Report of the Steering Committee for Efficiency Studies in Universities.*

*Journal of Management Studies*, (May 1986).

Judge, K., Smith, J., and Taylor-Gooby, P., (1983), 'Public Opinion and the Privatisation of Welfare: Some Theoretical Implications', *Journal of Social Policy.*, 12(4).

King, A., (1975), 'Overload: The Problems of Governing in the 1970s', *Political Studies*, XXVIII(2).

Kogan, M., (1974), 'Social Policy and Public Organisational Values', *Journal of Social Policy* 3(2).

Kogan, M., (1987), 'The British Experience', in Higher Education Group, The Ontario Institute for Studies in Education, *Governments and Higher Education - the Legitimacy of Intervention.*

Kogan, M., (1988), *Education Accountability*, Hutchinson Educational.

Kogan, M., and Henkel, M., (1983), *Government and Research*, Heinemann.

Kogan, M., and Terry, J., (1971), *The Organisation of a Social Services Department: A Blue-Print*, Bookstall Publications.

Kubr, M., (1980), *Management Consultancy: A Guide to the Profession*, ILO.

Laffin, M., and Young, K., (1985), 'The Changing Roles and Responsibilities of Local Education Chief Officers', *Public Administration*, Spring.

Langley, M., (1986), 'Comparative Studies' in Davies, R. U., (ed), *Watchdog's Tales*, HMSO.

Larson, M., (1977), *The Rise of Professionalism.*, University of California Press.

Layfield Committee Report, (1976), *Local Government Finance: The Report of the Committee of Enquiry*, Cmnd 6453, HMSO.

Lindblom, C. E., (1977), *Politics and Markets*, Basic Books.

Lindblom, C. E., and Cohen, D. K., (1979), *Usable Knowledge*, Yale University Press.

MacIntyre, A., (1981), *After Virtue*, 1st edition, Duckworth.

*Management Services in Government*, (1967-80)

*Management Today*, (1983).

McSweeney, B., (1988), 'Accounting for the Audit Commission', *Political Quarterly*, 59(1).

Minogue, M., (1983), 'Theory and Practice in Public Policy and Administration', *Policy and Politics*, 11(1).

Mitroff, I., and Kilman, R., (1978), *Methodological Approaches to Social Science*, Jossey-Bass.

Mueller, D., (1979), *Public Choice*, Cambridge University Press.

Neave, G., (1988), 'On the Cultivation of Quality, Efficiency and Enterprise: an Overview of Recent Trends in Higher Education in Western Europe, 1986-1988', *European Journal of Education.*, 23(1-2).

Neilson, A., (1986), 'Value for Money Auditing in Local Government', *Public Money*, June.

Nicholson, J. C., (1986), 'The Creation of the Audit Commission' in Davies, R. U., (ed), *Watchdog's Tales*, HMSO.

Niskanen, W. A., (1973) *Bureaucracy: Servant or Master? Lessons from America*, The Institute of Economic Affairs.

Normanton, E. L., (1966), *The Accountability and Audit of Governments*, Manchester University Press.

*O'Connor, J., (1973), The Fiscal Crisis of the State*, New York.

*Organizational Dynamics* (Autumn, 1983)

Ouchi, W., (1980), 'Markets, Bureaucracies and Clans', *Administrative Science Quarterly*, 25(1).

Ouchi, W., (1981), *Theory Z: How American Business can meet the Japanese Challenge*, Addison-Wesley.

Patton, M. Q., (1978), *Utilisation-focused Evaluation*, Sage.

Peet, J., (1988), 'The new witch doctors' in *The Economist*, 13 February.

Peters, T., and Waterman, R., (1982), *In Search of Excellence*, Harper Row.

Plant, R., (1970), *Social and Moral Theory in Casework*, Routledge and Kegan Paul.

Pollitt, C., (1986), 'Beyond the Managerial Model: the Case for Broadening Performance Assessment in Government and the Public Services', *Financial Accountability and Management*, 2 (3).

Pollitt, C., (1989), 'Performance Indicators in the Longer Term', *Public Money and Management*, Autumn.

Popper, K. R., (1966), *The Open Society and its Enemies*, 5th edition, Routledge and Kegan Paul.

*Public Money* (December 1984), 'The Audit Commission: a British Maverick'.

Ranson, S., (1980), 'Changing Relations between Centre and Locality in Education', *Local Government Studies*, 5.

Ray, C., (1986), 'Corporate Culture: the Last Frontier of Control', *Journal of Management Studies* 23:3, May.

Rein, M., (1976), *Social Science and Public Policy*, Penguin Books.

Rein, M., (1983), *From Policy to Practice*, Macmillan.

Rhodes, G., (1981), *Inspectorates in British Government*, George Allen and Unwin.

Rhodes, R. A. W., (1981), *Control and Power in Central-Local relations*, Gower.

Richards, S., (1987), 'The Financial Management Initiative' in Gretton, J., and Harrison, A., (ed), *Reshaping Central Government*, Policy Journals.

Rivlin, A. M., (1971), *Systematic Thinking for Social Action*, The Brookings Institution.

Robinson, A., and Webb, A., (1987), 'Parliamentary Responses to the Government's Efficiency and Effectiveness Initiatives' (unpublished paper).

Rossi, P., (1982), in House, E. R. (ed), *Evaluation Studies Review Annual, vol. 7*, Sage.

Rowbottom. R. W., Hey, A. M., and Billis, D., (1974), *Social Services Departments: Developing Patterns of Work and Organisation*, Heinemann.

St John-Brooks, C., (1986), 'Dual Role for the Audit Commission', *New Society*, 28 March 1986.

Schon, D., (1983), *The Reflective Practitioner*, Temple Smith.

Scriven, M., (1967), 'The Methodology of Evaluation', in *Perspectives on Curriculum Evaluation*, AERA Monograph No 1, 1967.

Scriven, M., (1980), *The Logic of Evaluation*, Edgepress.

Sharpe, L. J., (1970), 'Theories and Values of Local Government', *Political Studies*, XVIII(2).

Sharpe, L. J., (1979), *Decentralist Trends in Western Democracies: A First Appraisal.*, Sage.

Social Services Inspectorate/CHI/13, (1983b), Internal Paper.

Social Services Inspectorate, (1985), *Inspection of Community Homes*, DHSS.

Social Services Inspectorate, (1986), *Secure Accommodation for Children and Young Persons: Guidance for Local Authorities*. DHSS.

Social Services InspEctorate, (1987a), *Inspection of Secure Accommodation: Check List*. DHSS.

Social Services Inspectorate, (1987b), *Care for a Change?*

Social Services Inspectorate, (1987c), *Mission Statement*. DHSS.

Social Services Inspectorate, (1988a), *Family Centres*. DHSS.

Social Services Inspectorate, (1988b), *Health in Homes*. DHSS.

Social Services Inspectorate, (1988c), *Inspection of Cleveland Social Services Department's Arrangements for Handling Child Sexual Abuse*, Department of Health.

Social Services Inspectorate, (1988d), *Key Indicators*. Department of Health.

Social Services Inspectorate, (1988e), *Procedural Guide to Inspection.*

Social Services Inspectorate, (1989a), *Health in Homes.*

Social Services Inspectorate, (1989b), *Homes are for Living In*. HMSO.

Social Services Inspectorate, (1989c), *Managing Home Care in Metropolitan Districts*. Department of Health.

Social Services Inspectorate, (1989d), *Towards a Climate of Confidence*. Department of Health.

*Social Work Today*, (1970), 1(1).

Sprigg, J., (1986), 'Performance Measurement and the Use of Statistics' in Davies, R. U., (ed), *Watchdog's Tales*, HMSO.

Stake, R., (1982), 'A Peer Response. A Review of Program Evaluation in Education: When? How? To What Ends?' in House E. R. et al. (ed), *Evaluation Review Studies Annual*, 7.

Stevenson, O., and Parsloe, P., (1978), *Social Services Teams: the Practitioner's View*, HMSO.

Stewart, J., (1983), *Local Government: the Conditions of Local Choice*, Allen and Unwin.

Stoker, G., (1988), *The Politics of Local Government*, Macmillan Education.

Tomkins, C. R., (1986), 'Local Authority Audit under the Audit Commission and what it means to one private sector professional firm', *Financial Accountability and Management*, 2(1), Spring.

Tomkins, C. R., (1987), *Achieving Economy, Efficiency and Effectiveness in the Public Sector*, Kogan Page.

Toulmin, S., (1958), *The Uses of Argument*, Cambridge University Press.

Utting, W., (July 1978), 'The Role of the Social Work Service of the DHSS', *Social Work Service*, 16.

Walker, D., (1983), *Municipal Empire: The Town Halls and their Beneficiaries*, Temple Smith.

Watkin, B., (1978), *The National Health Service: the First Phase*, Allen and Unwin.

Webb, A., (1989), 'The Role and Work of the Social Services Inspectorate', in Gretton, J., and Harrison, A., (ed), *Health Care UK 1989*, Longman.

Webb, A., and Wistow, G., (1987), *Social Work, Social Care and Social Planning.* Longman.

Weiss, C. H., (1977), *Using Social Research in Public Policy Making*, D. C. Heath.

Whitehead, C., (1986), 'Housing Audit', *Public Money*, June.

Wholey, J., (1983), *Evaluation and Effective Public Management*, Little Brown.

Widdicombe Report, (1986), *The Conduct of Local Authority Business. Report of the Committee of Inquiry into Local Authority Business*, HMSO (and four research volumes).

Winch, P., (1958), *The Idea of a Social Science*, Routledge and Kegan Paul.

Winkler, J. T., (1981) 'The Political Economy of Administrative Discretion.' in Adler, M., and Asquith, S., (eds), *Discretion and Welfare*, Heinemann.

Young, K., (1989), 'The Challenge to Professionalism in Local Government', *Policy Studies*, PSI.

## Legislation

Boarding out and Charge and Control Regulations, (1988)

Children Act, (1989)

Children and Young Persons Act, (1933)

Children and Young Persons Act, (1969)

Community Homes Regulations, (1972)

Criminal Justice Act, (1982)

Education Reform Act, (1988)

Local Authority Social Services Act, (1970)

Local Government Act, (1988)

Local Government Finance Act, (1982)

Registered Homes Act, (1984)

Secure Accommodation Regulations, (1983 and 1986)

# Index